New Orleans

INSIGHT *City* GUIDES

Edited and Produced by Martha Ellen Zenfell
Principal Photography by Ping Amranand
Editorial Director: Brian Bell

A P A
PUBLICATIONS

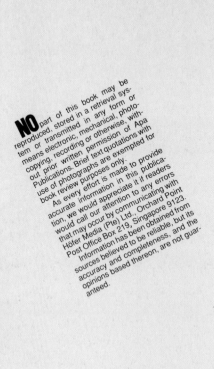
New Orleans

First Edition
© **1992 APA PUBLICATIONS (HK) LTD**
All Rights Reserved
Printed in Singapore by Höfer Press Pte. Ltd

ABOUT THIS BOOK

New Orleans is the most cosmopolitan of provincial towns," wrote Charles Dudley Warner in 1881. Over 100 years later, the same is still the case. New Orleans is the place to find French food, sophisticated nightlife, hot attitudes and cool jazz, all contained within an area so tiny – the French Quarter – it can be walked end to end in a matter of minutes.

Such a fascinating city was bound to attract the attention of Apa Publications, whose award-winning Insight and City Guides cover more than 140 destinations. The guides' reputation lies with their blend of frank reporting and bold photojournalism – a formula guaranteed to extract the best from a city.

Pleasure is business

When New Orleans came around in the expanding catalogue of American destinations, **Martha Ellen Zenfell**, Editor-in-Chief of Apa's USA titles, nabbed it for her own. With a sister who had lived in the suburbs near Lake Pontchartrain, and with a best friend who still calls a Creole cottage in the 9th Ward "home," she knew about the city. As project editor of Insight Guides to the Greek Islands, Bermuda and New York City, Zenfell knew about the books. It was time to put the two together.

One of the most important choices in an Insight Guide is who to use as principal photographer. Some of Apa's finest were clamoring for the job, but **Ping Amranand** was the obvious choice. Born in Bangkok and now based in Washington, DC, Amranand photographed Insight Guides to both Paris and the Bahamas, the two destinations many

feel New Orleans most closely resembles. "The combination of European and Caribbean influences makes New Orleans unlike any other city I have visited in the United States," he says now. Also, "I don't think I have been anywhere else (in America) where as much energy is devoted to the pursuit of pure pleasure."

Pleasure is business in the case of **Syndey Byrd**, the local photographer whose music and Mardi Gras images complement those of Amranand's. Byrd's pictures appear in many publications; her standing in the musical fraternity is so firm that she will probably be awarded that rare accolade, a jazz funeral, when the Pearly Gates are beckoning.

Music also got the better of **Honey Naylor**, who wrote all of the "Places" chapters in this book. A Louisiana native who once traipsed off to New York with the idea of becoming an actress, Naylor found that New Orleans, like the smell of greasepaint, gets under your skin and doesn't go away. Dixieland and *café au lait* lured her back home, and Naylor now lives and writes from her French Quarter apartment.

"In New Orleans I enjoy a sense of place and historical continuity, conditions which are absent in much of urban America," says historian **Clive Hardy**. The son of an Englishman and a New Orleanian, Hardy worked for Tulane University, was a consultant at the Louisiana State Museum, and established the Archives and Manuscripts department at the University of New Orleans.

New Orleans also gives a sense of place to **Errol Laborde**, who wrote the introduction to this book, and the essay on Mardi Gras. As well as being the author of two books pertaining to the city, he is associate publisher and editor of *New Orleans* magazine. Midwest-

Zenfell

Amranand

Naylor

Hardy

Laborde

erner **Tim Harper** ("Governors and Other Grievances") is a lawyer and journalist who writes about economics for publications like *Time* and the *International Herald Tribune*. He once almost took a teaching job at Loyola University, but ended up instead in London. Harper was the project editor on Insight's guide to another political town, Chicago.

Iris T. Kelso was named by a television series as one of the five most influential women in New Orleans. A political columnist for the *Times-Picayune* newspaper, she has covered state and local government since 1954, making her ideal to chronicle the ups and downs of life in the 20th century.

Kalamu ya Salaam is a writer and editor as well as a music producer. His editorial credits include being the modern jazz editor for *Wavelength* magazine; his producing talents include two recordings by Ellis Marsalis, with whom he is also collaborating on a music autobiography. Salaam served for four years as the executive director of the New Orleans Jazz & Heritage Foundation, and wrote the essay "Let the Good Times Roll."

"New Orleans is a storybook city, where one can step straight from the pages of a novel to the streets where it actually occurred, " says **Susan Larson**, who penned the essay "A Confederacy of Writers." She should know, having been a bookseller, a novelist, and now the book editor of the *Times-Picayune*. "The city dazzles the eye even as it breaks the heart."

Or feeds the stomach. What other American town would devote two hours every day to broadcasting about food ? This particular radio program is hosted by **Tom Fitzmorris**, editor and publisher of *Menu* magazine and responsible for our feature "What's Cookin'." Born on Mardi Gras, Fitzmorris has never left town for more than a month at a time.

Home-made jambalaya and astute observations are just two of the contributions made by **Lisa Shroyer**, the best friend in the 9th Ward mentioned earlier. Shroyer and project editor Zenfell, both Southern girls, met many years ago and founded a friendship based on music and running away. Shroyer ("the only nine-year-old I ever met with a sense of irony") eventually headed for New Orleans while Zenfell ended up in that other town of contemporary music, London. Shroyer and her husband **David**, Director of Retention and Special Programs at UNO and the writer of this book's piece on Mardi Gras Indians, lent Zenfell reference books, a brass bed in their home below a wooden ceiling fan, gave tips on authors and offered hours of invaluable guidance. Many, many thanks.

Southern hospitality

Beverly Gianna, Director of Public Relations at the Greater New Orleans Tourist & Convention Commission, also contributed time and enthusiasm, answering what seemed like a million questions, organizing tours, and responding to difficult requests without once losing her charm or efficiency – a thoroughly modern Southern woman. Thanks, too, to **Christine DeCuir**, and to **Milly Spear** of the TLC Company, who took our photographer around town with the tender loving care her company's initials imply.

In the London editorial office, the finishing touches to the book were aided by the combined and capable skills of **Dorothy Stannard**, **Madeleine Nicklin**, **Mary Morton** (who also compiled the index), and **Jill Anderson**.

Harper

Kelso

Salaam

Larson

Fitzmorris

History

Features

Maps

TRAVEL TIPS

Compiled by Honey Naylor

*For detailed information
see page 257*

As a matter of geography and politics New Orleans is very much an American city. But to understand New Orleans properly, it is important to realize that, in terms of character and personality, it is more than just American or just a city.

In many ways New Orleans is an island, with the river curving around one side, Lake Pontchartrain and its marshes on another, and located along the nation's southern rim by the Gulf of Mexico. Like an island it tends to have a style of its own, including its own dialect. Its celebrations, though influenced by places near its borders as well as by the ships passing through, are also distinctive.

In some ways New Orleans might even be considered to be the northern-most isle of the Caribbean, a crescent-shaped piece of territory that seems as though it were pushed from the sea into the womb of Louisiana by some ancient hurricane. As in most Caribbean spots, there is a black majority in New Orleans, though a European heritage and white economic power.

See the world: Like the Caribbean, it also has a native music form, a tradition of Carnival celebrations, poverty, yet a wealthy social class, voodoo, and a form of cooking that is as hot and spicy as the passions of both the islands and the city. See New Orleans and, in some ways, you see the world.

See New Orleans and you're also likely to see some type of celebration, many of which reflect different parts of the world. Festivals, in general, reign all year long in New Orleans. Next to Mardi Gras, the biggest festival is the New Orleans Jazz Fest, which is spread over two weekends in late April and early May. But sometimes it is the smaller celebrations that can be the most charming.

New Orleans, being a port city, has a substantial ethnic heritage. St Patrick's Day

is celebrated by the Irish here, as it is everywhere else where the Irish settled. The only difference is that the local version has a Mardi Gras touch, including floats. And whereas in Mardi Gras trinkets are thrown from the floats, the St Patrick's revelers also throw cabbage and potatoes.

Two days later the local Sicilians celebrate St Joseph's Day by building altars to their patron saint. Many of the altars are built in homes as repayment for favors granted to

those who prayed to St Joseph for help. St Joseph is also honored by the city's black community. By tradition, the Mardi Gras Indians – "tribes" of blacks who wear glittery American Indian costumes on Mardi Gras – make one appearance outside Carnival, and that is usually on a weekend near to St Joseph's Day. Some black families also build altars to the saint. New Orleans, of course, is a living altar to the god Music and on weekends during the fall various black marching groups enliven their neighborhoods with spontaneous brass-band parades.

By reputation, however, if not by fact, the

Preceding pages: hidden faces of New Orleans; home bass; the river, the Quarter and beyond; Jackson Square; a procession to the Pearly Gates; twin peaks. <u>Left</u>, wedding bells. <u>Right</u>, belle and bow on Bourbon Street.

groups of people with which New Orleans is most identified are the "Creoles" and the "Cajuns," both terms that are frequently misused and misunderstood. New Orleans, by its heritage, is a Creole city, but, despite what some natives think and what some brochures may suggest, it is not strictly Cajun.

A "Creole," as the term was originally used in the city, was any native-born person whose family was directly linked to either France or Spain. During the next two and a half centuries that term would blur and become less relevant as the population of New Orleans increasingly comprised American hybrids rather than first-generation Europe-

ans. The word "Creole" would come to describe just about anything that had some link, albeit distant, to New Orleans itself. Thus a locally grown species of tomato is known as the "Creole tomato," a version of the popular soup, gumbo, is called "Creole gumbo." When applied to people in modern New Orleans, the term is most often given to those within the black community whose ancestry traces back to the union of slave women who served as mistresses to French gentlemen. They constitute an important part of modern New Orleans.

The so-called "black Creoles" tend to have fairer skin than most other American blacks. They generally have French names, and their families tend to have more wealth than the rest of the black community. They have been the business leaders within black New Orleans and, in recent years, an increasing number of the city's leadership has been from that group of people. New Orleans, once a Creole city, is becoming a Creole city again – only the definition has changed.

"Cajun" is a little less complex although the word seems to be equally misused. The original Cajuns were French who had settled in Nova Scotia on the northeastern Canadian shore. During the 1700s, they were displaced by the British and moved to France, but, failing to settle, they headed back to North America. The largest group of them settled in southern Louisiana. As the section of Nova Scotia from which they originally came was known as "Acadia," the word "Cajun" evolved to describe them. If there is a Louisiana town that can truly be called "Cajun" it is Lafayette – about 120 miles west, as the crow flies, from New Orleans.

The Cajuns are known as a fun-loving people who have their own music and dance form. Cajun cooking is known for its spiciness. New Orleans' prominence in modern Cajun history lies in being the home of Paul Prudhomme, the rotund Cajun chef who has created a new era of Cajun dishes and popularized them around the world. Prudhomme's version of blackened redfish became such a rage that the Gulf of Mexico was almost depleted of the fish.

Adding to the ethnic confusion are the many residents of Louisiana whose ancestry is French and who think they are "Cajun," but who in fact are not. They are the descendants of early settlers who came directly from France and who were part of no particular great migration other than the movement west. They are technically not Cajuns, at least not according to blood and history, although they are by spirit and personality.

When people of different types share one island, however, they develop some similarities. New Orleanians are, for the most part, united in:
● thinking that they are a unique people and that nobody else really understands them;

- being overwhelmed by snow or cold weather, which they seldom experience;
- expecting their food to be spicy;
- celebrating Mardi Gras (even if that means leaving town for the holiday);
- being fascinated by politics;
- rooting for their frequently beleaguered professional football team, the Saints.

Like the inhabitants of tropical islands, New Orleanians tend toward life at a leisurely pace, and it is that pace that is one of the most endearing characteristics of the city. It is a town that has never been in a hurry. Sometimes that has worked to its advantage. New Orleans, for example, was

Water continues to nourish the city, even when its economy is weakened. New Orleans' port is not what it was in the days before railroading when steamships lined the waterfront. Nevertheless, it is still one of the busiest in the world.

But if shipping is in the middle of an economic struggle, another industry, tourism, has increased dramatically. Paddle wheelers that once carried bales of cotton along the Mississippi now carry groups of visitors instead. Nearby, the European architecture of the French Quarter has been preserved, but behind the walls there is still a living, working neighborhood.

not in a hurry to modernize at a time when other cities were tearing down old buildings and plowing across their waterfronts to make way for expressways. Because of that, New Orleans preserved its French Quarter and maintained its river's edge, which today is the center of recreational and leisure development. The city is discovering that, when done correctly, what serves the tourist can serve locals as well. Developments such as the new Aquarium of the Americas draw both to the waterfront.

Left, service with a smile. **Above**, heavenly music.

The city itself is also showing signs of life, although it is troubled by the maladies of modern cities everywhere. In a sense, New Orleans might be compared to Venice and other grand old romantic cities of the world that sometimes suffer by comparison to their economic and political roles in previous centuries, but that nevertheless survive.

The truth is that great cities are immortal because there is so much to them worth preserving. If New Orleans ceased to exist there would be a need to create something to take its place. Most people, after all, yearn for an island.

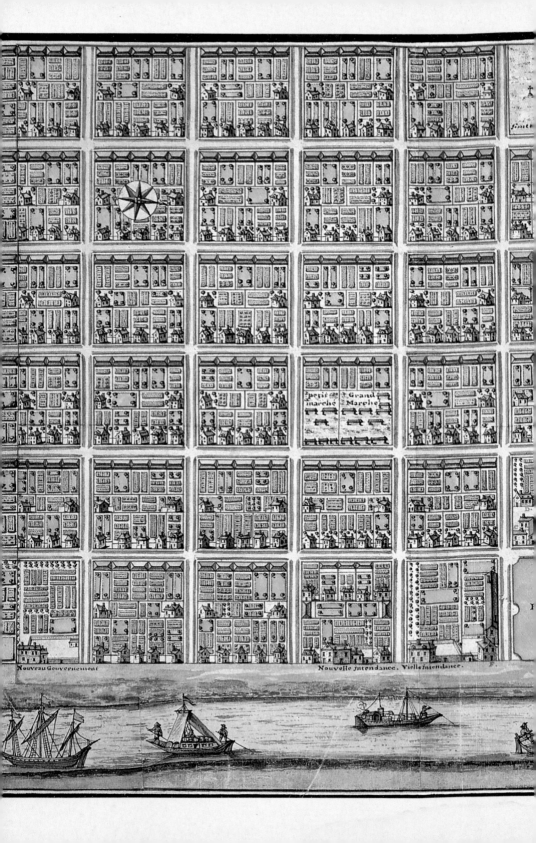

Nouveau Gouvernement

Nouvelle Intendance. Vieille Intendance.

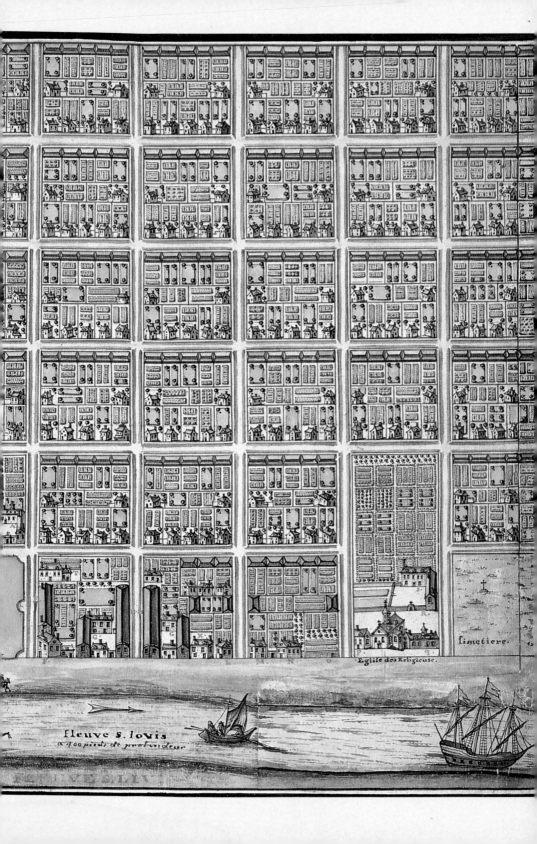

Eglise des Religieuse.

simetiere.

fleuve S. lovis
a 400 pieds de profondeur

On April 9, 1682, at a site on the Mississippi River about 90 miles below present-day New Orleans, the French explorer Robert Cavalier, Sieur de la Salle, and 53 followers erected a cross and a column and proclaimed the region drained by the great river a possession of Louis XIV. Spanish adventurers had skirted and even passed through what is today Louisiana since the early 16th century, but they had come as soldiers of fortune seeking only the quick wealth of gold and silver. Finding none, they had moved on leaving nothing to mark their passage. La Salle, however, and the other French explorers who shortly followed in his lead, were mainly intent on establishing a colonial empire for the greater glory of their king.

Two years after he first sailed down the Mississippi and claimed the vast heartland of North America for his sovereign, La Salle returned to the region to establish a settlement at the mouth of the great river. Sailing into the Gulf of Mexico, his small flotilla missed the river's mouth and ended in Matagorda Bay, Texas. La Salle spent the next two years in a futile search for the river. His quest ended only when he was murdered by his own men.

War and financial problems prevented further French efforts to establish control over the lower Mississippi Valley until 1697, when the Treaty of Ryswick brought France a respite from war and permitted Louis XIV to once more consider his North American empire. He commissioned an expedition under the command of the Canadian, Pierre le Moyne, Sieur D'Iberville, to establish a colony on the Mississippi and secure French interests in the region. Consisting of two warships and two small coastal vessels called *traversiers*, Iberville's expedition sailed from Brest in late October 1698.

Following stops at Santo Domingo and Pensacola Bay, the small flotilla finally dropped anchor in early February at Ship Island, about 12 miles off the Mississippi Gulf Coast. In the months that followed, Iberville established a headquarters for the colony on Biloxi Bay, at the site of present-day Ocean Springs, Mississippi. During the following spring he established a second fort, this time on the Mississippi River near the present town of Phoenix. Named for de La Boulaye, it was the first French settlement in present-day Louisiana.

Progress in securing the region for France was slow, however. Wars and Louis XIV's profligacy consumed French energies for the better part of the next decade and a half, and Louisiana remained on the periphery of French concerns.

Mississippi Bubble: Then, in 1715, with the death of the king, Philippe, Duke of Orleans came to power as Regent for Louis XV, the five-year-old great-grandson of the deceased Sun King. For Louisiana this changing of the guard at Versailles would be important. Included in the Regent's coterie of friends was the then up-and-coming Scottish financial wizard and bon vivant, John Law. Under the Regent's sponsorship, Law devised a get-rich-quick scheme that included the extravagant promotion of Louisiana as a source of great riches for the easy taking. Later dubbed the Mississippi Bubble, the scheme eventually contributed to the virtual bankruptcy of France, but not before it had two important consequences for Louisiana. The first to happen was the population of the colony increased dramatically, rising from about 400 in 1717 to about 8,000 in 1721.

The second significant consequence was the founding of the city of New Orleans. In 1717, Law's Company of the West determined that a town named in honor of the Regent, the Duke of Orleans, should be established 30 leagues above the entrance to the river at a spot which could be reached by the Mississippi and by Lake Pontchartrain. The town was founded and later governed by Jean Baptiste le Moyne, Sieur de Bienville, Iberville's younger brother and his natural

Preceding pages: Plan de la Ville de la Nouvelle Orleans, 1755. Left, Robert Cavalier proclaims the region a possession of France in 1682.

successor when the explorer died, having previously accompanied Iberville on his frontier expeditions.

Work to clear the forest and dense cane breaks that covered the area began in the early spring of 1718, but progress was slow, and when a great flood caused havoc with these initial efforts there was some consideration given to a different location. The project had produced little more than a small clearing and some 35 or 40 haphazardly situated huts and cabins when Adrien de Pauger, an engineer, arrived in late March of 1721 with a plan. Working under the burdens of bureaucratic impediments and natural

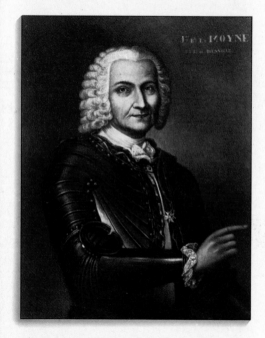

obstructions, Pauger and 10 soldiers managed in a few weeks to clear a sizable swath close to the river and lay out a grid pattern of streets in the clearing.

Much of the building that occurred over the next year and a half was destroyed on September 11, 1722, when the area's first recorded hurricane destroyed some two-thirds of the structures that had been erected in the interim. The basic plan of the city had been established, however, and it dictated the configuration of the rebuilding that quickly followed the storm.

Black slavery had existed in Louisiana from the colony's earliest years, but it was only in 1719 and 1720 that large numbers of black slaves began to arrive in Louisiana. By 1724, these slaves had become so numerous that Bienville felt compelled to promulgate the *Code Noir* for their regulation. Originally drawn up at Versailles for the care and governing of the large slave population in Santo Domingo, the *Code Noir* was designed not only to regulate slave conduct, but to protect slaves from injustice and other ill-treatment. Thus, while it prescribed such harsh penalties as branding and mutilation and even death for stealing or running away or striking a white, it required that masters properly feed and clothe their slaves and allow them respite from work on Sundays and Holy Days.

Other important provisions stipulated that slaves be instructed in Catholicism; that concubinage with slaves and marriage between blacks and whites were forbidden; and that slaves were prohibited from carrying weapons, owning property, and congregating. It also decreed Catholicism the state religion and ordered the expulsion of Jews from the colony. Perhaps most interesting of the Code's numerous provisions was one that granted freed slaves the same rights, privileges and immunities as those enjoyed by the freeborn.

Bienville, for all his long service and considerable accomplishments in establishing French control in the lower Mississippi Valley, seemed always to be at odds with other administrators in the colony. By 1724, it was concluded that criticism of his administration was sufficiently serious to warrant a full investigation. Bienville was recalled to France, but the political and religious discord that plagued the colony was not resolved by his removal. In fact, the respect of the Indians for the French, which Bienville had established and skillfully managed over many years, deteriorated rapidly following his departure. The situation finally boiled over on November 28, 1729, when Natchez Indians surprised Fort Rosalie on the bluff at Natchez, killing about 250 colonists and slaves, and taking captive perhaps another 450 women, children, and slaves.

Political and religious discord in the

colony accelerated. Men of influence decided that Louisiana was a poor investment and petitioned Louis XV to accept its retrocession. The king agreed, and Louisiana was returned to the Crown. Bienville was summoned from retirement to once more govern the colony. But by 1733, conditions in New Orleans were precipitous. Money and provisions were in short supply, and morale among administrators and colonists had sunk to a new low.

Fortunately, at least two events gave some promise of a brighter future. A small contingent of Ursuline nuns arrived in New Orleans in August, 1727, to establish a school for

effect only after time, however, and, for Bienville, faced with such immediate problems as the growing hostility among the Indians, the ladies were scant comfort.

In an attempt to subdue the openly belligerent Chickasaws, and no doubt intimidate and bolster French prestige among tribes that might be wavering, Bienville mounted two campaigns. In the first of these in 1736, miscalculation and delay turned the operation into a bloody French defeat and withdrawal, leaving French prestige among the Indians even further diminished. Four years later another move was made against the Chickasaws, but sickness, heavy rains and

girls and to care for the sick. The period also witnessed the arrival of several shiploads of young marriageable women of good character. Because the government supplied each of these girls with a chest of clothing and linens, they were called *les filles à la cassette*. Dubbed "casket girls" by later generations, their presence, like that of the Ursulines, added an element of social stability to what was then a raw frontier community. This benign influence would have its

Left, Sieur de Bienville, founder of New Orleans. **Above**, trading with the Indians, *circa* 1720.

delays intervened, and in the end, Bienville decided to call off the campaign and offer a negotiated peace. For once happenstance favored the French. The Chickasaws misinterpreted Bienville's intentions and sued for peace themselves. The end result, however, was less than a French triumph.

For Bienville this failure decisively to defeat and subjugate the Chickasaws climaxed years of seemingly intractable frustrations. Aging and depressed by what he viewed as his personal failure, Bienville tendered his resignation and in 1743 left Louisiana for France, never to return.

As it happened, events were already occurring in Canada and Europe that would drastically alter the future course of Louisiana's history. In the 80 years since La Salle had claimed the vast region for Louis XIV, the colony had never shown a profit. Entrepreneurs, joint-stock companies, and two French monarchs had all lost fortunes in attempting to develop it. With the loss of Canada by 1760, Louis XV and his ministers were determined to be rid of Louisiana so that they might concentrate their efforts on saving France's West Indian islands.

Spanish cousin: By the secret Treaty of Fountainbleau signed in 1762, Louis XV

DON ALESSANDRO O'REILLY

gave New Orleans and the portion of Louisiana lying to the west of the Mississippi River to his cousin, Carlos III of Spain. This news was received with dismay, particularly in New Orleans, where a mass meeting was held and several of the city's prominent citizens harangued the crowd with inflammatory speeches. A petition urging the king to rescind the colony's transfer was hastily approved, and a wealthy merchant, Jean Milhet, was appointed to carry it to Louis XV at Versailles. But to no avail.

Word of the French Crown's refusal to reclaim Louisiana provoked much huffing and puffing in the streets and taverns of New Orleans, but the bluster of the populace soon subsided. For a small group of the colony's elite, however, the prospect of Spanish rule remained anathema. The merchants and public officials who had prospered under the lax and often corrupt administration of French rule, felt threatened by any change in the status quo, and Spain had a reputation for strictly administering colonies.

On March 5, 1766, Don Antonio de Ulloa, accompanied by a few officials and some 80 soldiers, landed at New Orleans during a driving rainstorm. His reception by the colony's senior officer, Captain Aubry, and other local officials was formal, courteous, and, at least superficially, friendly. A small and not very attractive man with a grating voice and a nervous manner, Governor Ulloa, then aged 50, was regarded as one of Europe's leading scientists. A conscientious and industrious man, he was, unfortunately, also singularly lacking in diplomacy and any form of social grace.

While most of his efforts to improve the condition of the colony and its inhabitants were largely successful, at least some of his actions further antagonized the small clique of malcontents. The growing disaffection of the citizenry for Governor Ulloa and his administration finally turned into open rebellion on October 27, 1768, when the Spanish cannons in New Orleans were spiked during the night. On the following day a number of the city's merchants and planters drafted a petition calling for the expulsion of Governor Ulloa and other Spanish authorities, while a mob of several hundred roamed through the streets shouting obscenities and threats against the Spanish authorities. On October 29 the Superior Council met and issued a decree ordering Ulloa and his troops to leave the colony. Apparently realizing the futility of remaining in New Orleans, Ulloa sailed for Cuba.

Some nine months would pass before Spain reasserted her authority over the colony. As the principal official on the scene during the interim, Captain Aubry forwarded reports on local conditions to his own government at Versailles and to the Spanish authorities in Havana. Conditions of turmoil and instances of near violence were common themes in these communications, with the onus for such conditions falling on Ulloa in Aubry's reports to Versailles, and on local French officials in his separate reports to Havana.

The torpor that envelops New Orleans during the hot summer months was suddenly broken on July 24 by word that a Spanish armada of 24 ships had entered the river and dropped anchor. The large size of the Spanish fleet left no doubt that the Spanish Crown meant to assert its sovereignty in Louisiana. The next day at a large public gathering in the Place d'Armes, Captain Aubry announced in the afternoon, the loud bang of a signal cannon startled the curious who had thronged the levee and muddy streets since early morning. A cadence of snare drums followed, interspersed with barked commands in Spanish, as some 2,600 Spanish troops marched in close precision down gangplanks across the low levee and into the Place d'Armes.

Down with the French: A brief ceremony ensued during which the flag of Bourbon France came down and that of Bourbon Spain went up. The ceremonies concluded with shouts of *Viva el Rey* from sailors high in the fleet's riggings and the thunderous

the impending arrival of General Alejandro O'Reilly and his forces. He advised the citizenry that immediate and complete acquiescence to Spanish authority was imperative and warned that any defiance of that authority risked severe consequences.

Three weeks later, all 24 vessels of O'Reilly's fleet had completed the tedious upriver voyage to New Orleans and lay moored opposite the Place d'Armes. At five

Left, Nouvelle Orleans became a Spanish city under General O'Reilly. **Above**, a pre-renovation Place d'Armes.

reverberations of a salute from the ships' cannon. The provincial populace of New Orleans had witnessed a spectacle that none would forget. Three days later, after reviewing reports by Ulloa and others, and interviewing several local officials, O'Reilly ordered the arrest and trial of 12 leaders in the revolt against Don Antonio de Ulloa. Six were condemned, and five of these – one having previously died in a scuffle with his jailers – were ordered hanged. When no hangman could be found, O'Reilly ordered the shooting of the condemned men. The executions were carried out the next day in the courtyard of a barracks located near the present site of the Old Mint Building.

Over a period of a few months, O'Reilly instituted a wide range of changes and reforms. For the colony as a whole, he annulled the French laws that had previously governed and substituted Spanish law, while in New Orleans he replaced the old French Superior Council with a Spanish *Cabildo*, or municipal council. He organized a competent militia and improved the city's fortifications and public structures. To better the social and economic condition of the citizenry, he set prices for food and essential commodities to prevent profiteering and

THIS ALLEY IS NAMED IN MEMORY OF THE SPANIARD ANTONIO DE SEDELLA ALSO LOCALLY KNOWN AS P. ANTOINE WHO WAS RECTOR OF THE CATHE-DRAL FROM 1785 AND FROM 1795 TO 1829.

abolished import and export duties to encourage trade. He also ordered a census, which revealed that New Orleans had a population of almost 3,200 persons of all conditions and backgrounds. Perhaps most important of all, O'Reilly wisely left the customs of the local populace undisturbed, a practice which his followers would continue and build upon.

While generations of New Orleans school-children have been instilled with the notion that General O'Reilly was a cruel tyrant and have been taught to refer to him as Bloody O'Reilly, the evidence does not sup-

port such harsh reprobation. Indeed, contrary to popular belief, O'Reilly's handling of the revolutionaries and the several changes which he inaugurated laid the foundation for a greater degree of well-being and prosperity than ever previously enjoyed by Louisiana or its capital, New Orleans. During half a century of French rule, New Orleans and the majority of its people managed to do little more than survive. Under Spanish rule New Orleans and its people prospered as never before.

Realizing the importance of trade as a basis for any future prosperity, a blind eye was often turned to the colony's illicit commerce with the British in West Florida and towards smuggling in general. The incipient prosperity that resulted from this benign oversight was further advanced when the governor lowered duties on imports and exports, and initiated regulations that permitted trade with France and the French West Indies, and the duty-free purchase of slaves for a period of 10 years. These actions fostered a general improvement in the economy, which, in turn no doubt, contributed to the lessening of the tensions that initially existed between the local populace and the new Spanish authorities. In addition, any resentment the city's elite bore towards the Spanish for O'Reilly's punishment of the rebellion's leaders soon subsided as successive and successful leaders married into prominent local families.

Expansion: The nascent commerce that had been previously nurtured blossomed during the administration headed by General Don Esteban Rodriguez Miro. Great quanties of goods came down the river from the American settlers in the Ohio country and the Northwest Territory. As the transshipment port for these goods, New Orleans in the late 1780s was on the verge of an economic cycle of prosperity that would continue and expand, with only minor setbacks, for the next three-quarters of a century.

A census published during Miro's first year as governor revealed that the colony's population had almost doubled under the Spanish and that New Orleans had a population of about 5,000. To govern this population Miro issued a series of regulations entitled *Bando de Buen Gobierno*, or Proclamation of Good Government. Viewed from today's perspective, perhaps the most interesting of the Proclamation's strictures was one that forbade the wearing of finery by women of color and required that they cover their heads with a *tignon*, a local form of madras turban.

In 1788, New Orleans suffered the first of two catastrophic fires that taken together would destroy virtually all of the city that had been built by the French. The 1788 fire began in the early afternoon of Good Friday, March 21, when a candle on the altar of a private chapel in a home on Chartres Street

Street was the most notable and the only one that still stands today.

Under Miro's direction a program of rebuilding was quickly begun, and within months, public and private structures were rising from squares of charred desolation. Where formerly there had been a provincial French town, there arose a powerful Spanish town. Where there had been residences separated one from another, there now arose buildings joined by a common wall so that the appearance from the street was one of a continuous façade. Masonry rather than wood became more common as the principal building material and ceramic tile replaced

fell against some drapery. Because of a strong wind and the refusal of religious authorities to permit the ringing of church bells on Good Friday, fire fighters were not alerted quickly, and the fire was soon out of control. By evening between 800 and 900 structures had been consumed, with only a few buildings still standing along the river and on the western fringe of the town. Of these, the Ursuline Convent on Chartres

Left, the Spanish embarked on ambitious building schemes. **Above**, Ursuline Convent was the sole survivor of the 1788 fire.

shingles as a roofing material. Perhaps the most notable change was the introduction of an inner courtyard or patio into the plan.

The change in the city's appearance, which began with the rebuilding after the fire of 1788, continued under Miro's successor, François Louis Hector, Baron de Carondelet, who took office on January 1, 1792. Under Carondelet's leadership the economy of the colony and in particular its capital, New Orleans, continued to expand. An able administrator, Carondelet was responsible for a number of innovations and physical improvements that altered not only the city's appearance but also its social environment.

Among the most important of these initiatives were the establishment of a corps of armed and uniformed night watchmen to patrol the streets from dusk to dawn; the installation of oil lamps at street corners to facilitate night traffic; and the digging of a drainage canal from the rear of the city to Bayou St John. Later improvements to the canal, which followed the roadbed of present-day Lafitte Street, soon converted the canal to a major waterway for commercial traffic between the city, Lake Pontchartrain, and the eastern Gulf of Mexico. It would remain an important means of trans-

portation and commerce until well into the 20th century. Carondelet can also be credited with establishing and editing the colony's first newspaper, the *Moniteur de la Louisiana*. He gave his blessing to the colony's first theater, which opened in New Orleans during the fall of 1792. There was no question that the city was changing: what had been little more than a small town was becoming an urban and urbane place.

The revolutionary spirit that swept over France in the early 1790s not surprisingly evoked a sympathetic response in the French Creoles (i.e., persons descended from the original settlers) of New Orleans. These feelings finally boiled over in 1793 with the execution of Louis XVI and the declaration of war between Spain and France. In New Orleans, the singing of the "Marseillaise" and other revolutionary songs and talk of republicanism became commonplace. Fearing the worst, Carondelet issued a proclamation that forbade the singing of such songs, the reading or distribution of any printed materials about events in France, and even conversation on the subject.

For a time Carondelet was successful in suppressing anti-royalist and republican sentiments, but early in 1795 these feelings flared anew. Mobs roamed through the streets destroying property and shouting threats against Spanish officials. By forming an alliance with the local landowning and wealthier classes, Carondelet once more managed to dampen the revolutionary fervor. He also worked to enlarge these conservative classes by encouraging the nobility fleeing France to settle in the colony.

In 1794, on the Feast of the Immaculate Conception, December 8, New Orleans experienced a second major conflagration when children playing in a courtyard on Royal Street accidentally ignited some hay. A strong wind fanned the fire, and in a little over three hours, more than 200 buildings were destroyed. While fewer structures were lost than in the 1788 fire, the monetary loss was far greater. Determined to prevent such fires in the future, Carondelet instituted a building code with the requirement that all structures of more than one story in the built-up part of the city be constructed of adobe or brick and have tile roofs. While intended as fire prevention measures, these provisions hastened the changing appearance of New Orleans, which increasingly took on a Spanish flavor. The Cabildo and Presbytère, which flank the St Louis Cathedral in what is now Jackson Square, are prominent examples of Spanish-influenced buildings that were begun after the fire of 1794.

It would not be long, however, before time began to run out for the Spanish in Louisiana.

Above, Baron de Carondelet. Right, a Creole courtyard in stained glass.

The rise of Napoleon Bonaparte to First Consul of France was the impetus for the decline of the Spanish in Louisiana. Having consolidated his power at home, Napoleon turned his attention to the acquisition of an overseas empire. To this end he pressured Spain to cede Louisiana back to France.

While the retrocession was accomplished by the Treaty of San Ildefonso, which was signed on October 1, 1800, the actual transfer of control over the colony was postponed until the insurrection then raging in the French colony of Saint-Domingue could be quelled. The revolutionary ideas that Carondelet had so feared as potentially dangerous to the well-being and stability of Louisiana had, indeed, ignited a blood bath on the West Indian island that Napoleon regarded as essential to his plans for an overseas empire.

Word of the retrocession reached President Thomas Jefferson, who viewed French control of New Orleans as a threat to the essential egress of American goods produced in the upper valley. In an effort to avoid the necessity of having to seize the city, which some influential members of Congress increasingly favored, Jefferson sent Secretary of State James Monroe to approach the French about the purchase of New Orleans.

Even before Monroe arrived in Paris, Napoleon had determined that the colony could not be held and that it was in his best interest to sell not only New Orleans but all of Louisiana to the United States. Negotiations took a little over two weeks. In the end, a price equivalent to $15 million was agreed upon and official documents for the transactions, dated April 30, 1803, were signed during the first days of May.

Word of Louisiana's sale to the United States reached New Orleans in mid-August. The city's populace, already bewildered and

Preceding pages: procession of the "Mystick Krew of Comus." **Left**, raising the American flag in Jackson Square, 1803.

more than a little anxious in the contemplation of the colony's transfer to France, received the news with less than enthusiasm. The arrival of Napoleon's emissary, Pierre Clement de Laussat, in late March had stirred considerable anxiety.

In addition to the general apprehension which any citizenry might feel if faced with the prospect of such change, there were the more specific concerns of at least two important groups in the local community. The religious were fearful that Laussat might introduce the anti-Catholic measures then prevalent in France; indeed, the Ursulines were so panicked by the prospect that they left for Havana. Another group made uneasy by Laussat's arrival were the émigrés from the French Revolution who feared the imposition of republicanism, which they considered evil incarnate.

American transfer: If New Orleanians felt little or no enthusiasm for the idea of being governed by the United States, the new status at least relieved their foreboding over Laussat and a return to French rule. For his part, Laussat was chagrined. As the newly appointed Colonial Prefect of Louisiana, he had come to New Orleans to build an empire for France, and now, only months later, he learned that his assignment had been changed to that of liquidator for a major part of the empire. In accord with his new role, however, Laussat formally received the colony from Spain on November 30 and three weeks later transferred ownership to the United States.

In both ceremonies the signing of documents took place in the Sala Capitular, a large room on the second floor of the Cabildo, while the more public observances of changing flags and military salutes were performed in the Place d'Armes. In the first transfer, Governor Salcedo, assisted by the Marquis de Casa Calvo, represented Spain, and in the second, William C.C. Claiborne and General James Wilkinson represented the United States.

At the time of Louisiana's transfer to the

United States, New Orleans was a small, provincial town of just over 8,000 people with blacks accounting for slightly more than half of the population. More than half of the latter were slaves, but the number of free blacks was substantial. Creoles of French, African, and Spanish descent were in the majority, but there was also a significant element with other origins. Physically, the town consisted of about 1,300 structures situated almost entirely in the area that is today called the *Vieux Carré* or, more commonly, the French Quarter.

At the heart of the old town, facing the river across a large and mostly unkempt

square, then called the Place d'Armes, stood a twin-towered St Louis Cathedral flanked by a two-storied Cabildo and a partially constructed Presbytère. In addition to perhaps 10 commission houses, two or three small banks, and a half dozen general stores, there were numerous taverns, gambling houses, dance halls and billiard rooms.

The streets were unpaved, and what few sidewalks there were, were mainly of cypress planking. Open ditches flanking the street served as drains, but all too often they were clogged with garbage and unspeakable waste. Hard rains were the principal agent for flushing these ditches, but more often than not, they only inundated the streets and distributed the waste more widely. In dry weather clouds of dust coated everything and everyone with a layer of grime. When the stench became unbearable, and then only occasionally, slaves were put to work flushing the ditches.

On June 19, 1812, just seven weeks after Louisiana's admission to the Union, the United States declared war on Great Britain. For the next two and a half years the war would go badly for the United States with even its capital being sacked and burned in the fierce summer of 1814. However, except for a British blockade at the mouth of the Mississippi, Louisiana and New Orleans remained largely unaffected. Then, in the final weeks of the war, New Orleans became the scene of the only major American victory of the entire conflict.

Aware that the British were assembling a large force in Jamaica for a probable campaign against Louisiana, the Federal government in November, 1814, ordered General Andrew Jackson to proceed to New Orleans. Jackson arrived in the city with a small force on December 1, just nine days before a massive British fleet from Jamaica dropped anchor close to the entrance to Lake Borgne. Consisting of 50 vessels and an army of 10,000 troops under the command of General Sir Edward Pakenham, it was a force sufficient to give pause to even so undauntable a general as Jackson.

Pirates on pay: Since his arrival in the city, Jackson had worked feverishly to prepare a proper defense. He had ordered the immediate redeployment to New Orleans of troops in Baton Rouge, Natchez and Mobile; ordered the positioning of artillery at strategic approaches to the city; and ordered old fortifications strengthened and new ones built. With an offer of full pardons from the governor, he also enlisted the services of the notorious privateers Jean and Pierre Lafitte and several hundred of their followers.

On the morning of December 28, General Pakenham ordered a reconnaissance in force to test Jackson's defenses, but after suffering heavy casualties and making no gains, it retreated. Then on New Year's Day, the

Americans decided to celebrate the occasion with a full military review on the field behind their line. As bands played, various units of what may have been the strangest looking army ever assembled marched up and down, with banners flying. Consisting of general citizenry of all conditions and classes, regular army troops, ill-trained militiamen, free men of color of various shades, roughhewn privateers, and a few Indian warriors, it was a true panoply of American frontier democracy. In the middle of the ceremonies British cannon suddenly commenced a bombardment, and all turned to confusion as the ragtag ranks broke and everyone raced

shot and ball cut large swaths through the close ranks that continued without flinching to press forward. Finally, Jackson's riflemen opened a continuous fire that riddled the British ranks. Units dropped back and reformed and then moved forward once more. Suddenly, however, units began to break up as men turned and ran. Reportedly, Pakenham was riding forward to rally the troops when he was shot from his horse. It was at this point that British General John Lambert ordered a retreat that marked the end of the Battle of New Orleans.

Widely differing casualty figures have been given for the battle of January 8. A

helter-skelter back to the breastworks. Quickly overcoming their discombobulation, the Americans returned the fire and an artillery duel commenced. It inflicted very little damage on the American line and broke off about one o'clock when the British guns finally went silent.

At about six o'clock on the morning of January 8, British units in tight formation began a steady-paced advance on the American lines. American artillery firing grape-

Left, the Battle of New Orleans. **Above**, 10 duels in one day were once fought in City Park.

participant on the American side put American casualties at 71, including 13 dead. The British placed their dead at 858 and wounded at 2,468, with many missing. While authorities differ on specific figures, all have agreed that American losses were very small and British losses horrifically large. For the families of the British dead their loss must have seemed especially poignant. A peace treaty between Great Britain and the United States had been signed at Ghent, Belgium, on December 24 – two weeks before the battle.

Under United States sovereignty, New Orleans entered upon an era of extraordinary prosperity that would last, with only brief setbacks, for some 57 years. This prosperity and the expansion that it fueled were the result of several factors, the most important of which was the city's location at the entrance to the Mississippi River. Because the Mississippi and its tributaries during this period served as the primary means of commercial transportation for the vast Mississippi valley, and because virtually all goods entering or leaving had to pass through New Orleans, the city became a sort of tollhouse for the region. Arriving from upriver, the products of the valleys were reloaded at New Orleans to oceangoing vessels for shipment

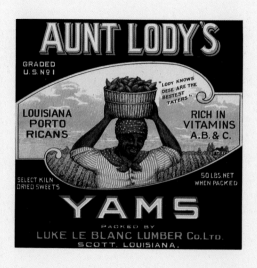

to the East Coast and Europe. Handling this transshipment required an army of factors, insurers, shippers, stevedores, and the like, with each extracting a toll.

Steamboat's a-comin': A second factor which contributed to the city's burgeoning economy was the advent of the steamboat. Up to 1812, shipping on the river was by keelboat and *radeau*, a form of flatboat, with propulsion by sail, oar, and pole. Such craft worked reasonably well when moving with the current, but were less than satisfactory when moving against it. The problem was solved by the coming of the steamboat,

which converted the great river from a one-way to a two-way artery of commerce. Although the steamboat failed to make New Orleans a major entry point for imports, it played a significant role in the city's becoming a port of entry for some half-million immigrants in the period before 1860. Ships carrying cotton, sugar, and other goods from New Orleans to such ports as Liverpool, Le Havre, and Hamburg quickly found a profitable return cargo in the Irish, French, and German immigrants seeking cheap passage to the promise of the New World. Only a few of these immigrants would remain in the city, the great majority journeying upriver in quest of cheap land and a new life. In doing so, they provided a profitable passenger market for steamboats returning upriver after depositing their cargoes in New Orleans.

While the number of European immigrants settling in the city remained relatively small in comparison to the number who passed through, it was sufficient, when coupled with the large influx of Anglo-Americans and their slaves, to quickly balloon the local population. Thus, the city's population grew from just over 8,000 in 1803 to 41,000 by 1820, and better than double again by 1840 to make the city the fourth largest in the nation. This growth in population would continue unabated up to the outbreak of the Civil War, with the 1860 census recording a populace of just over 168,000. Blacks by then no longer outnumbered whites as they had until 1830, but still remained a large segment of the total population that included about 11,000 slaves.

Although Anglo-Americans from across the South and East Coast constituted a majority in this great influx, there were other sizable groups, the most notable being the Irish, the Germans and, not least, the French. Where only a few years before there had been woods and bogs and plantation fields, roadways were now being cut, lots cleared, and buildings erected as landowners subdivided their properties which bordered on the original city.

Prior to the Louisiana Purchase, most New Orleans Creoles had had little contact with Anglo-Americans except for the rustics who arrived in the city by keel and flatboat. Having sold their cargoes these men, who were roughhewn by any standard, often spent at least a few days in rowdy carousing along the riverfront before departing for their upriver farms and communities. Not surprisingly, such individuals and their behavior left a not very flattering impression on the Creoles.

The Anglo-Americans who arrived in New Orleans after 1803 were, in the main, a very different lot. Businessmen, lawyers, doctors, bookkeepers, and such, they were the newly emerging American middle class, better educated and, of course, far more polished than their frontier countrymen. Almost to a man they had come to make their

ability to speak French impede their fulsome capacity to communicate their disdain for the locals and their ways. For their part the Creoles responded to real or fancied slights by the Americans much as any indigenous people might: with trepidation, diffidence, resentment, and occasional hostility. Conversely, courtesy, and friendliness on the part of an individual American usually elicited a like response from the average Creole.

French disdain: The French immigrants from the continent and Saint-Domingue regarded the local Creoles with as much or even more disdain than the Americans. To these Frenchmen the city's French Creoles

Left and **above**, Louisiana's burgeoning economy was influenced by the invention of steamboats.

fortunes in what was fast becoming the El Dorado of the American West. In brief, they were more given to industry and hustle than to drunken brawling.

Even so, for the Creoles these newcomers and especially their rapidly growing numbers posed a threat. To begin with, they didn't speak French or show the slightest inclination to learn how. *Mon Dieu*, on occasion they even voiced the opinion that it was a backward impediment! Nor did their in-

were bumpkins. But the Americans were the real threat to the city's Gallic culture, and the recognition of this fact by the two French-speaking groups quickly led to their alliance against the common enemy. Because the foreign French were generally better educated and more worldly than the "country" Creoles, they became the leaders of this particular alliance.

With this leadership the coalition soon became a political force in the city and state and for many years successfully promoted legislation favorable to its constituencies, while simultaneously thwarting American interests and ambitions. But time and circumstance were not on the Creoles' side. With each passing year more Americans came into the city and state, and as their number increased their power grew.

Signs of New Orleans' expanding prosperity were everywhere. In the early 1830s, Samuel J. Peters, a native of Canada, and some fellow entrepreneurs formed the New Orleans Canal and Banking Company to construct a canal from the rear of the newly emerging American enclave, centered around the suburb Faubourg Ste. Marie, to Lake Pontchartrain. Just as the Carondelet Canal served the commercial interests of the

Vieux Carré, the new canal would serve as a quick route to the American sector for lake and coastal steamers and luggers delivering cargoes of lumber and other building materials and agricultural products. The work of digging the canal, which had to traverse a vast cypress swamp, fell to newly arriving Irish immigrants who were desperate for work. In the process many thousands of them died of cholera, yellow fever, and malaria.

Less than a mile upriver from this new canal, American businessmen in 1833 incorporated three small hamlets to form the city of Lafayette. Here, those American businessmen, who made fortunes by brokering and shipping and otherwise handling the cotton, sugar, and other products that passed through the port, built palatial homes surrounded by lush gardens. Here, also, many of the poor Irish who worked on the new canal would live with their families of four and five and even more to a room in small cottages or tenements close by the river. For many years, Magazine Street served as the town's principal thoroughfare separating the Irish section, now called the Irish Channel, from the wealthier area which was eventually dubbed the Garden District, an appelation still used today.

Three cities in one: By the mid-1830s, American influence had grown to a point where it seriously challenged the power wielded by the coalition of foreign French and Creoles. An indication of this growing American power came in 1836 following a court case in which a Creole charged with killing an American in a duel was acquitted. Angered by the court's verdict and determined to break the coalition's control of the city council, the Americans persuaded the state legislature to withdraw the existing city charter and issue a new one dividing the city into three municipalities, each governed by its own board of aldermen and a recorder.

The new charter still provided for a single mayor and a city-wide board of aldermen composed of representatives from the three municipalities, but this fourth board was only authorized to regulate matters of interest to all three municipalities. Under this 1836 charter the old Vieux Carré became the First Municipality, the new American sector above Canal Street became the Second Municipality, while the Third Municipality was composed of all other areas of the city not included in the others.

A large and conspicuous segment of the local population that had no voice in the government of the city were the free people of color. They could not vote or hold office or serve on juries or in the militia. In general, however, they had more legal rights than free blacks in most other Southern states or even some Northern states. They did have access to the courts for redress, and they could own and bequeath property, including slaves.

While most were small tradesmen, more than a few were capable entrepreneurs and some amassed considerable fortunes.

While the laws were generally restrictive of the rights and privileges granted to free blacks, they were often not enforced. The famous quadroon balls that openly controverted a law prohibiting blacks from intermingling with whites in public places were an example of such permissiveness. (A quadroon is a person of mixed blood, one-quarter black.)

Laws governing slaves were if anything even more restrictive, but these, too, were seldom enforced. Thus, while the law pro-

how central this peculiar institution was to the city's commerce and culture were the slave auctions held annually during the late winter and early spring. The most famous of these were held in the great halls of the St Louis and St Charles hotels. Here dealers, speculators, merchants, and planters gathered to bid for slaves brought in from the various showrooms and holding barracks throughout the business district. In addition to these large annual auctions, by 1860 there were some two dozen slave markets in the city, which catered throughout the year to the needs of planters and others.

By the mid-1840s, New Orleans had be-

hibited slaves from owning or carrying guns, many did so with the full knowledge of their masters. There is also considerable evidence that, at least in New Orleans, free blacks and even many slaves were anything but obsequious or particularly submissive in their dealings with white people. More than one visitor to the city remarked on the sight of "impudent" slaves lolling in groups on street corners.

Perhaps the most poignant reminder of

Left, plantation slaves. Above, city store specializing in domestic servants.

come one of the nation's great cities. Indeed, if taken with the several communities that were then closely linked to it by rail and were soon to be annexed, it was one of the nation's first great metropolitan centers. Its streets and sidewalks were paved with cobble and flagstone, and illuminated by gas light, the latter having been introduced in 1834 by James Caldwell, an English actor, entrepreneur, and political leader in the American Second Municipality. Caldwell was also a leader in establishing the English-language theater in New Orleans with the erection of his American Theater in the Second Municipality. Illuminated by gas and seating 1,100, it easily rivaled the already well-established St Philips and Orleans theaters which catered to a primarily French-language audience in the First Municipality.

Further evidence of the Americans' growing leadership and dominance in the city came with the establishment in the Second Municipality of a public school system. Until then education of the city's young had been pretty much hit-and-miss, with a handful of small private and parochial schools or individual tutors providing instruction for children of the well-to-do. Based on a Massachusetts model, then considered the best in

stance of support for black education by any Southern state.

Perhaps the most conspicuous monuments to the city's affluence in the last two decades before the Civil War were its palatial hotels, which featured accommodations the equal of any in the world. Except for the St Louis Exchange Hotel, which was located in the Vieux Carré on the site of the present Omni Royal Orleans Hotel, all of the city's six or seven major hotels were in the commercial section of the American Second Municipality. The most famous was the St Charles, which stood on the site of the present Place St Charles office building.

the nation, the system was quickly adopted by the other municipalities.

Children of slaves and free people of color were excluded from the system and would have to wait another 25 years before war and Union occupation finally initiated the beginnings of public education for the city's blacks. In the meanwhile, a number of small private schools continued to educate children of the free blacks, and in 1847 a group of free blacks established a school for that community's indigent orphans. Shortly after its founding, the school received some state funding, which was probably the first in-

Built at the same time as the St Louis Exchange Hotel, it was regarded by contemporaries as an American response in the rivalry between the Anglo-Americans and the alliance of Creoles and foreign French.

That the Americans had gained the upper hand in this rivalry became patently obvious in 1852 when the city's three municipalities were reunited under a single board of aldermen and mayor. The newly built Second Municipality Hall (today called Gallier Hall) on Lafayette Square was chosen as the seat of the new city government. As if to cap their economic and political dominance, the

Americans, in 1857, captured the public's imagination with a Carnival parade that would serve as the model for all of the city's future pre-Lenten celebrations.

Carnival coup: Carnival had, of course, been celebrated in New Orleans since its earliest days by masked balls and public cavorting in the streets. During the Spanish period and the early years of American rule it had been discouraged because of rowdy behavior caused by prohibitions against masking. But these laws, like laws prohibiting rain, were not particularly effective. However, by the early 1850s, the celebration had become increasingly disorderly and se-

but very grand, effervescence by its old French heritage. Between 1847 and 1851 the *tout en somme* that centered on the old Place d'Armes in the Vieux Carré was completely refurbished and given the formal Second-Empire appearance that it retains today. The Cathedral was rebuilt, the Cabildo and Presbytère were heightened by the addition of mansard roofs, and the Pontalba apartment buildings were constructed on the up and down river sides of the square, which itself was enclosed with a fence and laid out as a formal garden. This magnificent reconstruction was given the name Jackson Square.

But even as the city reached its zenith in

Grand Ball of his Royal Highness, Rex, King of the Carnival, at Exposition Hall, February 25th.

rious consideration was once more being given to the possibility of outlawing it. Then on Mardi Gras night in 1857, a group of Americans calling themselves the Mistick Krewe of Comus put on a torchlight parade that recast carnival in the mode that it still follows today. The Americans had won not only the political and economic contest but the cultural contest as well.

Even as Anglo-American eminence was asserting itself, the city was treated to a final,

Left, invitation to the ball. **Above**, society celebrated in style.

the 1850s, the foundation of its prosperity and eminence had already been eroded for some two decades as a result of factors over which it had no control or, indeed, of which it was not even aware. This reversal of fortune had begun in the 1830s when the Erie Canal began to divert the commerce of the upper Midwest to the East and New York, but the loss was not at first noticeable. By the early 1850s, however, the railroads reached Chicago and the rate of such diversion to the East accelerated. New Orleans had lost its exclusive patent as the tollhouse of the great Mississippi Valley.

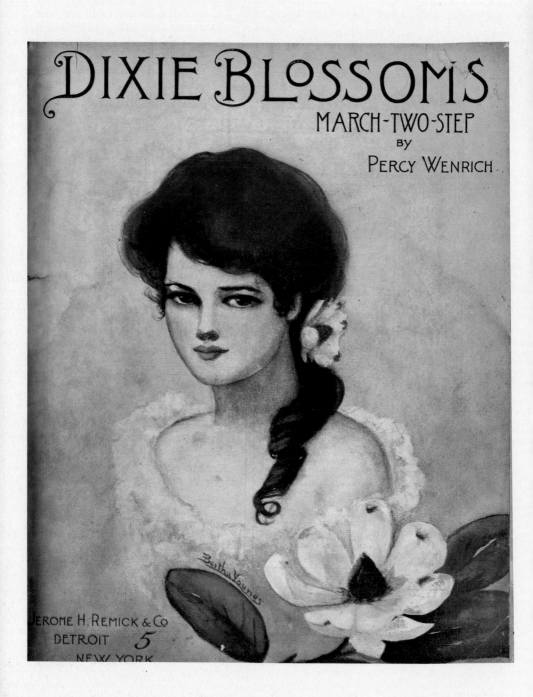

Historians and others initially blamed the Civil War for New Orleans' economic decline in the postwar years. In truth, the Civil War had little to do with this reversal of fortune. New Orleans, in fact, weathered the War Between the States far better than most Southern cities.

Many New Orleanians had little or no initial enthusiasm for the idea of secession from the United States of America. The city's merchants and bankers had strong economic and social ties to the North and were cool to the idea, as were the city's many German immigrants who certainly had more affection for their newly adopted country than for any theoretical Southern nation, especially one with slavery, which was anathema to them.

With Abraham Lincoln's selection as president, however, public sentiment began to shift. Urged on by such pro-secession leaders as Benjamin Morgan Palmer, firebrand pastor of the city's First Presbyterian Church, and the state's two senators, Judah P. Benjamin and John Slidell, the public quickly succumbed to secession fever, and on January 26, 1861, the state legislature adopted an Ordinance of Secession taking Louisiana out of the Union.

Sartorial rebels: In the weeks that followed, the city was alive with the talk of war and frenetic preparations for soldiering. Units were formed and open fields became parade grounds. Because there were no regulations governing uniforms at the time, the style, color, and cut of such garments usually reflected the taste of the well-to-do gentlemen who had decided to raise and lead the unit. The sartorial result was occasionally incongruous and often startling. The war's hostilities commenced on April 12 when a New Orleans Creole, General Pierre Gustave Toutant Beauregard, ordered the bombardment of Fort Sumter in Charleston Harbor.

Preceding pages: French Market and the Red Store, *circa* 1829–50. **Left**, the word "Dixie" originated in New Orleans.

New Orleans, however, would only begin to experience the war's effects six weeks later, when Federal naval forces blockaded the mouth of the Mississippi. Inflation set in, and economic chaos followed as prices soared and the value of money plummeted. But no further Federal action against the city occurred for almost 11 months.

Finally, toward the middle of April, 1862, word reached the city that a large Federal fleet had been sighted approaching forts Jackson and St Philip, some 66 miles below the city. News that an artillery duel had begun between the forts and the fleet kept the city in a state of near panic until April 24 when word came that the Federal fleet had run the gauntlet between the forts and was approaching the city. Pandemonium ruled. Realizing that the city could not be defended, local Confederate forces abandoned it, and with their departure chaos took over: warehouses were burned, boats were sunk at their moorings, and mobs roamed the streets looting and terrorizing the law-abiding.

With his fleet arrayed in the river in front of the city, local Flag Officer David G. Farragut demanded that the city be surrendered to the Yankees. To Farragut's surprise and probably chagrin, the mayor of New Orleans refused, and for the next several days there was a standoff. Farragut finally threatened to bombard the city, but then relented after meeting with a delegation of the city's foreign consuls. This *opéra bouffe* was finally resolved on May 1 when a large Federal force under the command of Major General Benjamin F. Butler landed and promptly arrested Mayor John F. Monroe.

In the days that followed, Federal troops were subjected to numerous insults by the women of New Orleans. By May 15, the situation had become intolerable and Butler issued his famous Order No. 28, which warned that any woman insulting a Federal officer or soldier could expect "to be treated as a woman of the town plying her vocation." The order apparently had the desired effect in New Orleans, but proved to be a public-relations blunder with politicians, preachers, and other social arbiters in Europe and the South calling it despotic and an affront to Southern womanhood. Three weeks later, Butler again came under a storm of criticism when he had William Mumford hanged from the portico of the US Mint in the Vieux Carré for tearing down a United States flag from the same building.

These incidents, and the fact that some of his officers profited from the sale of Confederate property seized under the Federal Confiscation Act, unleashed a storm of criticism of Butler. While Butler is still regarded by many New Orleanians as having been a

thoroughgoing scoundrel and ogre, historical evidence does not support such a judgment. There is evidence that Butler profited from some illicit dealings in hot cotton, but not that he stole any silver, a popular local legend which gave rise to the nickname "Silver Spoons" Butler. In truth, Butler kept a tight rein on his men, and there is no record of serious looting by his troops, such as occurred elsewhere in Louisiana under Generals Nathaniel P. Banks and Ulysses S. Grant. If anything, Butler's administration was honest, efficient and – when judged as a military occupation of an enemy city – mild.

On July 23, 1864, a state constitution was adopted which abolished slavery; established a public school system for all children regardless of race; and authorized the legislature to grant suffrage to individuals who paid taxes, had served in the military, or were intellectually qualified. This last, in effect, permitted the enfranchisement of blacks. The convention also adopted a resolution that allowed for its reconvening in the future. The first legislature to meet under the new constitution unanimously ratified the Thirteenth Amendment, which abolished slavery, but failed to enfranchise blacks.

Lieutenant Governor J. Madison Wells initially gained some favor with whites by his friendly attitude toward ex-Confederates. This attempt to curry favor with former soldiers backfired on Wells, however, when radical white Republicans and the Union Radical Association of mainly French-speaking Creole blacks refused to recognize his administration.

Asserting that Louisiana by its act of secession had lost its statehood and become a territory, these dissidents held a convention of their own and nominated Henry Clay Warmoth, a young man from Illinois, for territorial delegate to Congress. In the election that followed, blacks voted for the first time and to no one's surprise Warmoth, who ran unopposed, was elected. To almost everyone's surprise, however, Congress refused to recognize him. In the meanwhile ex-Confederates grew increasingly bold in their drive to regain power and exclude Radical Republicans, blacks, and former Unionists such as Wells from any role in city or state governance.

Alarmed by this growing assertiveness of the former Confederates and unhappy with Governor Wells, the Radicals called for the reconvening of the 1864 convention to revise the constitution. If the legislature would not enfranchise the blacks, the Radicals would do it by constitutional emendation. Called for July 30, 1866, at the Mechanics Institute, which stood where the Fairmont Hotel stands today on University Place, the convention itself was poorly attended, but attracted large throngs which milled about in the nearby streets.

The meeting began quietly enough at about 1 p.m., but almost immediately adjourned for an hour to collect absent members. Trouble began during the adjournment when a parade of blacks with an American flag and a band heading for the Mechanics Institute attempted to cross Canal Street. Hecklers in the crowd shouted taunts and catcalls and rowdies jostled several of the marchers. Suddenly two shots were fired and pandemonium followed; police and hooligans from the crowd charged the black marchers, who fled to the Mechanics Institute. For a time those in the building held the mob in the street at bay, but suddenly the

the latter. Following an investigation, General Sheridan placed the blame for the riot and killings on Mayor Monroe and Chief of Police Thomas E. Adams. Some months later a Congressional investigation came to much the same conclusion.

The rioters won the battle in New Orleans, but lost the war in Washington. Their actions furnished much of the impetus for the Reconstruction Acts, which Congress passed over President Andrew Johnson's veto in March, 1867. By these acts, Louisiana and other states of the former Confederacy were placed under military rule until new state constitutions could be fashioned to meet

barricaded doors were breached. Those inside were shot or clubbed even as they attempted surrender. Others, jumping from windows to escape, were quickly run down and shot or beaten senseless.

Federal troops from Jackson Barracks arrived to restore order sometime shortly after 3 o'clock, but by then the riot was over. Casualty figures vary slightly but an army report placed the number of wounded at 146 and the dead at 38, with blacks totaling 34 of

Left, Major General Benjamin F. Butler. **Above**, a funeral in the woods, 1860.

with Congressional approval. In New Orleans, General Sheridan, acting under this new authority removed a number of public officials including Mayor Monroe. He also replaced the governor and called for elections to authorize a constitutional convention and, if so authorized, to select delegates.

The vote for a constitutional convention was overwhelmingly favorable, and on November 23, 1867, the elected delegates were called to order at noon in the Mechanics Institute. Three and a half months later, on March 9, 1868, the convention adjourned after adopting a constitution that not only enfranchised the blacks, but contained civil rights clauses designed to prevent discrimination in a wide range of public activities. It also disenfranchised many of those who had been active in the Confederacy.

Realizing that the state's white Democrats would not willingly submit to rule by Radical Republicans and their black allies, Warmoth, now the new governor, got the legislature to create a police force that would be under his control. To do this the legislature combined the parishes (counties) of Orleans, Jefferson, and St Bernard into a Metropolitan Police District with a constabulary administered by a board appointed

lic corruption were, as the governor himself said, "the fashion."

Infighting over the spoils of office, and to a lesser extent philosophical differences, eventually led to an open split in the state's Republican party that pitted Warmoth and his followers against the Radical Republicans, both black and white. This resulted in numerous ugly disputes that came to a head during the election of 1872. Following a vicious campaign in which both sides committed all manner of election fraud, returning boards on each side claimed victory.

Two governors: The impasse remained, and on January 13, 1873, New Orleanians wit-

by the governor. It was, in effect, the origin of today's state police. The idea for such an agency was regarded at the time as progressive and was popular all across the country during the second half of the century. Under Warmoth's authority, however, it served mainly as an armed extension of the governor's office assuring Warmoth's control over the body politic and his own perpetuation in office.

While venality was no invention of Governor Warmoth or his administration, it certainly flowered during his tenure. Bribes, swindles, theft, and all other manner of pub-

nessed inaugurations for two governors. William Pitt Kellogg's inaugural ceremonies for the Radical Republicans began a little before noon in the Mechanics Institute, while John McEnery's commenced for the Democrat and Liberal Republicans about an hour later in Lafayette Square. *The Daily Picayune* covered both events, but its reportage left no doubt about its partiality. Under the headline "LEGAL GOVERNMENT IN LOUISIANA," it described McEnery's inauguration as a "great and propitious event" before "large and enthusiastic crowds." The Kellogg ceremonies, on the other hand, were reported as taking place in a "bayonet citadel on Dryades Street... surrounded by a dusky mob." Finally, on May 22, President Grant recognized Kellogg's government as the legal authority of Louisiana. Presidential recognition and the force that it represented, gave Kellogg's regime a degree of stability.

Two years later, Louisiana was once more treated to the spectacle of two inaugurations for the governorship, with Stephen B. Packard taking the oath at the St Louis Hotel and Francis T. Nicholls at St Patrick's Hall on Lafayette Square.

Nicholls immediately commissioned General Ogden's White League as the state's

too often, bloody clashes, they also witnessed an extraordinary physical expansion of New Orleans, in part at least, as a direct result of such strife. An example of this last was the 1870 annexation of Jefferson City, an incorporated town that extended above New Orleans between Toledano and Joseph streets. When the town's officials refused to recognize the authority of Governor Warmoth and his Metropolitan Police, the governor had the legislature enact a bill that redrew the boundaries of New Orleans to include the upriver community as well as the village of Algiers on the west bank of the Mississippi. This permitted Warmoth to ap-

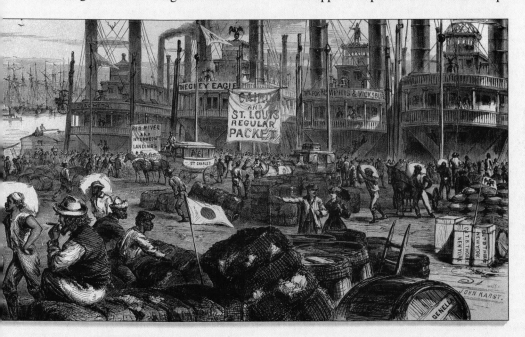

militia. These actions and President Grant's refusal to intervene resulted in a general desertion among Packard's followers and by late March his government was little more than a paper entity. The end of the Packard government came on April 24 when Federal troops guarding his statehouse were removed and Nicholls' government took possession of the building. Reconstruction in Louisiana had ended.

While these closing years of Reconstruction were marked by civic acrimony and, all

Left and **above**, the first and last port of call.

point any officials necessitated by the incorporation. Four years later, the city again expanded when it annexed the town of Carrollton, a short distance upriver from what had been Jefferson City. The erosion of the city's economic base, which began in the 1840s and '50s with the diversion of upper valley commerce via the Erie Canal and railroads, was accelerated by the war and the postwar boom in Northern railroad building. By the end of Reconstruction the impact of this economic realignment was painfully apparent throughout much of New Orleans, where business was at a standstill and much of the population was unemployed and in utter despair.

During the 1880s, however, the city began to experience a quickening in its commercial life. This upturn resulted from several factors, the most important being the growth of foreign trade through the port and the emergence of the city as a major distribution center for the South. The first of these, the growth in foreign trade, was made possible by the construction of jetties at the river's mouth during the late 1870s. A few years later in the early 1880s, railroads linked New Orleans with the rest of the nation for the first time, and the economic synergism that re-

sulted from these two forces gave the city a greater prosperity than it had experienced in almost a quarter of a century of industry.

The local economy was further buoyed during these years by a steady growth in the cotton and sugar industries. As the nation's leading center for the distribution of these commodities, the city extracted a percentage of the value from every bale of cotton and hogshead of sugar that its pressers, refiners, factors, insurers, shippers, and army of laborers handled. Further sustaining this economy were the city's numerous foundries, mills, machine shops, cooperages, and

similar prosperous manufactories that created and maintained much of the equipage used by these industries.

Not surprisingly, this quickening of commercial activity stimulated a degree of optimism in the business community that hadn't been felt since the halcyon years of the late 1850s. New Orleans was not alone in this new found buoyancy which, under the catchphrase the "New South" was then enjoying much currency in the counting rooms of the region. In New Orleans, its leading exponent was Major E. A. Burke, railroad executive, state treasurer, and flamboyant editor of the city's *Times-Democrat* newspaper. More than anything else, Burke's remarkable gift of the gab persuaded the city's business and political leadership that their financial salvation – indeed prosperity – lay in a world's fair. With such assurances Burke managed to garner about $2 million in loans and gifts from federal, state, and city governments, and corporate sponsors.

Unfortunately, incompetent management and Burke's ever more grandiose expansion of the project quickly consumed most of the original capital so that the fair was all but bankrupt when it opened belatedly and largely unfinished on December 17, 1884, as The World's Industrial and Cotton Centennial Exposition.

While the opening day's ceremonies attracted a crowd of about 14,000, attendance thereafter dropped off precipitously. Press reports about its numerous shortcomings and unfinished condition were no doubt responsible for a large part of this decline, but Burke's overly optimistic projections had created expectations beyond any possible fulfillment. In any event, the poor attendance contributed significantly to a $500,000 debt when it finally closed on June 1, 1885, with only about one quarter of the originally projected attendance.

Like so many grandiose schemes before and since, the New Orleans exposition of 1884–85 ended as a failure. Above and beyond its large debt, it accomplished none of the goals promised by its promoters. It brought no significant new industry to the city and stimulated no noticeable increase in port activity. Nor is the popular assertion that it stimulated residential development in the upriver path to its site persuasive. In a city where high and dry land was scarce and mainly in the natural levee adjacent to the river, a growing population made such development inevitable. The exposition did have a legacy, however, but it was one which its promoters did not anticipate, and which none would recognize at the time. Indeed, it would only become apparent many years after the exposition had long since been forgotten by most of the citizenry.

This other America: That legacy was tourism, or more specifically, the tourist industry. The city had attracted a steady trickle of visitors since the 18th century, but these had been mostly wealthy individuals in search of the exotic, and their fleeting presence had no impact on the city. The exposition would mark the beginning of middle-class or mass tourism, a phenomenon that would eventually, in our own time, affect the city and its unique culture.

Actually, the inception of mass tourism in New Orleans evolved from a combination of factors with the exposition as a catalyst. Bored by a fair that promised much but delivered little, journalists sent to cover the event turned instead to writing about the city itself and its notably different culture. A spate of articles describing the quaint old city and its unusual ways soon appeared in Northern newspapers and national journals where they aroused the curiosity of a burgeoning middle class just then beginning to enjoy paid vacations and the pleasure of travel. New Orleans would experience no immediate surge of tourists as a result, but the message had gone out about "this other America," a strange, exotic place, unlike anywhere else in the country, and what had been a trickle of visitors increased to a steady flow that grew substantially with each passing year.

The city still had problems, however. The establishment in Louisiana of legalized racial segregation in the last decade of the century had great consequences for New Orleans and, indeed, the nation over the long

Left and <u>above</u>, trade expositions introduced New Orleans to early tourists.

term. Ironically, the legal sanctioning of segregation resulted from a challenge by a New Orleans Creole of color to the state's Jim Crow law requiring separate seating arrangements on trains.

Throughout most of the 1870s and '80s, political parties and factions of all stripe courted the black vote, but in 1890 the political winds in Louisiana shifted when the state legislature passed an act requiring separate accommodations for blacks and whites on railroads operating within the state. It was this law that Homer Adolph Plessy, the New Orleans Creole of color deliberately challenged when he took a seat in a "whites only"

car of an excursion train in the early summer of 1892. Plessy was summarily arrested, tried, and convicted of violating the state's separate accommodations law. Four years later on appeal to the United States Supreme Court, Plessy's conviction was sustained in a ruling that came to be known as the "separate but equal" doctrine.

It was this doctrine that would serve as the legal foundation for segregation in New Orleans and the rest of the South for the next 60 years. It would also serve as a stimulus for the disenfranchisement and all but complete removal of blacks from any part in the political process. This was accomplished by the state Constitutional Convention of 1898, which included property and educational qualifications that effectively removed or barred most blacks from the voter registration rolls. To prevent the disenfranchisement of the many whites who did not possess such qualifications, the Convention confected the notorious "Grandfather Clause" whereby an individual was exempt from such requirements if he, his father, or grandfather had been entitled to vote before January 1, 1867. The cruel irony in all of this is that it was largely the work of dedicated reformers who almost certainly believed that their actions

tion resulted in considerable notoriety at the time and is today very much remembered by romantic New Orleanians.

Storyville: In an attempt to control prostitution, which was then boisterously unrestrained and city-wide, the Flower administration in 1897 enacted an ordinance that restricted such activity to a relatively small area of about twenty city blocks located just beyond the city's old French Quarter. Nicknamed Storyville, much to the chagrin of Sidney Story, the silk-stocking councilman who authored the restrictive ordinance, the district flourished for some two decades, during which its fame became worldwide.

were genuine reforms and in the best interest of the city and state.

Many of the same individuals had been prominent in the Citizens League, a reform group that had been the driving force behind the 1896 election of Mayor Walter C. Flower, a well-to-do cotton broker. Flower's major accomplishment in office was the reorganization of city government under a new charter and the establishment of a civil service system for municipal employees. While these and other reforms enacted by Mayor Flower have long since been forgotten, at least one reform of the Flower administra-

Indeed, in an attempt to satisfy the erotic inclinations of visiting men who flocked to the district, directories, known generically as "Blue Books," were issued with names and addresses of individual prostitutes and illustrated advertisements with none too subtle texts for the more fashionable establishments. These are much prized by collectors today whose passion for such items often approaches the veneration accorded relics during the Middle Ages.

Above, Storyville ladies. **Right**, detail from the painting the *Absinthe House*.

ABSINTHE

Oscar Wilde apparently said of it: "After the first glass, you see things as you wish they were; after the second, you see things as they are not; finally, you see things as they really are, and that is the most horrible thing in the world."

The liquid to which Wilde was referring was absinthe, the fashionable yellow-green, dangerously potent liqueur whose hallucinogenic qualities produced some of the most influential art of our time. Manet's *Absinthe Drinker* and Degas's *L'Absinth* are testaments to its intensity. Van Gogh, it is said, was introduced to it by Toulouse-Lautrec; one of his drinking buddies was fellow artist Gauguin. Picasso was highly influenced by absinthe during "the Blue Period" and later produced his sculpture *The Glass of Absinthe.*

Absinthe was a bitter drink, with an alcoholic strength of about 19 over proof, made of aromatic herbs that grew on the slopes of the Swiss Alps, such as aniseed, liquorice, coriander, and fennel. Its essential component was the herb wormwood, which induced a curious, dreamy state of intoxication appreciated by artists and fashionable society. Absinthe's commercial appeal was recognized by Henri Louis Pernod, who, in 1805, built a factory in France and began to export it.

The drink soon caught on in New Orleans, the "Paris of North America." Its appeal was confirmed when the Juncadella mansion on Bourbon Street was turned into a coffeehouse. The bartender hired was a Spaniard from Barcelona, Cayetano Ferrér, who had already achieved recognition among the *bon ton* of local society for his skills in the bar of the old French Opera House. In 1874, when Ferrér became the leaseholder of the French Quarter mansion, the name of the coffeehouse was changed to the "Absinthe Room," in honor of his most popular drink. The fame of the refreshment parlor grew, and the entire Ferrér family joined in to serve growing numbers of customers. The name was changed again, this time to "The Old Absinthe House."

The establishment's centerpiece was a long bar, with a fountain that slowly dripped water into the spirit glasses. This approximated the French method of serving the liqueur, which was to pour, drop by drop, about 2½ ounces of water into every ounce glass of absinthe. Water added slowly turned the green liquid the desired shade of yellow; water added quickly produced an inferior, less dry, taste.

Even in the latter case, the spirit was too dry for some customers, usually women. As a sweetner, water was dripped over a lump of sugar before mixing with the spirit. The sugar was placed on a special spoon that rested on the rim of the glass. These perforated spoons, "absinthe spoons," are now much in vogue as collectors' items.

The drink was celebrated in many parts of the US, with New Orleans playing a leading role. To cope with the searing summer heat, it was often served as a frappé. Absinthe's fame was repeated in France, where the cocktail hour became known as *l'heure verte*, in honor of the liqueur's distinctive color. But the drink's notoriety also grew. Wormwood was addictive, and the drink's image suffered due to its proximity to drug-related crimes. In 1905, a Swiss farmer named Jean Lanfray shot his two daughters, his wife, and then attempted to shoot himself. It was heard at his trial that Lanfray had earlier drunk six quarters of wine, six brandies, and two absinthes. The judge ruled that the farmer was suffering from "absinthe-induced delirium." Lanfray subsequently hanged himself in jail.

This scandal was the turning point. The drink was banned – in Switzerland in 1905 and by ruling of the United States Senate in 1912. To counter the attack, outraged members of the New Orleans Absinthe Association devised a legal alternative, which they produced for 22 years after the ban.

Today, the clear-colored pernod and pastis are recognized as weaker substitutes to absinthe, its wormwood element long removed. The Old Absinthe House on Bourbon Street is still a popular watering hole, although the drinks it now dispenses are less heady than in previous years. The original bar, its marble pitted by water marks from the dripping faucet, is located in another tavern farther down Bourbon Street.

New Orleans in the early years of the 20th century saw changes that would forever affect its future. The emergence of jazz as the city's distinctive contribution to American culture, the construction of a drainage system that converted a swamp to reasonably dry ground, and an end to the only legalized prostitution district in the nation were landmark events. The drive to save historic buildings in the French Quarter also began in these early years.

Jazz came of age during the era of Storyville, the legalized prostitution district created by city ordinance in 1897. For another 20 years, New Orleans-born musicians like King Oliver, Louis Armstrong, and Jelly Roll Morton would play in the taverns around the city and in some of the bawdy houses that made up this rough and rowdy area around Basin Street. Storyville came to an end during World War I, closed down by the Secretary of the Navy when military authorities complained. But by that time jazz had already made its way upriver to St Louis and Chicago. Prostitution, though illegal, survived in houses run by well-known madams into the 1950s, but open prostitution was no longer the best-known characteristic of the city.

In the swim: In the early 1900s, New Orleans, which is below sea level, was still a swamp. It suffered constant flooding, even in the French Quarter, which is on relatively high ground. Famous restaurants in the French Quarter frequently had to close their doors because of water in the dining rooms. But in 1913, a young engineer and authentic genius, A. Baldwin Hood, invented the pumps that lifted the city out of the mud. Defying the existing laws of hydraulics, the miraculous machines were called the Wood Screw Pumps. Using these powerful pumps to lift the water, the city's Sewerage and Water Board constructed an underground

Preceding pages: Canal Street crowds. <u>Left</u>, the original streetcar named Desire. <u>Right</u>, the Saint Charles Hotel.

drainage system with more than 120 miles of canals carrying the water to Lake Pontchartrain. It became the world's largest draining system and was copied by the Dutch, who bought Wood pumps to drain their Zuider Zee. Today, the city has possibly more miles of canals than Venice.

Local projects were put on hold in New Orleans as elsewhere in the country after April 16, 1917, when the US declared war on Germany. World War I had begun. Ameri-

can involvement in the war, however, was so brief that, even though American troops were trained at military institutions in New Orleans and Louisiana and war materials were shipped through the port, the war had no overwhelming impact on the city.

The 141st Field Artillery of New Orleans, one of the country's oldest and most famous artillery units, sailed for France on August 26, 1918, but never saw action. The regiment was in Brittany when, less than three months later, the troops got word that the Armistice had been signed.

It was after World War I, in the 1920s, that

private citizens began an effort to save the French Quarter. By the 1920s, the Vieux Carré had become a slum. The old Creole families, descendants of the early French and Spanish settlers, had long since moved out. Poor Italian immigrants crowded into the 18th-century townhouses and cottages that formed the historic district. The famous Pontalba Buildings on Jackson Square were decaying apartment blocks. Centuries-old buildings were being bulldozed for parking lots. Iron grillework was being pulled off historic buildings and sold.

A fledgling preservation movement began in the 1920s as private citizens sought some

way to halt the destruction. Finally, in 1936, a state constitutional amendment created the Vieux Carré Commission with broad police powers to protect buildings of architectural and historic value. It was the first commission of its kind in the United States.

The Works Progress Administration, a federal agency President Franklin Roosevelt created to provide jobs during the nation's Depression, contributed to the reclamation of the Vieux Carré. It restored the Pontalba Buildings and the French Market in the late 1930s. Even the city's businessman-mayor, Robert Maestri, backed the preservation movement. Maestri, a millionaire with little formal education, was not impressed by history, but he did love the French Quarter. Maestri was of Italian descent, and by that time the Quarter had become known as "Little Italy." Besides, New Orleanians needed the jobs the WPA projects provided.

Roosevelt poured federal money into New Orleans after Louisiana's best-known governor, Huey P. Long, was assassinated in September, 1935. Long, elected governor as the Depression loomed in 1928, was a savior to some and a tyrant to others. He became a threat to Roosevelt after becoming a US senator, attacking Roosevelt and advocating his "Share The Wealth" program. Many thought he would run for President. New Orleans was a center of anti-Long sentiment, but the family cast a long, important shadow over local politics for years to come.

Maestri, a rough-cut diamond, was immortalized in New Orleans political lore with one story. President Roosevelt visited New Orleans in 1937 and was honored at a luncheon at Antoine's restaurant. As the president feasted on Antoine's famous dish, Oysters Rockefeller, Maestri turned to the president and asked, "How ya like dem ersters?" Many older New Orleanians still pronounce "oysters" as "ersters" and "oil" as "erl." It is a dialect that sounds quite like the one often heard in Brooklyn, New York.

War stops carnival: World War II galvanized the city from December 7, 1941, the day the Japanese attacked Pearl Harbor, to V-J Day, when the Japanese signed surrender documents on September 2, 1945. Because of New Orleans' exposed position as a port city, army troops were moved into the city to protect highways, water purification plants, and other vital facilities on the Sunday the Japanese struck Pearl Harbor. German submarines operated in the Gulf of Mexico, south of New Orleans in 1942, sinking 12 allied ships in one month. Mardi Gras was cancelled for only the third time in 115 years. Rationing, war work, and air raid drills became a way of life in the city. Over 5,000 servicemen from Louisiana died or were killed in action during the war.

Mardi Gras and Louisiana-style politics resumed with the war's end. A dashing young Army colonel, Chep Morrison, home from the war, ended Mayor Maestri's 10-year reign. He returned just in time to become the reform candidate for mayor. With a group of women spearheading the reform movement, Morrison was elected mayor in an upset victory in 1946. He would remain in office until 1961, when President John Kennedy appointed him Ambassador to the Organization of American States.

In those 16 years, New Orleans became a modern city. With construction funds up during World War II, Morrison consolidated railroad lines to bring them into one terminal and constructed overpasses and underpasses into the 1950s. Lavish gambling houses flourished in adjacent parishes. Another scar on Morrison's record was his failure to provide protection for the handful of black children who integrated two New Orleans public schools under court order in 1960. Unruly crowds gathered at the schools and harassed federal marshals as they marched the children into the schools.

Nevertheless, Morrison changed the face and the outlook of New Orleans. He brought the city into the 20th century. After his wife, Corinne, died in 1959, he was also a source of constant gossip. He was a ladies' man and among his conquests, if only for a time, was

to move traffic over the remaining tracks. He introduced modern planning methods to city government, launched a youth recreation program that became a model for the nation, and built a new City Hall as part of a governmental complex on Loyola Avenue.

Morrison was not a die-hard reformer. His police department was corrupt. Illegal lotteries, scattered houses of prostitution, and racehorse handbook operations continued

Left, Maison Blanche: "the leading and most progressive department store in the South." Above, St Charles Avenue palms are now gone.

Zsa Zsa Gabor, the Hungarian beauty and Hollywood jet-setter. They were immediately attracted to each other when Zsa Zsa went to City Hall to receive a key to the city on a visit to New Orleans in 1959. Zsa Zsa later said she was in love with Morrison, but he was not rich enough to marry. Morrison died on May 23, 1964, when a private plane carrying him, a woman friend, his young son, and her son crashed into a Mexican mountainside. All passengers were killed.

Victor H. Schiro, the city's second mayor of Italian descent, was named to succeed Morrison in 1961, and later was elected to two terms in office. He distinguished his first year in office by providing police protection for children entering integrated public schools. It was also Schiro who first put forth the idea for the Superdome, the mushroom-shaped structure that marks the city's skyline and attracts major sports events like the Sugar Bowl. Schiro brought forth the idea as a campaign gimmick when he ran for his second term in 1966.

It was during the Schiro administration that Poydras Street, now the city's main business thoroughfare, was widened and paved. The street is now lined with the city's major skyscrapers. Most of these newer

would have damaged the historic district irreparably. Visitors to New Orleans unknowingly benefit from that decision and honor Schiro's successor, Maurice Landrieu, when they visit the Moonwalk on the Mississippi River just across from Jackson Square. Landrieu changed his name legally to his nickname "Moon," when he entered the political arena. Landrieu succeeded Schiro in 1970.

The Moonwalk was the first project of the young administration. The walk, giving visitors and local citizens access to the river, was first of all just a dirt pathway with a few street lights. With federal money, the present im-

buildings went up during the boom years of the oil and gas industry in Louisiana in the late 1970s and early 1980s. Some of the plushest buildings have few tenants now that oil prices have plummeted and the entire industry is depressed.

New Orleans saw another preservation movement around this time that benefited the French Quarter. Again, it was private citizens who led the movement. With court suits and protests, they blocked construction of an elevated expressway that would have run along the riverfront in the Quarter. Even its advocates now agree the expressway

posing stairway was built, the walkway was improved, and the Moonwalk became a New Orleans landmark. Landrieu also established the pedestrian mall around Jackson Square. He was the first mayor to fully realize the potential of the tourist industry. Landrieu's other enduring legacy was bringing black citizens into full participation in city government. He had been elected with a solid black vote. He brought blacks into decision-making jobs in City Hall for the first time.

With the growing black population and voter registration in the city, blacks elected one of their own with the help of a segment of the white business establishment in 1978. Ernest N. Morial, known by his nickname, "Dutch," became the city's first black mayor in May, 1978. An appeals court judge and a leader in New Orleans' civil rights movement, Morial was the first mayor to have to confront the city's declining revenue base. One of his attempts to diversify the city's economy was the establishment of an industrial district that is just now beginning to develop in eastern New Orleans.

He also emphasized tourism and the French Quarter. Brass plaques on the sidewalks of the Quarter bear Ernest Morial's name. They commemorate a large

Besides fond memories for local citizens, the fair is credited with many local improvements made in the fever of enthusiasm that took place in the year before it officially opened. It had residual benefits. Among them are some luxury hotels, including the world-class and very English Windsor Court, the Riverwalk market, the extremely successful Convention Center, and the attractive pedestrian malls leading to the riverfront fair site.

Morial died suddenly and dramatically on Christmas Eve, 1989, as he was leaving a friend's home where he had been watching football on television. He suffered a heart

paving and sidewalk-construction campaign done to prepare the Quarter for the expected influx of visitors during the New Orleans world's fair in 1984. The fair, held at the site now occupied by the Riverwalk marketplace on the Mississippi River, failed to attract large numbers of visitors nationwide. It was a financial flop, but an enormous success with local citizens, who bought tickets and visited it repeatedly for its jazz music, its Cajun dancing, and its Italian Village.

Left, movies like *The Big Easy* kept the city in the public eye. **Above**, even GIs go for Dixie beer.

attack brought on by an asthma attack. Black leaders from all over the nation joined the Morial family, the city's political community, and thousands of his followers for the funeral march and the funeral mass at St Louis Cathedral. A dynamic but somewhat abrasive man, Morial remains a beloved figure in the black community and achieved a grudging respect in the white community as his accomplishments were recalled at the time of his death.

A city councilman and former state senator, Sidney Barthelemy, became the city's second black mayor with a landslide vote and support from the white community in 1986. He won a second term in 1990. Along with other mayors around the United States, Barthelemy struggled with the city's financial problems and with a spiraling increase in crime. But he promoted the city's riverfront developments, including the Aquarium of the Americas and the adjacent Woldenberg Park on the riverfront. He backed a third expansion of the extremely successful Convention Center near the river as well as a European-style gambling casino. New Orleans has now become a major tourist and convention city, even outside the month of Mardi Gras.

Movie mystique: The tourist and convention industry has helped sustain the city through its economic slump resulting from the near collapse of the state's oil and gas industry. Tourism leaders see boom years ahead. Movies like *The Big Easy*, which deals with police corruption, and *Blaze*, the story of former Louisiana Governor Earl Long's affair with a strip-tease artist starring Paul Newman as Long, have created a new mystique for the state and its largest city. Part of the Oliver Stone movie *JFK*, telling the story of a New Orleans district attorney's investigation into the assassination of President John Fitzgerald Kennedy, was filmed in New Orleans.

New Orleans today suffers from the problems that plague most American cities along with its own economic recession. But it remains a city that tourists enjoy and local residents love. A drive or streetcar ride up St Charles Avenue or a stroll through the French Market are as popular with natives as with visitors. Mardi Gras and the spring Jazz Fest are considered largely local events, although they attract visitors from all over the world. New Orleanians are inveterate diners-out and are harsh critics of restaurants that fail to meet their standards.

Dedicated New Orleanians often say New Orleans is a good city to visit, but it's even better to live there. It is this blend of tourist and local support that they believe will protect their city through its hard times – and perhaps for another 200 years.

Right, Cajun band at a local nightspot.

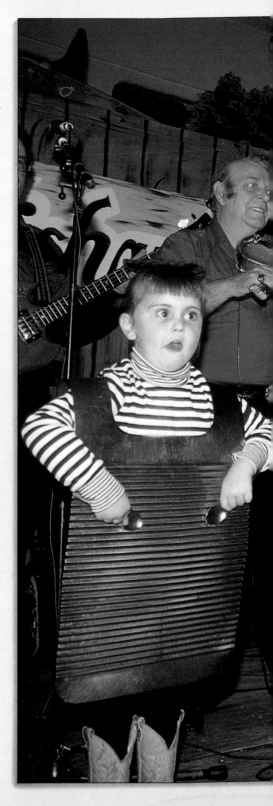

As a Carnival town, New Orleans is often called the City that Care Forgot. Politically, it might be characterized as the City that Forgot to Care. But that's not quite true. This is a city that cares, but in its own way.

Food, football, and politics are the major topics of conversation in New Orleans, though not necessarily in that order. Locals tend to regard all three as popular sports, though food is usually the only one they participate in personally. Politics remains essentially a spectator sport; its ups and downs are followed and commented upon by the general populace, but it isn't of sufficient interest to warrant the direct involvement of the man or woman in the street. The lack of grandiose displays of grassroots actions or attitudes in New Orleans may be a symptom of the city's diffuse character. There are many strongly identifiable racial and ethnic backgrounds: Cajun, Creole, African, French, English, Spanish, German, and Italian. But even within these groups there is little history of concerted community action.

The many different factions, and their frictions with other groups and with each other, are part of the reason that the author A.J. Liebling back in the 1950s called Louisiana "the westernmost of the Arab states," and compared the politics of New Orleans with those of Beirut. From politics to social clubs, it's not part of the local character to unite – or at least not to stay united for very long – in a common cause. Rather, it is part of the New Orleans tradition for members of a group to squabble among themselves, and then for some of the members to break away and form their own rival group.

Breakaway groups: In recent years, these breakaways have led New Orleans to have two groups of zoo supporters, two opera guilds, two ballet companies, two cancer societies, and more splintered political factions than anyone could care to count. Even the family connections for which New Orleans is known – people who work for Uncle Wardell or with Cousin Bubba – often fracture to the point that brothers and cousins end up operating competing restaurants or working for competing political fiefdoms.

This diffusion is natural in a metropolitan area that is itself administratively and politically divided, with three principal parishes making up what is generally known as New Orleans. Orleans Parish is the city proper, with a black majority population. St Bernard

and Jefferson parishes are predominantly white suburbs whose residents work in the city but pay few taxes for its support.

Because of the widespread skepticism toward politicians, people in New Orleans typically try to give them as little money to spend as possible. Some say New Orleanians simply hate to pay taxes, but it would be more accurate to say New Orleanians hate to give their money to politicians. While the United States grew out of the notion that there should be no taxation without representation, New Orleans seems to believe that the ideal political situation is representation

Left, former governor Huey P. Long. **Right,** Paul Newman as Earl Long in *Blaze*.

without taxation. Candidates that propose even modest tax increases, no matter how badly more money is needed for the public coffers, do not get elected in New Orleans.

In recent years, various exemptions have allowed up to three-fourths of the local homeowners to avoid paying any property taxes at all, even though the assessments are among the lowest of any major US city. In any given year, the local tax bills for people in New Orleans are likely to be one-third of those for the residents of Boston or Chicago.

Perhaps this is because taxation is historically connected with power, and New Orleanians are suspect of political power.

The fact that there are six publicly funded police forces and five different government agencies that cut the grass, provides comforting reassurance that no one is really in control. Some of this mistrust of power must date back to the days of Huey Long, the self-styled "Kingfish" who was elected governor of Louisiana in 1927 and erected what has been described as the closest thing to a dictatorship in American history. The Kingfish was a populist who spoke to and for the little people. Under his motto, "Every man a king," Long improved the roads, built hospitals, provided free school books for children,

and expanded social welfare programs.

Long, who also served as a US senator from Louisiana, also had another motto, "*L'Etat, c'est Huey.*" During his heyday, Long put a brutal hold on the processes of democracy in Louisiana through his vast political patronage system. It wasn't enough for a fellow Democrat under Huey to be broadly loyal; to get a job, or keep one, Democrats had to prove their loyalty again and again, in terms of time and money and whatever else the Kingfish required. He brooked absolutely no opposition or dissension, no matter how well-intentioned.

Here's a classic example of the way the Kingfish operated. In 1935, he approached Frank Costello, a New York gangster, and invited Costello to bring slot machines into New Orleans. The Kingfish promised no interference from local authorities. In exchange, Costello had to split the profits of the illegal gambling with Long, who planned to use the money to provide more welfare programs for the blind and disabled. The slot machines did come in, but only lasted a few months: Long was shot and killed later in 1935 by the son-in-law of a political opponent, a man who had been denied a job.

Huey Long, age 42 when he died, continued to cast a long shadow over Louisiana politics, even as his younger and more colorful brother Earl took up the populist mantle and served three terms as governor. Earl Long, immortalized in Liebling's fascinating book *The Earl of Louisiana*, once got into a fight with a political opponent in an elevator and almost bit the other man's ear off.

Like his brother, Earl Long used unorthodox methods to achieve his often laudable goals, and both brothers were given to making offhand segregationist remarks to white crowds while promoting programs to help blacks. Earl Long once found the state legislature reluctant to approve his recommendations for better health-care facilities in black areas, so he made an issue out of the fact that some blacks and whites were being treated under the same clinic roofs. The legislature promptly approved the money for more black facilities and staff.

Earl Long, reputed to holler, "That's a damn lie!" to deny his very public extramarital affair with the stripper Blaze Starr, showed signs of insanity in his later years in life, apparently due to a series of small strokes. At one point, state officials acting with the blessing of his wife, Miz Blanche, committed Earl Long to a state mental hospital. But a lawyer-crony went to court to seek his release, and the Earl, still the governor, fired the state officials who might have testified that he was indeed crazy. The Long legacy continued in Louisiana politics, most notably in the form of Huey's son Russell, a long-serving and influential US senator who was known for populist stands but also for serving special interests such as the oil, gas,

contributor to the economy in Breaux' district and also to his own campaign funds. A reporter asked Breaux if this act meant his vote could be bought. The congressman said no, but "it can be rented."

The more liberal strains of the Long legacy have not been totally lost in New Orleans, however. Hale Boggs, the popular US House Majority Leader killed in a 1972 plane crash, and his wife Lindy, who succeeded him and held his congressional seat for nearly two decades before stepping down, were both New Orleans politicians known for their honesty, integrity, and humanity. Other noted city politicians included

sugar, and shipbuilding industries.

More recent examples of the Louisiana style in national politics can be seen in politicians such as John Breaux, a Democratic congressman who voted with the Republicans when then-President Reagan made broad social services cuts in the federal budget. It was widely known that Breaux had been won over by the Reagan administration's promises of price supports that would help the sugar industry, which was a great

a pair of mayors in the 1970s and '80s, Moon Landrieu and Ernest "Dutch" Morial, the city's first black mayor. Their administrations did much to revitalize New Orleans.

But Landrieu and Morial, like subsequent mayors, were and continue to be handicapped by New Orleans' haphazard system of financing its public services. Over the past 100 years, some agencies have been deemed by the state government to be too important to leave to the local New Orleans politicians, so they were established outside City Hall.

An example is the Sewerage and Water Board, whose duties include keeping the

Left, Earl K. Long served three terms as Louisiana's governor. Above, Long with JFK.

water out of a city that was built below sea level. Because the board raises its own money through a separate property tax not connected with the city's general operating funds, it has had plenty of money in recent years – none of which it wants to share for other city services. The Sewerage and Water Board had enough money to build itself a modern new headquarters that some liken to the offices of a prosperous brokerage firm. City Hall, meanwhile, remained a dusty and musty edifice of worn carpets, leaky pipes, and broken air conditioning.

The revenues for New Orleans' general city spending increased by barely 3 percent

between 1985 and 1992, a period when an increase 10 times that would not have been able to maintain services. As a result, services and payroll have been trimmed. Twenty percent fewer people work for the city today than in 1985. The few agencies with money are the ones that have been able, one way or another, to persuade city fathers to allow them to follow the Sewerage and Water Board example of having their "dedicated" tax revenues reserved for their use alone.

The city Recreation Department, on the other hand, has had its requests for budget increases rejected repeatedly by voters in

recent years. When funds for the Society for the Prevention of Cruelty to Animals were slashed to the point that New Orleans no longer had dogcatchers to collect strays, the SPCA said it might have to ask volunteer patrols of young men with rifles to hunt down the growing packs of semi-wild dogs.

New Orleans has a thriving charity scene, but it can take a lot for its residents to dig into their pockets. When Maxim Shostakovich, son of the late Russian composer Dmitri Shostakovich, resigned after five years as music director of the New Orleans Symphony, he said he hadn't been paid in a year. He received a standing ovation at his last concert, but no one organized a fund drive to raise money to keep him in his position.

Like other troubled US cities, many of New Orleans' civic money woes in the 1990s were precipitated by the federal government in the 1980s. A number of key city programs that were once funded by the federal government are suffering because of budget cuts imposed during the Reagan years. Local health care, for instance, has deteriorated to the point that syphilis is a near epidemic, and there is not enough staff to promote or carry out routine check-ups for children. Nearly half the kindergarten children entering New Orleans public schools have not had the standard immunization shots – free at local clinics, when staff is available – for common childhood diseases such as measles.

About 90 percent of the children in New Orleans public schools are black. Whites generally send their children to private schools, though a new program of higher-caliber "magnet" public schools is aimed at drawing white families back to the state educational system. While historically a city where blacks and whites often mixed more closely than in some supposedly liberal cities of the north, New Orleans changed when the federal government began building huge public-housing complexes. The "projects," as they are known, turned areas such as Desire, Lafitte, and Iberville into harsh urban ghettoes where local whites dread to tread. On the other hand, the city has entire neighborhoods dominated by a black professional and managerial class. Whites and blacks still mix fairly easily throughout New

Orleans, however, and a visitor would be hard-pressed to find any sign of racism among the casual everyday throngs of upper middle-class whites from the Garden District and blacks from the nearby housing projects who literally rub shoulders as they fill their trolleys at the big Winn-Dixie grocery store at the end of St Charles Street.

But race is still a simmering political issue for some. The symbol of the white backlash for much of the city is David Duke, the yuppie state legislator from the suburbs. Once a high-ranking Ku Klux Klan leader, Duke has tempered his rhetoric by using thinly-coded statements about "welfare,"

delay a decision so they can have a big meal at the city's expense before going home. As S. Frederick Starr noted in his humorous and revealingly affectionate book, *New Orleans Unmasqued*, this is a city where the people throw parties for politicians who are sent to jail, and then re-elect them when they get paroled. It's a city that sells more formal wear and fewer copies of the *New York Times* per capita than perhaps any other US metropolis. It is a hedonistic town, where flood, fires, disease, hurricanes, and politicians have all taken a turn inflicting their own peculiar brand of damage. It is a town where economic equality is elusive, but

"drug abuse," and "quotas" to build a following among whites who oppose affirmative action hiring and any government welfare program helping the black community.

For the most part, however, New Orleans remains a city of tolerance – tolerance for three Sazerac cocktails and a dozen oysters before lunch, tolerance for streets full of potholes, tolerance for sometimes brutal heat and humidity, tolerance for jurors who

Left, the city has little money to fund dogcatchers. **Above**, high-profile politician David Duke was once a high-ranking KKK member.

many blacks eagerly put aside any injustices to join in the whites' tradition of dressing up and marching down Canal Street with their floats every Shrove Tuesday.

Most New Orleanians share the attitude of Louis Armstrong, born in the city in 1900, who said he had seen too many of those famous brass-band funerals – a dirge on the way to the cemetery, a joyous blast of upbeat jazz on the way back – to be afraid of anything that might happen tomorrow. After all, no matter what tomorrow brings, everyone in New Orleans knows there's going to be another big party next year.

There are rituals and there are ritual watchers. Just who and how many get to watch which ritual is part of the complexity of New Orleans' Carnival celebration, a festival so deep in social significance that ritual watching and observing the ritual watchers can become rituals in themselves.

"I like Carnival because it extends the good mood left over from Christmas," says the captain of a group known as the Phunny Phorty Phellows. That this person is identified here by a title rather than a name is yet another part of the ritual because in the New Orleans Carnival, tradition has it that Carnival organizations are headed by a captain whose identity remains secret. Most of the organizations have their kings and queens, but the captain is, like the president, the real hand of power.

In her wisdom the captain hit upon a fundamental truth about the New Orleans Carnival, a truth that will be missed by most casual visitors: New Orleans, unlike most of the rest of the world, does not suffer from post-Christmas letdown because Twelfth Night (January 6), the date given by tradition as the last day of Christmas, is also the first day of the Carnival season.

Fat Tuesday: That first day, however, is not what the world has come to associate with Carnival. Instead, it is the Carnival season's last day – a movable date that was tailored by Christianity in order to put some religious significance to the pagan tendency to celebrate the arrival of spring. The Catholic church gave the celebration a spot on the calendar and a message. The spot was the day before Ash Wednesday, which is the first day of the solemn season of Lent. The message was essentially to celebrate today, for tomorrow you fast. Because this day was to be one of feasting it came to be known as Fat Tuesday or, as the French would call it, Mardi Gras.

Preceding pages: Mardi Gras monarchy; French Quarter festivities; cloaked in secrecy. **Left**, the Rex parade. **Right**, bejeweled beauty.

New Orleans, founded by the French, adopted this celebration with vigor. Ironically, as the church became more lax about its rules for Lenten sacrifice, the city began to experience the best of both worlds. New Orleans still celebrated the coming of the season of penance, but without having to do the penance. The city became adept at the feasting without the fasting.

For most people the most visual manifestation of Carnival is the parade. During the

two and a half weeks that precede Fat Tuesday, there are parades throughout the metropolitan area, with the best and biggest winding their way through the city's business district almost daily. The period from the Saturday before Mardi Gras through midnight of the big day is in effect a four-day weekend. During the late morning and early afternoon of Mardi Gras, the central event is the parade of Rex, King of Carnival. That night the season is drawn to a close as the group that began the parading tradition back in 1857, the Mystick Krewe of Comus, stages its procession. By midnight it is all over and the police are clearing the streets. Lent begins with the sanitation workers and cleanup crews doing their penance.

Although the parades and revelry of the season's last days are what most visitors will watch, this is like staring at a mask without fully seeing what is behind it. For most locals the Carnival season affects them in many different ways through many different rituals. Behind the mask, there are stories to be told. And Southerners love stories.

For some, these begin as early in the season as Twelfth Night. On that evening a group known as the Twelfth Night Revelers stages its carnival ball – traditionally the first

gets the slice containing the object is "King" or, as appropriate, "Queen," and has to buy the next king cake. At the ball of the Revelers, the cake takes on a more symbolic importance. Each of the slices has a silver bean in it, except for one, in which the bean is gold. The girl who receives that slice is the Queen of the ball and thus one of the first monarchs of the year.

"I grew up with it and I enjoy it," says the captain of one of the oldest (founded in 1884) high-society groups, the Krewe of Proteus. While the newer, less socially connected organizations tend to have fewer restrictions on their membership, the old

of the major society balls of the season. At one point in the ceremony a wooden cake is presented and each of the year's debutantes is served a wooden slice. This gesture is supposed to represent the eating of New Orleans King Cake, a flat, oblong Carnival confection sometimes covered with icing and sprinklings of colored sugar, which is big business for local bakeries.

Baked into the cake is an object, perhaps a bean, maybe a small porcelain doll, but most often a tiny plastic baby. King cakes are served at parties and in offices throughout the season, the tradition being that whoever

groups remain connected to old family names. In this man's case, participation in Carnival is part of his family heritage, which he himself has enriched. Besides being captain of a group he has received two of the highest honors that Carnival society can give, having been chosen at different times to be Rex, King of Carnival, and Comus, the whimsical god whose parade is the oldest.

There are approximately 40 Carnival balls held throughout the season, of which only a few are those of high society. At some of the balls the purpose clearly is to have fun, but at those of the nobility the main business is the presentation of debutantes and the perpetuation of the debutante tradition. To society watchers the Carnival season is not merely watching parades, but also watching the society pages of the daily newspaper, *The Times-Picayune*, to see which families were best able to snare the crowns for their daughters. Huey Long, the former governor, once spoke of his vision of "Every man a king." It may be that for some the truer ambition is every daughter a queen.

Those rituals of the Twelfth Night Revelers are performed before a relatively small group of people, in black tie and evening dress, who are there by invitation

through uptown New Orleans and into the business district. Banners hung from each side proclaim that "It's Carnival Time!" The Storyville Stompers, a traditional jazz band, is on board to provide music for the Phellows who have somehow mastered the ability to dance in the narrow aisle of a moving streetcar while in costume.

Early in the ride two king cakes are served: one to the male members and the other to the females. In the tradition of the Twelfth Night Revelers, those who get the slice with the foreign object become the Queen and the Boss (the Phellows' equivalent of King). Here the similarity ends, for these Phellows

only. Elsewhere, on the same evening another group will be staging its traditions in front of anyone who happens to be in its path. This is the Phunny Phorty Phellows, a reincarnation of a 19th-century Carnival group, who, these days, are not all fellows, not always 40 in number, although, sometimes, they are funny.

Their tradition is to charter one of the city's streetcars and announce the season's arrival. The trolley waddles along its path

Left, Diamond Man. **Above**, the Golden Age Carnival ball.

are not members of high society, but just folks out to glorify the trolley, the city, and its Carnival. "I also like Mardi Gras," the captain says, "because it is good for the city." She might add that it is also good for the spirit.

"I like Carnival for the spirit of it," says Maureen Detweiller, the special events coordinator for the city of New Orleans. "These are ancient rituals that we can still experience. There are not many things like that around today."

Purity, like virtue, faces many temptations. Carnival in its purist form shuns commercialism. To date, however, that bit of purity has been better preserved within the city than in the suburban areas where financially-troubled parading groups have sought corporate bailouts. Within the city, though, it is illegal for a parade to have visible commercial sponsorship. That applies to the participating vehicles and units within the parade as well. Those rules make the New Orleans celebration all the more attractive because it may be the only major festival in the world in which the costs are the burden of the participants and not that of the spectators, business, or government.

City Hall does assume the expense for

backing or the emotional commitment. Yet, where tradition stands, it is a fortress. Thus, according to the laws of tradition, all riders on Carnival floats must remain masked; the identity of the kings of several groups remains secret, as does that of the captain; there shall be no commercial advertising; and Carnival organizations are known as "krewes." There are more rules, many more. Some are unique to particular krewes; some just try to preserve, for one night at least, old-world manners, such as the proper way for a debutante to walk when being presented at the ball. No one takes the ceremonies so seriously that the ritual and pretense tran-

police, fire, and sanitation overtime, but those costs are easily justified by the dollars in sales tax that the event generates each year. They call it "The Greatest Free Show on Earth" and while that may be a bit of an overstatement there is something about Carnival that runs contrary to capitalist values. It is like a tranquil island in a sea of sharks.

The Carnival is governed by a basic code of law – it's called tradition. Those who care about Carnival the most worry about the erosion of tradition, especially as Carnival parades have been quickly imitated in the surrounding areas, but without the historic

scends into the real world. It is like wearing a mask, only to return to normality once it is taken off again.

But, oh, when the mask is on! "I like Mardi Gras because I can dress up and be anything I want to be," says Kathleen Joffrion, a local art director and artist. Joffrion, who in daily life has a penchant for fashionable dressing, creates her own makeshift costumes for Mardi Gras. One year her costume was based on an aqua-colored satin swimsuit worn over

<u>Above</u>, society in the swim. <u>Right</u>, Big Chief of the 9th Ward Hunters.

MARDI GRAS INDIANS

From late spring until Fat Tuesday of the next year, they scrimp and save, sew and weave to create – by hand – the ornate costumes of their rank and tribe. They are the Indians, the Mardi Gras Indians, and they form one of the most colorful subgroups within New Orleans' black community. The members of these "tribes" live in inner-city black neighborhoods and generally come from poor or working-class backgrounds. They spend enormous amounts of time, money, and effort to participate in distinctive neighborhood "gangs" that go by such names as Golden Blades, Yellow Pocahontas, and Creole Wild West.

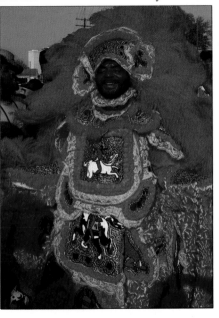

Both the intricate and elaborate bead work associated with the costumes of the uptown tribes, and the dazzling, more modern, sequined designs of the downtown gangs represent months of sewing. Tribe members often put aside other responsibilities in order to devote themselves wholly to fashioning their "suits." The designs, many drawn from magazine pictures of Native American clothing, are sanctified, literally, by their sweat.

The culmination of the months of work is when the "beautiful" Big Chief emerges from his house along with the members of his tribe on Mardi Gras morning, resplendent in a colorful headdress and hand-sewn suit that represents the Chief's most complete statement of visual cachet. His raiment is a dazzling challenge to that of every other Big Chief in New Orleans.

He'll be judged as the "prettiest," or not *as* pretty by the other chiefs he encounters, by the gang members who also "mask" in dazzling costumes, and by the neighborhood followers who celebrate the Indians as symbolically representing the dignity of all the residents of the black inner-city neighborhoods. Indeed, the Big Chief himself is most often from the workaday world of the longshoreman, warehouseman, bartender, hotel cook, taxi driver, or seaman.

The Big Chiefs and their Indian tribes have paraded through the byways of New Orleans' black culture since at least the 1890s (some say much earlier). The tradition reaches back to old and lost languages, back to a remembered or imagined tribal dignity, back to old values of courage and bravery, and back to non-Western concepts of male beauty, where the regal male plumage overshadows that of the female.

From 8 a.m. when the Big Chief comes out of his house until nightfall, the streets fill with the music of the chief and his gang. Everyone keeps rhythm with bottles, combs, sticks, tambourines, and drums, and second lines (a New Orleans tradition, meaning to follow the parade) with traditional responses to the leaders' chanting of dozens of well-known song lines from a vast oral repertoire that is as much a part of the shared black culture as the most familiar gospel refrains.

The rhythm sources are based on West African drumming and dancing. Although to unfamiliar ears the chants are rough-edged and unshapely, Indian songs and rhythms have been an important influence on New Orleans' jazz, rhythm and blues, and popular music at least since the 1930s, with a number of traditional Indian songs entering the popular recorded music repertoire.

In 1972, Bo Dollis, one of the most famous and most talented Big Chiefs, recorded an album of traditional Indian songs called *The Wild Magnolias*. He was backed up by the popular group the Meters. A few years later, the Neville Brothers recorded *The Wild Tchoupitoulas* with members of that particular tribe. Numerous other New Orleans recording artists before and since have recorded or alluded to the Indian songs, and various Indian groups are now a staple feature each year at the Jazz & Heritage Festival.

Come Mardi Gras, the invigorating chants and shouts are heard throughout the neighborhoods, in the streets, from balconies, and in and near the barrooms. The Indians sing and flaunt their finery until dark, when the spy boys, flag boys and, yes, even the Big Chiefs themselves, footsore, their necks and shoulders aching from the weight of their elaborate head-dresses, their voices hoarse, their eyes bloodshot from drink and lack of sleep, make their weary way home to re-emerge on Ash Wednesday in the working-class livery of the everyday world.

pink tights. Around her neck she wore a gold lamé clown collar, and to round off her outfit she had a pyramid-shaped hot pink cap, feathered butterfly wings, and yellow rubber gloves. On her feet were tap shoes. What was she supposed to be? "I don't know," she answered, "that's just what I had lying around the house."

As the story goes, the date that the French first arrived in the vicinity of what would be the city of New Orleans was March 3, 1699. It just so happened that this date was Mardi Gras of that year; so it can be said with some accuracy that from the moment the French arrived there has been Mardi Gras. With a history that is so ancient, at least by American standards, plenty of memorabilia relating to Carnival can be found around the houses of New Orleanians. This can include scrapbooks of family heritage as well as scraps of costumes. It includes yellowed family albums with pictures of the kids in their first Mardi Gras costumes or of relatives all dressed up for the one night they went to the ball.

Not all that is precious to Carnival is ancient. Carnival sometimes needs to bend with the breeze, adapt to the climate. Some innovations have managed to do this and still maintain the dignity of the past. In the early 1970s, two new krewes, Endymion and Bacchus, began to attract large crowds, both creating larger and more spectacular parades. Few groups have parade floats as innovative as those of Bacchus; no parade, perhaps none in the world, is as large as Endymion's, which has over 1,000 members. In 1987, the Lundi Gras celebration was created at which Rex, supported by music and fireworks, arrives by river to begin his reign on the day before Mardi Gras.

But what makes it all special, what makes the New Orleans Carnival different from being just another group of passing parades, is that loyalty to the past, preservation of tradition, appreciation for ritual. To those who really understand Carnival the season can be like a king cake – the fascination is not so much in the sugar coating, but in what is hidden inside.

<u>**Right**</u>, field of vision.

The conversations one most often overhears in New Orleans restaurants are not about politics or sport – they are about food.

Joe Cahn, director of the New Orleans School of Cooking, sums up the local attitude towards dining. He says, "In south Louisiana, food is not looked upon as nourishment, but as a wonderful way of life. We want to say 'Wow!' with every bite; to clap and cheer and make noises. With food, nobody is ever wrong, for it is the only thing in the world in which everybody is allowed to have a personal taste. To us, food is not only on the plate: it is also in the heart."

The key to enjoying New Orleans food is realizing that it is a separate cuisine, distinct from other American styles of cooking. It is very different even from traditional Southern cooking. New Orleans' Creole and Cajun food is America's most fully evolved regional cuisine; thick, worthy books were written on the subject over a century ago. These styles have long dominated local cuisine and probably always will. The differences between the two types of cooking can be summed up in one phrase: Creole is city; Cajun is country.

Rouxful cooking: Creole dishes feature rich, creamy sauces made with a *roux* and can be found in most restaurants. The fare served up under the name "Cajun," however, is likely to be a substitute for the real thing. Cajun food is typically cooked in a pot, slung together with ingredients to hand, extremely tasty – and very ugly. Too unattractive for diners paying lots of money, restaurateurs feel, and so the tendency is to dress the dishes up with superior ingredients, possibly improving the taste but diminishing the authenticity in the process.

All of this is changing, anyway. Cajun cooking of a sort *is* moving to the city, and Creole food is far spicier than it used to be, a tip passed on from its country cousin. In fact,

Preceding pages: muffuletta men. **Left**, Paul Prudhomme of K-Paul's Louisiana Kitchen. **Right**, drinks on the half shell.

the two styles have merged so successfully in the past few years that Paul Prudhomme, owner and celebrity chef of K-Paul's Louisiana Kitchen, calls this blended local cooking "Louisiana food," and leaves it at that.

Two indispensable elements of Creole-Cajun cooking are local to the southeastern part of the state. First are the great raw materials, especially seafood. Crawfish (only marine biologists and Yankees pronounce it "crayfish") exist in populations so

large that they are often shoveled into sacks right off the shore by lovers of shellfish.

The second essential element is the collective local taste. All Orleanians eat Creole-Cajun every day, to the near-exclusion of other styles of food. This is the taste which began with the original French settlers and was later modified by their Spanish successors. The hands-on practitioners of the art of Creole cooking have almost always been black – so the food shows a heavy Caribbean influence as well.

Creole-Cajun food is potent. There's more pepper, especially red pepper, than in other

American dishes. But beyond that there is an intensity of flavor from generous mixtures of salt, cream, butter, garlic, and herbs. An extremely common starting point in Creole-Cajun cooking is cooking "the holy trinity" in a *roux*. The trinity consists of onions, bell peppers, and celery; the *roux* is a blend of flour and some kind of oil.

But New Orleans cooking is never static. Some restaurants now dare to use no *roux* in any of their dishes – a policy that would have been considered heresy 10 years ago. An identifiable "nouvelle Creole" style has emerged, much lighter than the traditional cooking, but with flavors still intact.

look for excellent gumbo are the Gumbo Shop, Bozo's, and Bruning's.

Another popular, low-priced dish is jambalaya (pronounced *jum-bo-lie-ya*). Served on top of yellow rice, the best jambalaya consists of anything in the kitchen: sausage, vegetables, spices and, of course, seafood, dished up all together. Gumbo's only main rival in the soup department is turtle soup. Creole turtle soup is a far cry from the clear broth made with the chelonian elsewhere. Instead, it's a thick, chunky affair, powerfully flavored with lemon, cloves, *roux*, and the holy trinity.

The hardest decision one is faced with is

The most emblematic dish of Creole-Cajun cuisine may well be gumbo. The name comes from an African word for okra – a frequently used ingredient in the gumbo pot. The okra is mixed with all kinds of shellfish, sausages, and poultry. It is somewhere between a thick soup and a thin stew and lends itself to endless variation.

Most gumbo can be categorized as either seafood gumbo or chicken gumbo, although there are lots of hybrids. Many are thickened with a dark *roux*. Some of the best gumbo in New Orleans is "gumbo ya-ya," served at the restaurant called Mr. B's. Other places to

whether to begin a New Orleans meal with oysters, shrimp, or crab. (This is compounded in the spring, when crawfish are around too.) Raw oysters on the half shell are still easy to find, despite decimation of the oyster beds and some question about the healthiness of eating raw shellfish. The great oyster bars are those at Bozo's and the Acme Oyster House. Here you can stand and down the bivalves as they're opened, to the accompaniment of cold beer.

Oysters are also the subject of much creativity in the kitchen. Three oyster dishes in particular are worth trying. Oysters

Rockefeller were invented a century ago at Antoine's restaurant, where they're still delicious. The sauce is a mélange of puréed greens tinged with anise. Oysters *en brochette* are broiled or fried with bacon on skewers, then moistened with browned butter; this is a favorite at Galatoire's. The third great oyster speciality is found mostly in Italian restaurants, always under different names but always locally described as being "something like oysters Mosca." Here the oysters are baked in a drift of bread crumbs, garlic, olive oil, and herbs. The best are at Mosca's and La Riviera.

On the entrée lists of New Orleans restau-

overly "fishy." Pompano is best cooked with a minimum of fuss. Avoid *pompano en papillote*, in which the fish's flavors are overwhelmed by a thick sauce with several other seafoods in it, all baked in a paper bag that waiters love to open at the table. Also be wary of anything that even smacks of blackened fish. New Orleans' most famous culinary export can be delicious (as it is at K-Paul's, Brigtsen's, and a few other places) but it's usually terrible, a victim of crass commercialization.

A number of restaurants deftly grill fish over open wood fires, but usually it is fried. Even New Orleans classics like *trout*

rants seafood is king. A decimation of the city's two most popular fin-fish species – speckled trout and redfish – led to the popularization of a host of other superb Gulf fish: wahoo, *mahi-mahi*, red snapper, amberjack, grouper, flounder, puppy drum, mako shark, and yellowfin tuna, to name a few.

Arguably the best fish available from the waters near New Orleans is pompano. It has a smooth, textured, light gray flesh with just enough oil to make it rich without seeming

meunière are more often than not fried. So are soft-shell crabs, a marvelous local delicacy. Big specimens abound in the spring and summer, but soft-shells are almost always available fresh. You may run into soft-shell crawfish during the appropriate season, but these are almost always more interesting than good.

Crawfish in its more familiar guises is a far better treat. The two most familiar preparations with crawfish are as a thick, chunky bisque or *etouffée* (smothered with a light, spicy sauce) over rice. But during crawfish season (roughly Thanksgiving through the

Left, local labels from another era. **Above**, Arnaud's restaurant.

Fourth of July, with a peak in late April) the tail meat of these mini-lobsters is used in almost every imaginable way. The streets are literally strewn with the vivid orange/pink shells, cast away by outdoor diners and hunted down by stray cats.

Most crawfish are served in their whole form, boiled to a peppery distinction. Boiled crawfish is the apex of shirtsleeves Cajun gourmandise. Gigantic mounds are polished off by men, women, and children of every social stripe, leaving behind smaller mounds of shells and abandoned corn cobs. Even to the uninitiated, this activity quickly turns into a passion. The best places to indulge in

head and shells on (do not order them where the shells are removed) in a sauce of butter, black pepper, and a little garlic. It's a real mess to eat, but an unforgettable taste.

The city's strengths in the seafood department do not obviate red meat or poultry dishes. In fact, New Orleans is one of the best towns in America in which to eat a steak, taking a back seat to few other places. Prime beef is the rule, and the standard local way of serving a steak is with a bubbling butter-and-parsley sauce.

Recipes featuring chicken, duck, quail, and other birds all have their Creole versions. The most traditional of them is

boiled crawfish are Bozo's and Bruning's. All these places also turn out fine boiled shrimp and crabs, too.

The Gulf of Mexico near New Orleans is the source of most of the shrimp eaten in America. Eating shrimp here is like eating lobster in Maine: the best and freshest never get far from home. The premier Creole shrimp dish is barbecue shrimp – a complete misnomer, since there is no smoked aspect to the dish. It is the creation of the restaurant Pascal's Manale, whose cuisine exemplifies the merger of Creole and Italian styles. Barbecue shrimps are gigantic, cooked with the

chicken *bonne femme* – a roasted chicken covered with potatoes, onions, and garlic. This is at its best at Tujaque's and Antoine's. At Mosca's, they serve a superb platter of roasted chicken with all the garlic and olive oil you always wanted, but nobody would ever give you before.

Not all New Orleans' cuisine comes from restaurants. One of the most delicious "street foods" is a muffuletta, a sandwich extravaganza of Italian meats and cheeses, lavishly spread with olive salad stuffed between seeded buns the size of dinner plates. Near the French Market in the Quarter, several

Italian delis engage in friendly competition for the "original" or the "best" muffuletta. Another good lunchtime snack is the "po-boy," a submarine-shaped sandwich prepared on French bread and served "dressed" with a variety of meats – alligator is popular – and cheeses.

The classic New Orleans dessert is bread pudding. This is not the poor man's dessert one finds in most of America, but a rich confection with custard and cinnamon. As with gumbo, bread pudding has as many different forms and tastes as there are chefs who make it, but a few stand out. The bread pudding soufflé at Commander's Palace is in

by mules, of the Roman Candy Man. In 1915, Sam Cortese introduced New Orleanians to the taffy-like confection his family made in Italy, and it and they have been here ever since.

The essential adjunct to any New Orleans dessert is the dense coffee with chicory that Orleanians prefer. The chicory – originally a cheap herb extender of precious coffee, now added for its own distinctive taste – coats the sides of a mug with a visible, almost palpable, brown layer. In the cafés in the French Market, the coffee is cut with an equal amount of hot milk, yet it still packs a potent punch. This is always accompanied by a

a class by itself. The puddings at Arnaud's and Mr. B's, while more down-to-earth, are first-class.

New Orleans is also known for its handmade candies. In season, the fresh strawberries dipped in dark, or even white, chocolate are guaranteed to put on the calories. A perfect souvenir is a box of pralines (pronounced praw-leens), a sweet patty made with sugar, water, and nuts, with several variations available. One of the most common sights in the city is the white cart, driven

Left and **above**, Cajun cookin'.

beignet (pronounced *bin-yea*), a square-shaped pastry, like a doughnut without the hole, sprinkled with powdered sugar.

Wine lists in restaurants around town continue to improve. Consistently the best is that of Brennan's, which features lots of old vintages – especially Burgundys – sold at prices on the low side. Antoine's also has an extensive, reasonably priced cellar, strong on French wines. Commander's Palace led New Orleans into its appreciation of California wines and still maintains a fine list of them, along with a substantial array of French bottles. The Windsor Court Grill

Room has bought several private collections over the years and has a list full of rarities. Andrea's had the first decent collection of Italian wines in the area, and they still maintain an interesting selection. New Orleans' definitive wine bar, with some 50 wines offered by the glass, is Flagons, which is also a good nouvelle-Creole bistro.

The first cocktail: As the town that once did a roaring trade in the production of absinthe (*see box on page 59*), drink is no stranger to these famed streets. Pat O'Brien's, home of the potent Hurricane, claims to have the largest volume of liquor sales in the world. The first cocktail was supposedly invented in a pharmacy on Royal Street, by a Caribbean named Antoine Amedee Peychaud. Peychaud concocted "bitters" from a secret recipe that he later found went very nicely with brandy. He prepared this drink in an egg cup, which the French pronounced "huhk-tyay." This became "cocktay," and in time, "cocktail." Although New Orleans is known for its high-octane spirits, do not forget about Dixie beer, the local favorite and the only beer produced in the area. The brewery is located on Tulane Avenue and is open to the public for tours. The beer can be ordered in any local bar.

New Orleans has a problem in common with other places with a predominant indigenous cuisine: other cooking styles are crowded out. Even French and Italian cooking here is almost always heavily influenced by Creole tastes. But in this, as in many other cultural matters, the parochialism of the city leads to similar pleasures. Even though there has been a trendy sweep of pseudo-Cajun food emporiums which extend from coast to coast across America, you don't get that New Orleans taste anywhere but here in New Orleans.

Or, to quote Paul Prudhomme: "Nowhere else have all the ethnic groups merged to combine all these different tastes. And the only way you'll know the difference, honey, is to live 'em."

Details of restaurants can be found in the Travel Tips section in the back of this book.

<u>Right</u>, Susan Spicer of Bayona, one of *Food & Wine's* best chefs.

FAULKNER HOUSE

HERE IN 1925
WILLIAM FAULKNER,
NOBEL LAUREATE
WROTE HIS FIRST NOVEL
"SOLDIERS PAY"

THE BUILDING WAS ERECTED IN
1840 BY THE WIDOW OF
JEAN BAPTISTE LaBRANCHE
ON A SITE FORMERLY OCCUPIED
BY PART OF THE YARD AND
BUILDINGS OF THE FRENCH
COLONIAL PRISON

A CONFEDERACY OF WRITERS

"Don't you just love those long rainy afternoons in New Orleans when an hour isn't just an hour – but a little piece of eternity dropped into your hands – and who knows what to do with it?"

— Blanche DuBois, from
A Streetcar Named Desire

Long rainy afternoons are perfect for writing, and New Orleans has plenty of both. In this longtime haven for writers, visitors search out the haunts of Sherwood Anderson and William Faulkner, who were published in the literary magazine *The Double Dealer*, and Tennessee Williams, whose *Streetcar Named Desire* immortalized Stanley and Stella and Blanche. People with literary intentions want to walk the same streets their idols walked and drink in the same bars; some hope to write the same great books.

Writ large: The town's literary register reads like a *Who's Who* of American writers, with names like Walt Whitman, George Washington Cable, and Kate Chopin writ large across its pages. F. Scott Fitzgerald spent time here. The Beats made New Orleans a frequent destination, and William Burroughs, Jack Kerouac, and Allen Ginsberg all passed through town, chronicling their exploits for an entire generation. Charles Bukowski's early work was published by the French Quarter publisher, the LouJon Press, in the 1960s. Truman Capote, born in 1924, spent much of his life here.

Some visitors to the city decide to stay a while, taking a room in the French Quarter, settling in to write their own versions of the Great American novel, short story, play, or poem. Some of them make it, some of them don't. Some drift through, some stick around. It still happens.

Some writers grow up in New Orleans, leave for a while, and then come home to stay. Such was the case with best-selling novelist Anne Rice, who returned in 1988

after a 25-year exile in California. The First Street mansion Rice shared with her poet-painter husband and son is a frequent destination for sightseers, as well as the setting for *The Witching Hour*, Rice's saga of a family of Garden District witches.

Rice devotees prowl the city in search of the places featured in her *Chronicle of the Vampires* (the series that has brought her international acclaim), looking for the cemetery where Lestat took his long sleep, or for the Royal Street townhouse that was home to the vampire "family" of Louis, Lestat, and Claudia, the protagonists of *Interview with the Vampire*.

Perhaps better than any other writer, Rice's works evoke the sensuality and lushness of New Orleans. In an interview for *Lear's* magazine, she said: "Trying to come home, you run the risk of finding it pale in comparison to your memories, but New Orleans is such an intense place that I don't think memory can enhance it. For the first time, I'm actually able to write with the sound of the rain falling on the banana trees, the smell of the river breeze coming in the window; and every night, the twilight, the golden moment when the sky is shot with red and purple and gold, is just incredible. I don't think most people here appreciate the otherworldly quality of this city or understand the contrast that exists between Louisiana and the rest of the world. It's a place in the United States where you're not really in this country any more. It still is Third World, like being in the Caribbean."

New Orleans has been home to large numbers of women writers who have as their literary foremothers writers like Kate Chopin, whose *The Awakening* is now considered a feminist classic. Lillian Hellman (*Pentimento, An Unfinished Woman*), Sheila Bosworth (*Almost Innocent*), Patty Friedman (*The Exact Image of Mother*), and Ellen Gilchrist (*In the Land of Dreamy Dreams, Victory Over Japan*) are only a few of the many writers with ties to the city.

The mysterious side of New Orleans has

been a recurring inspiration. Chris Wiltz, for example, is the author of three mysteries set in New Orleans. Like Rice, Wiltz ventured to San Francisco, but she came home after only a year. Her romance with the city is ongoing, but she sees its less-benign side as well as its romance. "The past is written all over the face of the future in New Orleans," she said, "and darkness seethes beneath the atmosphere of bonhomie. Also, the living is easy here. Where else in the United States can you find an Old World city with built-in indolence? Writing requires a certain amount of indolence. Think-tank time, I call it."

Wiltz is part of a group of writers who

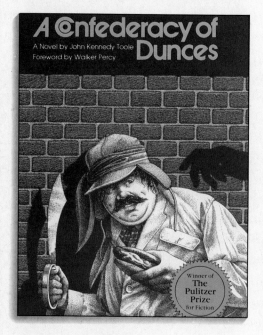

chronicle the dark side of the city. Former policeman James Colbert, O'Neill DeNoux, and John Dillmann have all written mysteries or works of true crime with New Orleans as their focus.

Transplanted writers have also made themselves at home here. Cleveland, Ohio native George Alec Effinger chose the Big Easy over the Big Apple in 1971. Science-fiction writer Effinger is one of the most prolific writers in the city, with some 16 novels to his credit. He has also won the Hugo and Nebula awards, the two most prestigious awards in his field. Why does Effinger stay in New Orleans? His response is quite down to earth. "I like the slow pace. It's much cleaner here than in New York, and everyone is so nice. And you can get around without a car. The food, the music, everything else that goes on here… this city has everything I ever wanted."

Perhaps New Orleans' most famous exile-in-residence is the Romanian poet Andrei Codrescu, known for his commentary on National Public Radio and for *A Hole in the Flag*, his memoir of the Romanian Revolution. Codrescu, who teaches at Louisiana State University in Baton Rouge, chooses instead to live in New Orleans, and occasionally he turns a sardonic eye on the city. Describing a convention of booksellers in an essay called *The Mind Circus is in Town*, he wrote, "I'm not here for my good looks either. My publishers have me shaking hands with the world. At night, we do what we do so well. We party. The moon is full, the velvety air of romantic old New Orleans caresses the exposed arms and legs of the swaying couples under the banana trees. The siren song of Café Brasil throws erotic shivers through the throng. Reading is the farthest thing from our minds."

Pulitzer prize: Despite its well-known literary heritage, not all writers have fared well in New Orleans. Thirty-year-old native John Kennedy Toole committed suicide in 1969, after despairing of ever seeing his work in print. After his death, Thelma Toole, the author's mother, haunted local bookstores and writers in quest of a publisher for her son's work. Finally, the amiable writer Walker Percy, the dean of Louisiana letters, took a look, liked what he saw, and recommended that Louisiana State University Press publish it. It did, and the book won the first posthumous Pulitzer Price for fiction. *A Confederacy of Dunces* offered a new and unique vision of New Orleans. The adventures of hulking Ignatius Reilly, pushing his Lucky Dog cart around the French Quarter and chronicling his philosophy on Big Chief tablets, captivated an international audience. Toole portrayed New Orleans from the inside out, talking the talk and walking the walk the way the locals do, and the world embraced his vision. *A Confederacy of*

Dunces has been published in 16 countries and has sold over a million copies.

A deep and abiding inspiration for many young writers is the work of Louisiana's presiding literary spirit, the late novelist and philosopher Walker Percy, whose *The Moviegoer*, published in 1961, virtually defined the existential quest of an entire generation. Percy's search for meaning in the increasingly barren modern landscape won him an enthusiastic following. Many disciples journeyed across Lake Pontchartrain in the hope of an audience with this extremely generous man.

In *The Moviegoer* Percy wrote, "The of highway." Inspired by a PEN award for a work about life in prison, he was determined to become a writer. After a period of great creativity, during which he wrote his critically acclaimed debut novel, *Homeboy*, a blackly funny and violent chronicle of prison life, Morgan died in a motorcycle accident in 1990. At the time of his death Morgan was at work on a New Orleans novel called *Mambo Mephisto*, in which he hoped to write "nothing less bold than the Mardi Gras novel as yet unwritten. A baroque and bustout tale of love foredoomed and sin unremitted spin between the bearded oaks, the streetcar lines, and lacework galleries of the Big Easy, a

search is what anyone would undertake if he were not sunk in the everydayness of his own life. This morning, for example, I felt as if I had come to myself on a strange island. And what does such a castaway do? Why, he pokes around the neighborhood and he doesn't miss a trick."

Writer Seth Morgan, whose search brought him into New Orleans at the end of a veritable orgy of drugs and drinking, liked to say that this was "the place where I ran out

Left and above, Toole's tale of a literate Lucky Dog vendor is published in 16 countries.

Gothic fable of helpless men and women who must 'in ignorance sedate roll darkly down the torrents of their fates,' gripped in the currents of those pasts which Faulkner taught are not even past but the stuff of the here and now, enigmatically shaping and informing the present." An ambitious plan from one who succumbed to the city's excess of temptation.

While the city has inspired great fiction, New Orleans has also nurtured a number of leading authors of nonfiction, among them Stephen Ambrose, author of multivolume biographies of presidents Nixon and Eisenhower, Carol Gelderman, biographer of Henry Ford and author Mary McCarthy, and Nicholas Lemann, whose bestselling *The Promised Land: The Great Black Migration and How it Changed America* was inspired by an awareness of race relations that began in his New Orleans childhood.

Of course writers do not exist in a vacuum; they need the support of their community in order to survive and prosper. Once lured South by cheap rents and an inviting lifestyle, writers have to *live* in the place they have chosen.

Walk into the Quarter's Napoleon House or the Café Brasil in Faubourg Marigny and

you will doubtless find a writer, leaning against the bar or hunched over a table, pen in hand. A week rarely goes by without an autographing or a reading in one of the city's many literary venues. The Maple Leaf Bar on Oak Street in Carrollton boasts the longest-running poetry reading series in the South. It began in 1979. Any Sunday afternoon at three o'clock, you can belly up to the bar, shove the beer bottles aside, and hear works-in-progress by local writers. Or, if you're lucky, you might arrive on a day when a well-known writer is reading.

The very private act of writing takes the public stage during the latter part of every March, when the Tennessee Williams/New Orleans Literary Festival celebrates the city's favorite playwright with a three-day extravaganza of plays, readings, panel discussions, and literary walking tours of the French Quarter. The Festival, international in scope, offers an appealing mix of new and established writers, and its book fair is a delight for every bibliophile.

Aspiring writers from around the country flock to the Big Easy in September for the New Orleans Writers' Conference. Sponsored by the Greater New Orleans Tourist and Convention Commission, the conference allows aspiring writers to meet editors, agents, and fellow authors for three days of workshops and manuscript evaluations. Some come just to soak up the atmosphere that has inspired so many before them.

Writers searching out the ghost of William Faulkner will want to visit Faulkner House Books, an elegant shop at 624 Pirate's Alley, off Jackson Square. The residence Faulkner shared with artist William Spratling, his co-author of the wicked parody *Sherwood Anderson and Other Famous Creoles*, has been lovingly restored, and the owners swear that they occasionally sense his spirit. Visitors may too, when they gingerly thumb through autographed first editions.

Writers come from near and far to visit the Maple Street Bookshops, the city's oldest local chain. Proprietor Rhoda Faust agrees that these are boom times for writers. "Writers come here because a lot of great writing has been done here and a lot of great writing has been *set* here and that's very appealing and confidence-inspiring. The same could be said of Boston, New York, and San Francisco, but New Orleans offers something more – a slower pace, less pressure, less competition within the community of writers. New Orleans is more tolerant than most cities, and it didn't become that way because it's politically correct. New Orleans has always been tolerant in a joyful way that seems more sincere. Writers seem to thrive in this atmosphere."

<u>Above</u> and <u>right</u>, Tennessee Williams, plus muse and myth.

COPING WITH THE MYTHS

Some cities make people go weak at the knees just thinking about them. Paris is one such city; New York and London, for all their attractions, are not. New Orleans is probably America's best contender in the *femme fatale* sweepstakes, a description given an airing by the writer George Sessions Perry in 1947: "In some ways gaudy old New Orleans very much resembles an alluring, party-loving woman who is neither as virtuous as she might be nor as young as she looks… a *femme fatale* who has known great ecstasy and tragedy but still laughs and loves excitement, and who after each bout of sinning, does duly confess and perhaps partially repent."

New Orleans has other labels, too: The City that Care Forgot; The Big Easy. Writers have inspired so many myths about the town and its residents that sorting out fact from fiction can be an uphill task.

Tennessee Williams, for instance, defined the archetypal Southern woman, perhaps for all time. His literary characters are invariably helpless, beautiful, neurotically dependent on men, and incapable of dressing in anything other than gorgeous peignoirs.

In fact, according to statistics published by the Department of Labor and the Census Bureau, far from being helpless, women make up 41 percent of New Orleans' workforce. Over half the women of working age have a job, and of all homes with households headed by women, around 40 percent hold the property in their own names. Women are now even captains of prominent Mardi Gras groups like the Phunny Phorty Phellows.

But then, New Orleans isn't a traditional Southern town, another popular myth. The city *was* the first Dixie-land: the term "dixie" originated before the Civil War, when the town still retained a prominent French influence. Because of the multilingual nature of the population, paper money was printed on one side in English, the other in French. Notes worth $10 became known as "dixies" because of the word *dix* (10) printed on them.

But even though it is located in the South, culturally and geographically New Orleans is an island. Proof of this is in the accent, which is not the slow, lingering drawl found in nearby Alabama, but the brisk, even brusque accent of farther north, probably due to the large number of Yankees and immigrants who made their homes here. Physically, the town remained an island for a very long time, as the first metropolitan bridge across the Mississippi River wasn't built until 1958. The city even fared fairly well in the Civil War, unlike the rest of the South.

Socially, New Orleans is known for food and jazz and Mardi Gras. Many people think that Mardi Gras is the best or even the only time to visit. In terms of pure entertainment, this may be the case. But as far as getting to know the city – its people and its way of life – Mardi Gras is one of the worst times to visit. Some hotels slap on a hefty "festival charge" and tables at popular restaurants are booked up a year in advance. Many residents leave town entirely, preferring to celebrate at one of the smaller festivals held throughout the year.

These festivals are numerous – on average around three every two weeks – giving rise to New Orleans' reputation as a nonstop party town. But life can be hard in the Big Easy, when money is scarce, when federal funds dry up, when schools and roads and education are neglected to the point of ruin.

The city faces serious, no-nonsense problems. Paint is peeling off its best-loved buildings, and the living are warned against visiting unaccompanied the cities of the dead, due to an increase in attacks on sightseers. The overall crime rate was 9,305 crimes per 100,000 in 1990, an 18 percent increase within a decade. Unemployment is escalating and, according to the latest available estimates, almost one in five households in the metropolitan area is at or below the poverty level.

New Orleans' romantic character is tailor-made for myths. It always was and always will be. Some of these tales, however, are similar to the decorative filigree that graces the balconies of French Quarter apartments – they're attractive, well-loved and durable as iron.

But they can also be full of holes.

10th ANNIVERSARY

NEW ORLEANS
JAZZ & HERITAGE
FESTIVAL 1979

In 1979, New Orleans R&B artist Ernie K-Doe mused, half in jest and half in earnest, "I'm not sure, but I'm almost positive, that all music came from New Orleans." If you qualify "all music" to mean "all authentic 20th-century American music" K-Doe's statement rings fairly true. The New Orleans music magazine *Wavelength* carries the quote on its masthead.

One reason 20th-century American music might well have begun in New Orleans is because the city developed as a major cultural force long before it was officially annexed into the US in 1812 as part of the Louisiana Purchase. By the 1830s, full opera productions in a world-class opera house were presented here.

New Orleans-born composer and concert pianist Louis Moreau Gottschalk (1829–69) toured and performed in both America and Europe, where he was feted by the likes of Chopin and Berlioz. Well before the Civil War and the cultural unification of America, New Orleans had developed a distinct identity as a "musical city."

Walkin' to New Orleans: The town was also the only location in North America where African musical culture was celebrated. Jazz's first great saxophonist, Sidney Bechet, traces his love of music back to an ancestor who danced in Congo Square. Duke Ellington celebrated Congo Square in his "A Drum Is a Woman" suite. So what is Congo Square, and why is it important?

Located in Armstrong Park near the French Quarter – and also called Beauregard Square – the field that became Congo Square was used in the early 1880s by the Oumas Indians to celebrate their corn feasts. As New Orleans grew, the field was turned into a public square. On weekends, Congo Square was the site of music and dance performed by enslaved Africans who were permitted to congregate there. Many white

Preceding pages: Ladies Zulu at the Jazz Fest. **Left,** around 300,000 people attend the festival each year.

New Orleanians were unnerved by these religious celebrations, which sometimes lasted for two full days and nights. In 1817 and for more than 20 years thereafter, the New Orleans city council limited the congregations to Sundays during daylight hours. After a brief interruption the congregations resumed in 1845 and lasted until the outbreak of the Civil War in 1861.

Old New Orleans was the only city which permitted slaves to sing in African languages, perform African dances, and use African instruments – notably the drum and the string instrument that became the banjo. The musical retentions of Congo Square contributed significantly to the development of jazz and popular American music. The New Orleans Jazz & Heritage Festival was founded in Congo Square.

Pre-Civil War New Orleans boasted an unmatched quantity of both African and European musical activity. But it was only after the Civil War that a distinctive American musical form began to develop. Prior to the abolition of slavery, the descendants of enslaved Africans generally did not have the opportunity to develop their cultural expressions publicly. During the post-bellum period (the Reconstruction era of 1865 through 1876), newly emancipated African Americans began to move into the major cities. The official census notes that between 1860 and 1880 the black population of New Orleans more than doubled, growing from 25,000 to over 56,000.

This was the period of SA&PC (Social, Aid & Pleasure Clubs), benevolent societies established to provide both entertainment and social support during times of illness, death, or economic hardship. These organizations were the network that hired brass bands to play at social functions ranging from picnics and parties to weddings, births, and funerals. No other American city had such a strong network of benevolent societies among African Americans of both the laboring as well as the professional and artisan classes.

Turn-of-the-century New Orleans was a mixture of peoples and cultural influences. Both the German and Italian immigrant communities had extremely strong musical traditions, which found expression in numerous outdoor venues. The German Oompah brass bands were particularly popular. Additionally, America as a whole was high-stepping to the parade beat of John P. Sousa, and New Orleans was no different.

Also, at that time New Orleans was the major gateway port to the Caribbean and Central and South America. There were numerous public ceremonies, all involving music, to welcome officials, dignitaries, and

sic in New Orleans brought with them more than simply a "jungle sound" which emphasized the "wild beating of drums" and "undisciplined intonations and timbres." Buddy Bolden, Jelly Roll Morton, Freddie Keppard, King Oliver and, above all, Louis Armstrong, also introduced the influential idea of outdoor processions.

Jazz began as music to accompany outdoor social activity and not as brothel music, as is commonly thought. The Storyville legend of jazz's birth is probably based on the fact that the music's first major composer, Jelly Roll Morton, spent his formative years playing ragtime piano in Storyville. But jazz

other important people. On a more mundane level, the pawn shops were awash with instruments left behind from the Civil War.

Although it might seem obvious that brass band music, which gave birth to jazz, would develop in New Orleans because of the city's cultural richness, the jazz band was not simply an extension of existing music, but rather a radical combination of African cultural antecedents and the technical demands of existing European musical cultural expressions. These diverse cultures produced a music that is distinctly American.

The African descendants who played mu-

bands did not generally perform in brothels; the founding father of jazz, Buddy Bolden, most often played in the streets of New Orleans or at Lincoln Park in the uptown section of the city.

Jazz autobiographies such as Louis Armstrong's *Satchmo* and Sidney Bechet's *Treat It Gentle* make clear the community basis of the birth of jazz as opposed to the mythical Storyville birthplace. It is ironic, however, that the closing of Storyville and the popularization of records, as opposed to live music, marked the end of the first major jazz period. Although the 1920s became known as the "Jazz Age" in America, by then most of the major New Orleans jazz musicians were performing and recording in Chicago and New York.

The first jazz recording was cut by Nick La Rocca's ODJB (Original Dixieland Jazz Band) in the Big Apple in 1917. In the 1920s, Louis Armstrong cut the first classic recordings of jazz in Chicago and New York. New Orleans itself was experiencing a downturn that coincided with the introduction of rigid segregation known as "Jim Crow."

It was not until the jazz revival movement of the late 1940s and early 1950s that musical attention was again focused on New

While Fats Domino played the piano and sang, trumpeter Dave Bartholomew, who grew up playing traditional New Orleans jazz, was the songwriter and producer. They have written well over 200 songs and crafted numerous hits. By the early 1960s, when the Beatles dominated popular American music, Domino and Bartholomew were the first American artists to dethrone the moptops from the number-one spot on the US charts.

Following on the heels of the Domino/Bartholomew duo was songwriter, pianist, and producer Allen Toussaint, who was single-handedly the most important creative force in the resurgence of local music during

Orleans. By the late 1950s the same synthesis that produced jazz produced another major development known as "rhythm and blues," or R&B. Although New Orleans was not the sole center for the development of this new musical form, the city did play a seminal role. The major focus of this resurgence was an ebullient pianist in the Fats Waller tradition, Antoine "Fats" Domino, the more flamboyant personality in a team known as Domino and Bartholomew.

Left, spiritual awakening. Right, "Fats" Domino was responsible for a 1950s musical resurgence.

the 1960s. Like composer and bandleader Duke Ellington, Toussaint had the ability to craft memorable songs to fit the individual talents of the people with whom he worked. From Ernie "Mother-In-Law" K-Doe and Irma "It's Raining" Thomas, to Aaron "Tell It Like It Is" Neville (currently of the Neville Brothers) and Lee "Working In The Coalmine" Dorsey, to bands such as the Meters, in many ways Allen Toussaint was a credit to the spirit of Jelly Roll Morton.

After the 1960s, the national impact of New Orleans music waned. However, the New Orleans Jazz & Heritage Festival was born soon after and grew to become the largest paid music event in the world with an annual attendance of over 300,000 revelers. Focusing on the unique musical styles of the region, the "Jazz Fest" (as it is popularly called) showcases and, in a number of instances, helps revive the careers of New Orleans artists.

The late 1980s saw a resurgence of national and international interest in New Orleans jazz artists, brought about mainly through the rise of jazz stars Wynton Marsalis, Branford Marsalis, Harry Connick Jr, Terrence Blanchard, and Donald Harrison. Wynton Marsalis, in particular,

the day-to-day life of the New Orleans black community. The city government does not economically support this important manifestation of black culture. Brass bands exist because the local community has made it a priority to fund them. After all, they play at parades, funerals, picnics, after baseball games, for private parties, wedding receptions, and similar social functions.

Visitors who come to New Orleans are often frustrated in their search to find "authentic New Orleans music." Invariably they are steered towards the French Quarter nightclubs and hotel lounges. Although there are fewer venues than in the past, the

has stylistically incorporated traditional New Orleans jazz into his composing and performing styles. Additionally, the resurgence of marching brass bands is garnering international acclaim. Led by the Dirty Dozen Brass Band, there are literally hundreds of young brass band musicians mixing the traditional repertoire and instrumentation with contemporary rhythms and songs.

These modern brass bands receive both the opportunity to develop, and economic support from the SA&PCs. Often this aspect is overlooked by those who are unaware of how deeply the brass-band scene is rooted in

real music still exists in the various neighborhoods. More often than not, you can hear these bands in small taverns on the weekends and in the streets at funerals.

The ambience of venue and audience is often just as important as who is playing. For those who have a particular interest in the brass band tradition, October through early December is the best time to visit. During this period, on Sunday afternoons, many of the SA&PCs hold their annual parades. Dancing in the streets is the order of the day.

Above, fringe performers at the Jazz Fest.

JAZZ FEST

At the New Orleans Jazz & Heritage Festival, it's likely a member of the Marsalis family will be playing. It could be Wynton on the Ray-ban stage, sharing a bill with the likes of Robert Cray or B.B. King. It could be father Ellis, a professor of music at the University of New Orleans, holding forth in the Jazz tent. It could be brother Branford, whose "Makin' Whoopee" always raises cheers. If a Marsalis isn't playing, chances are a Neville Brother will be.

Despite the enormous crowds that pour into the Fair Grounds during the two April weekends of the festival, the Jazz Fest feels like a family affair.

Neighbors greet neighbors at the stand selling crawfish po-boys or run into people they haven't seen for years at the children's tent. Attendance at Jazz Fest is 60 percent local people, 40 percent American or international, but the low-key ambiance of the world's largest paid music festival is one to be savored.

The hurly-burly around the main tent is like any big-city concert, where 20,000 spectators attempt to negotiate a few lanes of pedestrian traffic to catch a glimpse of big name stars. But over near the gospel tent or the Musical Heritage stage, people are stretched out on the lawn having picnics or dancing the *fais do-do*.

It is these minor stages that are the real attraction of Jazz Fest. It is a cliché, but also the case, that most of the finest jazz, gospel, and blues musicians in the world will make an appearance; if not this year, then sometime soon. As a result, the level of performance is exceptional. Even if the names of the people playing are unknown, the music is guaranteed to be high-stepping and hot.

Artists are likely to have local connections, like Eleanor Ellis, blues guitarist and vocalist, or C.J. Chenier, son of Cajun zydeco king, Clifton Chenier. The gospel singers often come from nearby high schools. With around 75 acts performing every day, it's impossible to make a poor choice.

That the music is of such consistently high standard is due, in large part, to the festival's founder, impresario George Wein. New York-based Wein, himself no mean pianist, staged the first jazz extravaganza, the Newport Jazz Festival, in 1954. However, his love of New Orleans' music extends back to his first entrepreneurial exercise, which was an evening of brass band and bebop music co-presented with New Orleans clarinetist Edmond Hall.

The first local festival was a humble affair, funded by a $10,000 bank loan and held in Congo Square. That year, 1969, there were apparently more musicians playing than audience in attendance. New Orleans' father-and-son team Arthur and Quint Davis joined with Wein in an uphill battle to fund the festival, but it was only years later, when the event transferred from Congo Square to the Fair Grounds, that the fest moved out of the red.

By 1983, Jazz Fest had become a major musical event and tourist attraction. Sponsorship, however, was still a problem. A noted cigarette company promised to underwrite the event if the name were changed to reflect its brand. The festival board refused, and the music played on without a sponsor. The following year, board members, described by Wein as "a gumbo of ethnic backgrounds and neighborhoods and interests," went all out for local sponsorship, and the rest is musical history.

Jazz Fest's economic impact on the city is considerable. According to a survey conducted by Cypress Research and Development Corp., a recent festival generated $59.4 million. Visitors spent around $19 million during their stay in New Orleans, plus an additional $7 million on hotels.

For music-lovers, the festival itself is a bargain. Tickets at the gate are so inexpensive that one social chronicler worked out that each act costs under 10¢ to see. Combine this with great food, sunshine, plus parades and free workshops throughout the day, and a good time is guaranteed.

The only drawback to the Jazz & Heritage Festival is if the weather on previous days has been poor. Straw spread over mud, which dries in the steaming swamp heat, means that indoor tents can be unbelievably smelly. Only music of such high quality could avoid the nose and go straight to the heart and feet.

According to the *Encyclopedia of Witches and Witchcraft*, New Orleans is the traditional American headquarters of voodoo. Along with Miami, the Big Easy is one of the few cities in the US where almost everyone will have some knowledge about the subject, even if it is little more than after-dinner conversation. There are thought to be around 50 million followers of voodoo around the world, although worshippers now prefer the term "verdoun" to voodoo, to distance their practices from the more lurid aspects of the faith. They believe that the work of various gods appear in all parts of everyday life and that pleasing (or appeasing) them will achieve spiritual prosperity. New Orleans' heyday as a spiritual center was the mid-19th century, although even today token *gris-gris* (voodoo charms, often a small bag) can be bought with very little effort.

Charming custom: The charms are the most obvious manifestation of the cult and have traditionally been used to attract members of the opposite sex, acquire money, achieve good health, or to ward off enemies. A genuine *gris-gris* (pronounced *gree-gree*) is one which is sacred by having been blessed with fire, water, earth, and air and which contains several ingredients, the number of which must not exceed 13. It can be used for good or evil purposes. Although the amulets bought in French Quarter tourist shops are innocent enough, there are still believers around. A local museum conducts "voodoo tours" for visitors and one (unconfirmed) report is that New Orleans policemen have been known to carry *gris-gris* for protection during their daily rounds.

In the mid-19th century, upper-crust Creoles pursued voodoo in much the same way that fashionable people of today latch on to the latest New Age development. It was a heated topic of conversation in the posh parlors of well-heeled New Orleanians, but

Left, Marie Laveau, voodoo queen. **Right**, an 1880s French newspaper gave an account of Louisiana sacrifices.

much more than mere lip service was paid to the practice. Superstitious Creoles scrubbed their front stoops with brick dust to ward off curses and called regularly upon witch doctors and voodoo queens. For the most part they sought advice on affairs of the heart and purchased love potions, powders, and oils.

For 19th-century tourists, no trip to the Crescent City was complete without a visit to famed voodoo queen Marie Laveau. The strange and exotic voodoo ceremonies drew

enormous throngs of thrill-seekers. Reporters frequently turned up to view the rites, and local newspapers of the period were filled with detailed, sometimes shocking accounts of voodoo conclaves and voodoo-related activities. But the ceremonies witnessed by the hordes and the reporters were often elaborate shows staged for the outsiders. Voodoo was a mysterious, secretive cult whose more sinister aspects were carefully shielded from curious eyes.

Voodoo originated in the African kingdom of Dahomey (now the Republic of Benin). *Vodu* was the religion of the

Dahomeans. The word vodu and its various forms – voodoo, voudou, vaudau, and even hoodoo – encompassed all aspects of the religion, including the gods, the cult, the cultists, and the rituals. One of the primary gods was Zombi (also called Damballah), which was a snake – usually a giant python. Among other things, the snake-worshippers believed that the first man and woman on earth were blind until the serpent gave them sight. The Bantu word *zumbi* means fetish, and the cult involved beliefs in sorcery and black magic. When voodoo arrived in New Orleans, the cultists incorporated some of the characteristics of the Catholic Church.

the cultists out to Bayou St John and Lake Pontchartrain. In 1817, the Municipal Council, fearful of voodoo-inspired slave uprisings, outlawed slave gatherings except on Sundays and in officially designated and supervised areas. Congo Square was one such legal meeting place. For many years the slaves gathered each Sunday afternoon in Congo Square (later renamed Beauregard Square, the plaza in Armstrong Park), chanting, beating their tam-tams, and dancing the Calinda and Bamboula. Congo Square drew large crowds of gawkers, but the activity there was mere window-dressing compared to the grotesque and orgiastic illegal rituals

Statues of the Virgin Mary and pictures of saints sometimes adorned voodoo altars, but the tenets of this particular religion bore little resemblance to Christianity.

The first organized voodoo ceremony in New Orleans is said to have taken place in an abandoned brickyard on Dumaine Street. It was probably presided over by Sanite Dede, the first of the great voodoo queens. (Voodoo was a matriarchy. The witch doctors and kings paled in comparison to the strong queens – always free women of color, never slaves – who reigned over the rituals.) Repeated police raids on the brickyard drove

that took place around the bayou and the lake. Most people in town knew it, and when word spread about a voodoo ceremony on St John's Eve, the roads leading to the designated site were clogged with sightseers.

For practitioners of voodoo, St John's Eve (June 23) was the most important night of the year. Eyewitness accounts of St John's Eve ceremonies on the lakefront include lurid tales of half-naked cultists whirling in fantastic dances around a huge bonfire and a boiling caldron into which they tossed live frogs, black cats, and the ever-present snakes. Congo drums were beat with the leg bones of buzzards and the crowd chanted "Li grand Zombi" as the reigning voodoo queen danced with the python. It was said that the voodooists ripped live chickens apart, and ate them, and that sometimes in the throes of a frenzied dance they clawed, bit, and drew blood from each other. The presence of small coffins at the torchlit rituals led to the belief, widespread among Creoles, that white babies were kidnapped and sacrificed by the voodoos. The majority of voodooists were black, but there are many stories of whites – particularly young women – who participated in the rites.

The two most famous names in local voo-

Creole homes spied and then sold him information. When Doctor John died in 1884, writer Lafcadio Hern wrote a flowery elegy that was published in *Harper's Weekly*.

The name Marie Laveau is, of course, legendary in New Orleans. There were at least two voodoo queens named Marie Laveau – mother and daughter – and possibly others. The first was a tall, handsome, and mean-eyed woman who was said to have been the illegitimate daughter of a wealthy white planter and a mulatto. The reddish cast of her skin indicated some Indian blood. In 1819, at the time of her marriage in St Louis Cathedral to Jacques Paris, a native of Santo

doo lore are Doctor John and Marie Laveau. A free man of color who claimed to be a Senegalese prince, Doctor John was an enormous man whose ebony face was marked with hideous tattoos. In the 1840s, he bought a veritable harem of female slaves and a house on Bayou St John. He exerted great power over the Creoles, who flocked to his house to purchase charms and have their fortunes told. He seemed to see into their homes and knew their innermost secrets. In fact, he did – the servants in many prominent

Left and **above**, **Voodoo Museum exhibits.**

Domingo, Marie was a devout Catholic. Paris mysteriously vanished shortly after the marriage, and she began calling herself the Widow Paris.

Working as a hairdresser, she listened to gossip and secrets while arranging the tresses of aristocratic white ladies. A few years after Paris vanished, Laveau became the mistress of a quadroon named Louis Christophe Duminy de Glapion, with whom she had 15 children. They lived in a cottage (long ago demolished) on St Ann Street between North Rampart and Burgundy streets. The disappearance of her husband

and her move into voodoo may or may not have been connected; in any case, by 1830 Marie was *the* voodoo queen and a force to be reckoned with. She is said to have eliminated other queens through the use of hideous *gris-gris*, literally "voodooing" them to death. One of her bad-luck charms was supposedly a small bag made from the shoulder of a dead body. The contents included bats' wings, cats' eyes, a rooster's heart, and an owl's liver. Keeping this company was a dried lizard, a dried toad (one-eyed), and the smallest finger of someone who was black and had committed suicide. Any unfortunate receiving such a potent gift would certainly

die. Everyone in the city was terrified of Marie Laveau; she is said to have had police and politicians in her pocket. She reigned over the Congo Square rituals, and danced with the snake at the Lake Pontchartrain rites, to which she extended invitations and charged admission.

Fantastic tales were told of the house on St Ann Street – that it contained a 20-foot python, mummified babies, skeletons, and two altars, one for "good luck" and the other for "bad luck." Marie retired in 1869, and her "luck" ran out in June, 1881. Long before her death, her daughter, born in 1827, had gained as much notoriety as Marie I, perhaps even more. Other queens reigned after these two women, but none ever had the power or the fame of the Laveaus.

The Laveau-Glapion tomb is in St Louis Cemetery No. 1, near the Basin Street entrance. The stark-white tomb is always adorned with burnt candles, flowers, and voodoo offerings. It probably holds the remains of the Widow Paris, and may also be the final resting place of the second Marie Laveau. Many believe that it is, but others maintain that Marie II, exiled by her family after the death of her mother, is buried elsewhere – in one of the "ovens" of St Louis Cemetery No. 2 and in at least three other cemeteries. Some say that her spirit is restless and cannot be contained.

Voodoo is scarcely the force it once was. It is not, however, dead. There are stores and small companies throughout America that stock voodoo accouterments, most with highly descriptive names – Love Oil, Courting Powder, Controlling Powder, Follow Me Drops, Boss Fix Powder. Believers still use the "mojo hand" – a small cloth filled with pieces of dead reptiles, birds, animals, or people – to "fix" (hoodoo) someone or something. The most popular and potent *gris-gris* is a root called "Johnny the Conqueror," also known as High John and Big John. Big John has turned up in several blues recordings, such as Bo Diddley's "I'm a Man" and Muddy Waters' "Hootchie Cootchie Man." Another voodoo-related blues tune is John Lee Hooker's "Crawling King Snake Blues." And in the 1960s, rock-and-roller Mac Rebennack, decked out in feathers and face paint, adopted the stage name Dr John.

Perhaps the most impressive proof that voodoo is still with us is in its use in modern-day medicine. According to the *Encyclopedia of Southern Culture*, voodoo is of increasing interest in Southern schools of medicine and psychiatry. Doctors in respectable medical schools have consulted voodoo doctors, especially with regard to the treatment of paranoid schizophrenics.

Above, Laveau's tomb is always adorned with offerings and graffiti. **Right**, Ava Kay Jones, Voodoo Museum priestess.

Residents of New Orleans are far too self-confident to take offense at this description of themselves written by Oliver Evans in 1959: "Hedonistic, complacent, extravagant where amusement is concerned, soft to the point sometimes of insincerity, tolerant to the point sometimes of decadence; but always vivacious, good-natured, well-dressed, and well-mannered – these are the characteristics of a typical New Orleanian. You might think, perhaps, that his vices outweigh his virtues; it depends on what you believe is important, but there is no denying that he is an easy fellow to get along with."

Although the city has many undeniably attractive neighborhoods, to most visitors New Orleans is the French Quarter. This area of 96 square blocks, laid out in a perfect grid by French engineers in 1721, encompasses what many people think about the city as a whole: that it is a town where an architect, a gourmet, or a roué is in hog heaven, according to that prolific scribe, Ibid.

Directions in this 1-square-mile area are governed by the flow of the Mississippi River. The lower Quarter is the area from Jackson Square to Esplanade Avenue. The upper Quarter lies between Jackson Square and Canal Street. If in doubt, aim for the spires of St Louis Cathedral, the centerpiece of the square, and then head out once again.

The French Quarter is not a polished place. Its buildings can appear shabby; its streets are sometimes dirty. It is overrun with tourists. On sultry summer nights, shambling hordes of out-of-towners, intent on guzzling as many Hurricanes as possible, maraud through the narrow thoroughfares as if it were a playground for demented youths. Others, in daylight hours, shop until they drop in the tacky souvenir emporiums that have replaced many of the small specialist shops. Some people, in fact, wonder what all the fuss is about when it comes to the French Quarter.

The answer can be found on the quiet side streets, in tiny cafés where all-day breakfasts with homemade biscuits can be bought for less than you thought possible. In the neighborhood clubs, where the melancholy sound of jazz mingles with the sweet scent of perfume. Or at dawn on a spring day, when the sun colors the old buildings with a glow so mellow that it cannot fail to lighten the step.

Some visitors mind the crumbling nature of the French Quarter, the faded buildings, and the sometimes eccentric behavior of its habitués. They prefer their attractions to have more gloss.

It all depends on what you believe is important.

Preceding pages: the French Quarter at dusk; Rebecca Lentz in her French Quarter residence; home security. **Left**, shoe shine near the square.

French Quarter

0.1 miles/ 160 m

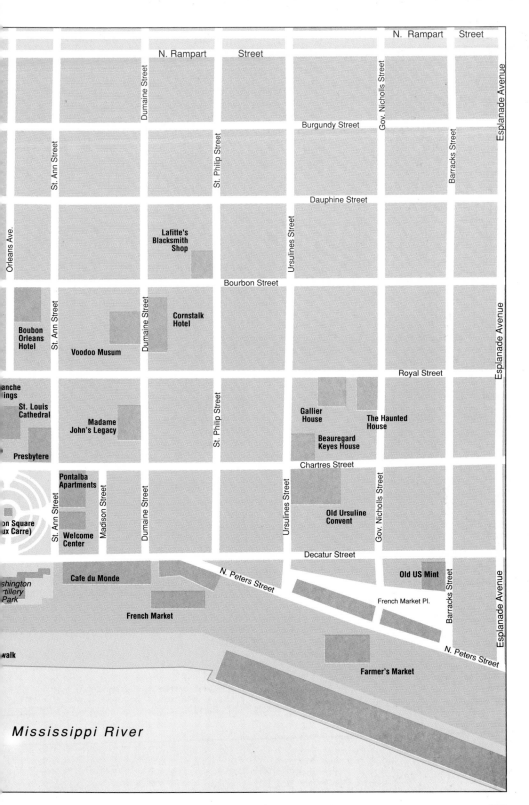

N. Rampart Street

N. Rampart Street

Dumaine Street

St. Philip Street

St. Ann Street

Orleans Ave.

Burgundy Street

Gov. Nicholls Street

Barracks Street

Esplanade Avenue

Dauphine Street

Lafitte's Blacksmith Shop

Ursulines Street

Bourbon Street

Dumaine Street

Cornstalk Hotel

Boubon Orleans Hotel

St. Ann Street

Voodoo Musum

Esplanade Avenue

Royal Street

anche ings

St. Louis Cathedral

Madame John's Legacy

St. Philip Street

Gallier House

The Haunted House

Beauregard Keyes House

Presbytere

Chartres Street

Pontalba Apartments

Madison Street

Dumaine Street

Ursulines Street

Gov. Nicholls Street

on Square ux Carre)

St. Ann Street

Welcome Center

Old Ursuline Convent

Decatur Street

Cafe du Monde

N. Peters Street

Old US Mint

Barracks Street

Esplanade Avenue

shington tillery Park

French Market Pl.

French Market

walk

N. Peters Street

Farmer's Market

Mississippi River

131

AROUND JACKSON SQUARE

Jackson Square is the centerpiece of the city's most famous attraction, the French Quarter. Also called the **Vieux Carré** (Old Square), the Quarter is the original colony of La Nouvelle Orleans. The buildings, most of which date from the early to mid-1800s, are small and colorful, with steep gables, sloping shingled roofs, dormer windows, and graceful fanlight windows. Many are painted in bright colors or pastels and festooned with ironwork galleries or gingerbread trim.

Surrounding the square is a flagstone pedestrian mall, which is the scene of circus-like activity. A black iron fence, which wraps around the park, is hung with paintings – the work of the many sidewalk artists whose easels are set up on the mall. Portrait painters, caricaturists, and landscape artists work, display their wares and await new business, seemingly oblivious of the jazz bands, tap dancers, clowns, and bongo players who provide day and night-time entertainment. In recent years, mime artists and fortune tellers have appeared on the scene to entertain visitors.

Broad flagstone carriageways behind black cast-iron gates sweep from the street to secluded courtyards with tiered fountains and masses of lush tropical plants. Strolling through the Quarter it is easy to imagine the place peopled with aristocratic Creoles, swashbuckling pirates, voodoo queens, and all manner of characters from the past.

The past is very much cherished in New Orleans. Street signs in the Quarter come in three languages: French and Spanish, in fond remembrance of colonial days, and English. It seems almost a shame that Italian is missing. At the turn of this century the French Quarter was an Italian neighborhood. The Vieux Carré Commission was established by the state legislature in 1936 to preserve the old colony.

Although the 19th-century buildings were here, the French Quarter as we know it did not exist until after World War II. The present Commission is composed of a group of dedicated preservationists who drive a hard bargain when it comes to exterior renovations. Still, the Quarter is hardly a polished and pristine place; it definitely has that "lived in look."

Bordered by **Chartres**, **St Ann**, **Decatur**, and **St Peter streets**, Jackson Square was known to the French Creoles as Place d'Armes and to the Spanish Colonials as Plaza de Armas. The park was originally a parade ground for the militia. The area around the drill field, with its church and government buildings, was the center of social, religious, and political life. Grisly public executions sometimes took place in the square, as well as various ceremonies and celebrations.

Today, the former parade ground is a landscaped park with splendid magnolia, palm, and banana trees, cultivated

Left, St Louis Cathedral. **Right**, mime attraction.

flower beds, and park benches. Rearing up in the middle of the park, looking as if it sprouted out of the flower bed that surrounds it, is American sculptor Clark Mills' imposing equestrian **statue** of **General Andrew Jackson**, for whom the park was renamed in 1856. It was America's first equestrian statue and stands as a monument to the hero of the Battle of New Orleans, fought on the green fields of Chalmette in 1815. Each January 8, on the anniversary of the famous battle, solemn commemorative ceremonies are held in the square. During more frivolous occasions, such as the French Quarter Festival and La Fête, food booths and music stages are set up along the green.

Facing the park, stately **St Louis Cathedral** rises above these earthy goings-on. Parishioners sometimes complain about the difficulty of keeping their minds on the spiritual with all the sensuous sounds emanating from the tap dancers and bongo players in the square. From time to time, to the delight of tourists, long white stretch limos with police escorts ease over the flagstones, bearing the wedding party of a wealthy socialite couple.

The first church on this site was a small wooden structure, designed in 1724 by Adrien de Pauger, the French engineer who surveyed the original colony. It was named for Louis IX, the 13th-century saint-king of France who fought in two Crusades. This first church was one of more than 850 buildings that went up in flames during the Good Friday fire of 1788. A wealthy Spaniard named Don Andre Almonester y Roxas bankrolled the construction of the new church, which was dedicated on Christmas Eve, 1794.

The present St Louis Cathedral dates from 1851. The stained-glass windows in the front of the church were gifts from the Spanish government. In 1964, the cathedral was elevated to the status of minor basilica by Pope Paul VI. Pope Jean Paul II visited New Orleans in 1987; in honor of the papal visit the mall

St Louis Cathedral interior.

in front of the cathedral was renamed Place Jean Paul Deux. Virtually every building in the French Quarter has its resident ghost, and the cathedral is no exception. A long-dead priest who had a robust appetite for earthly pleasures is said to amble around the aisles singing hymns and chanting.

Pirate Alley and **Père Antoine Alley** are flagstone passageways that cut alongside the cathedral and lead from the square to Royal Street. Romantics cannot stroll these cracked flagstones without imagining what life must have been like in 19th-century New Orleans. There are guides who tell of clandestine meetings in Pirate Alley, when Jean Lafitte and Andrew Jackson were planning strategy for the Battle of New Orleans in 1812. Alas, not only were the alleyways constructed in the 1830s, long after Lafitte and his fabled band of pirates had disappeared, but Pirate Alley was originally called Ruelle d'Orleans, Sud.

At 624 Pirate Alley, the present site of the **Faulkner House Bookstore**, William Faulkner wrote his first novel, *A Soldier's Pay*. **Cabildo Alley** is a short passageway that leads from Pirate Alley to St Peter Street (and a Haagen-Daz ice cream shop). Père Antoine Alley (originally Ruelle d'Orleans, Nord) was renamed for a Capuchin priest, Father Antonio de Sedella, who arrived here in 1779. He was much loved by the French Creoles, who called him Père Antoine.

Cathedral Garden – the backyard, as it were, of the cathedral – lies between Pirate Alley and Père Antoine Alley. Centerpiece of the Garden is a statue of the Sacred Heart of Jesus. The monument near the Royal Street gate was erected during the reign of Napoleon III to honor 30 French marines who gave their lives while serving others in a yellow fever epidemic. A peaceful, green park now, this was the scene of many a duel in the 19th century. This, and the Dueling Oaks in City Park, were two favorite spots in which to fight it

The Presbytère.

out, usually over the honor of some young lady.

Although its official name is Cathedral Garden, the park is sometimes called St Anthony's Square. The two historic buildings that flank St Louis Cathedral on Jackson Square are the Cabildo and the Presbytère. Both buildings date from the Spanish Colonial period and are now part of the Louisiana State Museum complex.

The **Presbytère**, on the right as you face the cathedral, was begun in 1795. The two great fires destroyed both of the smaller structures that stood on this site. The Casa Curial, as it was called by the Spanish, or Presbytère, to the French, was intended as a home for the priests who served the church, but has never been used for that purpose. A part of the museum complex since early in this century, the Presbytère houses changing historical exhibits. The odd-looking object squatting in the arcade is the Confederate submarine *Pioneer*, a relic of the War Between the States. In 1862,

the Rebs deliberately sank it in Lake Pontchartrain, lest it fall into the hands of the Yankees.

One of the most important structures in the city is the **Cabildo**. The building received its name from the Spanish governing council – that is, the *Cabildo* – which was housed here during the Spanish period. As he did with the Cathedral and the Presbytère, Don Almonester provided funds for the reconstruction of this building. Work began in 1795, but it wasn't fully completed until after the Americans took control of the city in 1803.

Much later, archaeologists discovered part of a wall from a 1750s police guardhouse that had been incorporated into the building. And it was in the room called the Sala Capitular on the second floor that transfer papers for the Louisiana Purchase were signed in 1803. When the Marquis de Lafayette made a ceremonial visit to the city in 1825, the Cabildo was his home away from home. In the 19th century, when the city was divided into three separate municipalities, the Cabildo served as city hall for the First Municipality. It later housed the Louisiana Supreme Court.

In 1988, 200 years after the monstrous conflagration that decimated the old town, a fire caused severe damage to the roof and upper floor, and the building closed for extensive repairs. Some of the museum's important exhibits – including a **death mask of Napoleon** – were moved to the Presbytère.

Another building in the Louisiana State Museum complex is the **Louisiana State Arsenal**, behind the Cabildo at 615 St Peter. This was the site of the *calabozo*, or prison, in the Spanish Colonial period. After the Louisiana Purchase of 1803, when the Americans gained jurisdiction, a state arsenal was built here. The building was headquarters for the Louisiana Legion, a militia unit, whose insignia and initials are worked into the wrought-iron railing on the Pirate Alley side of the building.

The twin buildings lining St Peter and

Cathedral Garden was a 19th-century dueling ground.

136

St Ann streets are the **Pontalba Buildings**, which were constructed in 1849 and 1850. Named for the colorful woman who financed and saw to their construction, they are among the oldest apartment buildings in the US.

The aforesaid woman was Micaela Almonester, daughter of the Don who financed, among other things, the reconstruction of St Louis Cathedral, the Cabildo, and the Presbytère. While still in her early teens, Micaela married her first cousin, Joseph Xavier Celestin de Pontalba, and moved with him to Paris. That the couple later divorced is undisputed, but the events surrounding the separation are murky. According to one version, Micaela's father-in-law objected to the divorce and, in a heated argument, shot and wounded her. She then wrenched the gun from him and shot him dead in the head.

Another version has it that the old baron shot her and, thinking her dead, turned the gun on himself. In any case, he died and she didn't. She obtained her divorce, returned a wealthy baroness to New Orleans, and threw herself into civic activities. By the mid-1800s, as the American Sector was growing more and more affluent, Micaela de Pontalba made up her mind to promote the French Quarter and create jobs for the Creoles. She financed the building of the two apartment houses, which, in the European style, have commercial establishments on the ground floor and living space on the upper floors. Her architects were the estimable James Gallier and Henry Howard, and the lady herself was often seen up on a ladder wielding a hammer and overseeing the work. The initials "A" and "P", for Almonester and Pontalba, are worked into the ornate ironwork of the balconies themselves.

Each building consists of 16 row-houses: 12 units facing Jackson Square, two facing Decatur Street, and two facing Chartres Street. The "lower" Pontalbas, on St Ann Street, are the property of the State of Louisiana, and the "up-

The Cabildo.

per" Pontalbas on St Peter Street belong to the City of New Orleans. ("Lower" and "upper" refer to the downriver and upriver sides of Jackson Square).

Though Jackson Square is one of the noisiest places in the city, the apartments in the Pontalbas are among the Quarter's most coveted. In the lower Pontalbas, the Louisiana State Museum maintains the **1850 House**, which gives visitors a chance to see how upper-class Creoles lived in the 19th century. In addition to the canopied beds and other antiques, the apartment exhibits a kitchen filled with old-timey things and a display of antique dolls.

Adjacent to the 1850 House, the **New Orleans Welcome Center** has a wealth of free information, including maps, pamphlets, brochures, and advice. The **Louisiana Office of Tourism** shares space with the New Orleans Welcome Center and provides helpful information to visitors who plan to explore other parts of the state.

This being New Orleans, the comcercial establishments on the ground floors of the Pontalbas are primarily shops purveying some form of food. There are three restaurants, a pastry shop, two ice-cream parlors, and a candy store – plus, of course, the food vendors winging it in the square.

Across St Peter Street from the Cabildo is a balconied pink stucco building that houses **Le Petit Théâtre du Vieux Carré**, the oldest continually operating community theater in America. It began in 1916 with a group called The Drawing Room Players that first mounted its productions in a private home and later moved to space in the lower Pontalbas. In 1919, the company moved to the present location.

The building that houses the theater is a faithful reconstruction of one that was completed on this site in 1797. The interior of the theater has a charming old-world ambience, and the inner courtyard is lovely. Each season between September and June the theater presents seven plays, including musicals, on its main stage, as well as performances for kids that are held in the Children's Corner.

Up the street from Le Petit, at 632 St Peter, a **plaque** notes that **Tennessee Williams** wrote *A Streetcar Named Desire* in an apartment in this building. Williams scholars say the playwright was inspired by the streetcar that used to rattle down Royal Street. Williams first arrived in New Orleans in 1939; many years later he bought a house on nearby Dumaine Street, and continued until his death to visit the city he called "my spiritual home."

Just around the corner from the theater, on Chartres Street, is yet another New Orleans institution. La Marquise pastry shop is a French pâtisserie with wonderful croissants, Napoleons, éclairs, coffees, and other delectations. There are a few tables in the two tiny rooms and a pleasant courtyard with umbrellas to shield against the sun's rays. La Marquise is a delightful interlude in anyone's day.

Le Petit Théâtre: the oldest continually operating community theater. Right, beads of contemplation.

THE RIVERFRONT TO THE FRENCH MARKET

Fringed surreys drawn by mules wearing silly hats and faded flowers are a common sight in the French Quarter. These half-hour carriage tours are a pleasant, old-worldly way to see the local sights, and the guides' spiels are entertaining if not necessarily accurate. An oft-repeated example of misinformation is that given by the carriage driver who solemnly informed his fares that the Presbytère in Jackson Square was the Presbyterian Church.

The pitch where the driver/guides ply their trade most avidly is **Decatur Street**, the busy thoroughfare between Jackson Square and the Riverfront. Restaurants, delis, and coffeehouses line its perimeters, which is fitting, for the street ends up near to the open-air food emporium, the French Market.

Just across Decatur from Jackson Square is **Washington Artillery Park**, a broad split-level expanse of concrete and cast iron. Steps and ramps lead from the sidewalk to a **promenade** with box trees and park benches. This is a superb place to get a picture-postcard overview of Jackson Square and the Mississippi River. Street performers are often out in full force entertaining the sightseers, and the mournful sound of a jazz trumpet is never far away.

From here you can walk down and across the Riverfront streetcar tracks to **Moonwalk**, a wooden walkway smack on the river. (It was named for former New Orleans mayor "Moon" Landrieu.) This is one of the finest places in town to watch the ever-changing parade of tugs, fanciful river boats, and serious cargo ships and tankers on the river. The best time of all is at sunset, when both the sky and the water are streaked with scarlet color.

Directly across the river is the residential section of Algiers. The great bend of the river at Algiers Point is the *bête noire* of river boat captains who must negotiate the sharp turn. Just upriver is the **Crescent City Connection**, which is the bridge from the east to the west bank of the river. At night the bridge, ablaze with yellow lights, looks like a long golden chain stretched across the river and reflected in the water. As an example of how the Mighty Mississippi wreaks havoc with directions here, the West Bank is due east of the East Bank. Quarterites love to relax on a Moonwalk park bench and dreamily contemplate their river. Oftentimes street musicians play here for tips, which can either enhance or destroy the mood, depending on the talent of the performer. Unfortunately, this is a pretty good place to be harassed by panhandlers. Shoeshines are also easy to come by in this area.

The large building on the riverside of Decatur at St Peter Street is the **Jackson Brewery** (also called the **Jax Brewery**). The restored structure, which dates from 1891, now contains a maze of specialty shops and restaurants, but for many years Jax Beer was brewed here. Jackson Brewery is connected to a sister property, the Jackson Brewery Millhouse, another restored building containing shops and eateries. A block along toward Canal Street is the third of the Jackson Brewery Corporation's festival marketplaces, called, interestingly, The Marketplace. Many of these restaurants offer superb views of the Mississippi River, with both indoor and outdoor seating.

The steamboat *Natchez* docks behind the Jax Brewery at the **Toulouse Street Wharf**. An authentic paddle wheeler, this great white floating wedding cake does delightful twice-daily calliope concerts as passengers board for sightseeing cruises. The wonderful off-key calliope wheezes out old-time tunes that can surely be heard throughout the southeastern United States, if not the entire Western Hemisphere. **Woldenberg Riverfront Park**, a 16-acre landscaped area with trees, statuary, and park benches, stretches along the river from the Jackson Brewery all the way to the Aquarium of the Americas in the Central Business District.

Food, not surprisingly, is nearby. **Café du Monde** is an open-air pavilion at the corner of Decatur and St Ann streets, on the downriver side of Washington Artillery Park. Open 24 hours and jammed with tables and chairs, the café is a New Orleans legend, as popular with locals as with tourists. The café has been on this spot for more than a hundred years. This is the place for *café au lait* and *beignets*, either to start the day, finish it, or help get through it. New Orleanians who've painted the town red usually stop here before heading home in the dawn's early light.

The *beignets* are heavily cloaked in powdered sugar, and more often than not so are the people trying to eat them. As is the case with many New Orleans foods, it's impossible to eat them neatly. But do try to avoid sneezing when a *beignet* is en route to your mouth, and remember that a sudden intake of breath prior to taking a bite usually results in an attack of coughing. The only other caveat is that it's very hard to eat just one.

Café du Monde is the upriver anchor of **the French Market**, a shopping complex with colonnades, arcades, specialty shops, and outdoor cafés. This is a great place to shop for gifts and souvenirs of the city. Shoppers of one kind or another have been doing business here since the early 1700s, when there was a trading post on this site. Today's street vendors are hardly a new phenomenon; only the styles and goods have changed.

In the old days, Sunday mornings in the French Market gave true meaning to the term "festival marketplace." The Creole shoppers haggled loudly over everything from ice cream to live chickens to jewelry, while vendors sang out clever rhymes to hawk their wares. An itinerant dentist would arrive with a brass band to drown out the howls of unanesthetized patients.

Café du Monde in the 1940s.

There are still bands playing in the French Market, but they're more for toe tapping and hand clapping than tooth pulling. Open-air cafés such as the Mediterranean and the Gazebo are great places to take in the sounds of Dixieland, and free concerts are regularly held in **Dutch Alley**. Schedules of free concerts are available at the **Dutch Alley information kiosk** at the foot of St Philip Street. Park Rangers at the **Jean Lafitte** National Historical Park Service's **Folklife & Visitors Center** in Dutch Alley offer free tours of the French Quarter and the Garden District, and can supply a wealth of information about the city and its environs.

One thing which isn't lacking in New Orleans is information about Jean Lafitte himself. Or perhaps we should say disinformation – so many legends abound concerning this pirate/patriot that even the spelling of his name is in dispute, being variously Lafitte (with one "f") or Laffite, with two "f" and one "t". The most romantic amalgam of

these various tales is that Jean Lafitte was a 19th-century French buccaneer and smuggler who attacked Spanish ships sailing near New Orleans. Lafitte's brother Pierre sold black slaves to "quality households" around town, including the nuns at Ursuline's convent. Jean received a presidental pardon for his smuggling activities for aiding Andrew Jackson in his war against the British, but, born to be a sinner, he soon returned to piracy. This time Lafitte attacked American, rather than Spanish, ships. Hotly pursued by the US Navy, he sailed away in his favorite ship, *The Pride*, and was never seen again. How much of the tale is true is anyone's guess, but this is how legends are made.

The **Farmer's Market** is the downriver link in the French Market's chain of shops. Farmers from the surrounding areas have been bringing their fresh produce to this site for more than 160 years. Sightseers and locals cram the aisles of the open-air shed, picking

Garlic in sepia.

through bins of fresh fruits, vegetables, garlic, and pecans. There are also booths piled with wallets, jewelry, and other nonedible market goods. On weekends, a huge open-air **Flea Market** takes place at the rear of the Farmer's Market, a popular social as well as shopping event. Tables and booths spill into the streets, loaded with everything from one-of-a-kind junque to just plain junk. Many newcomers to the Quarter are able to furnish their apartments almost exclusively from items bought at the Flea Market. The market is now a peaceful place indeed compared to what occurred on this site between the years 1840 and 1870.

In those days, Gallatin Street was a two-block stretch along the riverfront docks between Barracks and Ursuline streets. Lined with brothels and gin mills, Gallatin Street was among the toughest, meanest places in the world. Murders, mutilations, and mayhem went with the territory, and those who valued their lives steered clear of it.

Thoughtful policemen avoided it like the plague. One of the bars is said to have been decorated in a mortuary motif. Bartenders were dressed up like undertakers, liquor bottles were stored in little coffins, and drinks were spiked with creosote. Not so much as a trace of Gallatin Street remains today, not even the name.

At the point where the Farmer's Market trickles into Barracks Street, *A Streetcar Named Desire* is on display in the backyard of the Old US Mint. A tribute to Tennessee Williams' world-famous play of the same name, the restored car is from the old Desire streetcar line that inspired the playwright. The Desire line is no longer running; only a bus carries that name. Think how theatrical history might have been changed if there had never been such a streetcar line: "A Bus Named Desire" just doesn't have the same flair.

The **Old US Mint** itself, which fronts on Esplanade Avenue, houses exhibits of two phenomena identified with the

Cajun fishmonger in the Farmer's Market.

146

Big Easy city – Mardi Gras and jazz. The **Mardi Gras exhibit** is ablaze with sparkling gowns, crowns, scepters, and other carnival paraphernalia. Across the hall, the **jazz exhibit** contains a well-documented history of this famous tradition, as well as sheet music and instruments used by famed musicians, including one of Louis Armstrong's first trumpets and also one of his white handkerchiefs. The building houses an excellent jazz archive, which is available free to *bona fide* researchers.

The Mint, a massive three-story Greek Revival structure, was constructed in 1835 on the site of an old Spanish fort. One of the first regional branches of the United States Mint, it produced about $5 million a month in coins. However, it was in operation for less than 30 years; the mint was closed in 1862 when Union forces occupied New Orleans during the War Between the States.

As part of a development called Riverfront 2000, the Audubon Institute (which administers both Audubon Zoo and the Aquarium of the Americas) is extending Woldenberg Park downriver to Esplanade Avenue. The park will be a valuable asset to the community, providing more open space and a plant conservatory. In addition, a plan has been proposed by the New Orleans Center for Creative Arts (NOCCA) to open a facility in the area of the **Mandeville Street Wharf**, next to the plant conservatory. There is controversy here about how the riverfront should be developed, but the possibility exists that this area could in years ahead rival the Riverwalk/Spanish Place development located upriver.

At Esplanade Avenue, the **Riverfront streetcar** begins its breezy ride alongside the river. These "Ladies in Red" consist of seven vintage streetcars painted red with gold trim as a historical reference to the old French Market line which followed the same route. They carry around 5,500 people every day, and are a great way to get home.

Jazz Museum in the US Mint.

ROYAL STREET

In the 19th century the intersection of Conti and Royal streets was the banking center of the French Quarter. The police station now occupies the porticoed Greek Revival mansion at 334 Royal Street, but it was built in 1826 as the Bank of Louisiana. Its handsome gate and fence were modeled after those at Lansdowne House in London.

Across the street is a balconied building that once housed the Old Bank of the United States. Nearby, at 403 Royal, are the premises of the old Louisiana State Bank, the last work of architect Benjamin Henry Latrobe. He designed the Bank of Pennsylvania in Philadelphia and later contributed to the United States Capitol in Washington, DC.

Money, as you may have gathered, is the keynote to Royal Street. Enjoyment of its pleasures is enhanced if you happen to have a lot of it, for this is the place to find upscale boutiques and fine restaurants, or that perfect "gentleman's gift," a hand-tooled snuffbox from one of its antique emporiums. For those without bank notes to spare, window shopping on Royal Street is pretty pleasant, too. Just as a visit to New Orleans isn't complete without a visit to Bourbon Street 'round midnight, a trip to the French Quarter isn't complete without a stroll along Royal.

World-famous **Brennan's** restaurant is located at 417 Royal. This building was constructed around the turn of the 19th century as a residence for the maternal grandfather of French Impressionist painter Edgar Degas. Shortly thereafter it was bought by the Banque de la Louisiane, and the initials "BL" were worked into the wrought-iron balcony that fronts it.

Directly across the street from Brennan's, occupying the entire 400 block, is a deserted, neglected white marble building surrounded by wonderful old magnolia trees. Locals usually call it the "old **Wildlife and Fisheries building**," a reference to a former tenant. When the city purchased this whole square at the turn of the century as a site for the Civil Court Building, buildings razed to make way for it included the former site of Antoine's restaurant. Many New Orleanians think this fine baroque building would be an ideal place for a casino. The front steps of the building presently provides a stage for various street performers.

At the corner of Royal and St Louis streets, the posh **Royal Orleans Hotel**, called locally the "Royal O," sits on a historic site. The fabulous St Louis Hotel, designed by noted architect J.N.B. dePouilly, opened here in 1838. Much has been written to describe the splendor of this opulent property, with its great cupola, columns, and graceful archways. One of the archways was incorporated in the Royal O, which was built in 1960.

In the lobby of the present hotel is a large painting of the St Louis Hotel,

Preceding pages: cornstalk fence, Royal Street. **Left**, sunshade and flagstone. **Right**, former bank at 403 Royal.

which boasted – besides an exchange and, of course, guest rooms – public baths, a bank, and shops. (Incidentally, the Esplanade Lounge in the lobby of the Royal O is an elegant place to enjoy pastries, flaming coffees, and piano music in the evening.) Running through the lobby of the old hotel was the St Louis-Toulouse stretch of the Exchange Passage, also designed by dePouilly.

Exchange Passage led from the Merchants Exchange Building at Royal and Canal (the site now occupied by the French Quarter Holiday Inn) through the center of three blocks, including those in the 400 block of Royal where the old Wildlife and Fisheries building now is, and eventually to the Cabildo, which was in those days the city hall. The route was well-trod by Creole businessmen who had city business to transact and who attended the slave auctions that were held at the St Louis Hotel. (The auctions took place between noon and three in the afternoon, and the ac-

commodating manager of the St Louis Hotel bar, Philippe Alvarez, served free lunches to anyone stopping in for a drink during that time.)

The only remaining sections of Exchange Passage (now called **Exchange Place**) are from Canal to Conti streets and from St Peter to Pirate Alley. That latter segment is now **Cabildo Alley**; as part of Exchange Passage it led to city hall. The "Fencing Masters' Houses" at 618 and 620 Conti housed the studios of… well, fencing masters. (Fencing lessons were, of course, *de rigueur* during the era of many duels.)

During the day, when Royal Street is blocked off to vehicular traffic, itinerant musicians and other performers take to the middle of the street to entertain passers-by. The most popular "stages" are the corners of **St Louis, Toulouse, and St Peter streets**. The quality varies, of course, but the majority are quite good. There is an outstanding ponytailed piano player, who rolls his upright around, parks it, and sits down to **Hotel bedroom**.

152

play ragtime. Banjoists and guitarists are much in evidence. A black female contralto, whose voice is rich and mellow as she belts out acappella spirituals, can be heard clearly from up to three blocks away.

In the middle of the block, between St Louis and Toulouse streets, is the courtyard of the television studio WDSU. In the early 19th century, two famous cabinetmakers worked in New Orleans: François Signouret and Prudent Mallard. Their ornately hand-carved canopy and tester beds, armoires, and tables can be seen in historic homes all over the state. This house, with its courtyard, was built for Signouret in about 1816. The courtyard is lovely and open to the public during business hours.

Across the street and down the block from WDSU, the **Historic New Orleans Collection** is pretty much what the name says it is: a collection of maps, documents, and memorabilia to do with the history of New Orleans. The **Williams Gallery** on the ground floor

has changing exhibits of regional art, and there is an excellent research library here. The building itself, which surrounds a lovely courtyard, was erected in the late-18th century as a residence for the Merieult family. According to Stanley Clisby Arthur in *Old New Orleans*, Napoleon Bonaparte, anxious to secure a political alliance with Turkey, made repeated attempts to purchase Catherine Merieult's mane of blonde hair, for the sultan of Turkey required a blonde wig for one of his sultanas. A fortune, and even a castle were offered, but each time Catherine rejected the emperor's request. This home was one of the handful of structures that survived the fire of 1794 and tours are well worth the nominal fee.

Another property that boasts a spectacular courtyard is the **Court of the Two Sisters**, a restaurant in the 600 block. Named for two sisters who had a variety store here in the late 1800s, the restaurant does a jazz buffet every day. Next door, the building that houses the

Royal wheels.

Old Towne Praline Shop (which makes some of the best pralines in the new town) also has a lovely courtyard. In the 1800s, the famous coloratura soprano Adelina Patti stayed in this house, which was then a private home, during the time she was appearing in the opera.

A souvenir shop presently occupies the ground floor of **New Orleans' first skyscraper**, which was built at 640 Royal between 1795 and 1811. An atmospheric old party with peeling pinkish-gray facade and wrought-iron balconies, this house is known variously as the Pedesclaux-LeMonnier House; 'Sieur George; and the First Skyscraper. The initials "YLM" worked into the balcony railing stand for Dr Yves LeMonnier, for whom the house was originally built. George Washington Cable, a 19th-century New Orleans novelist, used this house as the setting for his short story 'Sieur George. Some say that the fourth floor was added sometime after the house was built, in order for it to retain its "tallest" title.

The **corner of St Peter and Royal** is said to be the most photographed place in New Orleans. The **Royal Café** is housed in one of the Labranche Buildings, which were built around 1840 and are notable for their exquisite cast-iron galleries. There are actually 11 **Labranche Buildings** – separate three-story row houses – lacing down the 600 block of St Peter Street to Cabildo Alley. Cast iron was introduced in New Orleans in 1850; these buildings originally were undoubtedly festooned with simpler wrought (handworked) iron.

At 717 Orleans Street, a few steps from Cathedral Garden, massive white paneled doors open onto the lobby of the Bourbon Orleans Hotel. From the lobby a spiral staircase leads to the mezzanine and the restored **Quadroon Ballroom**, which is today a handsome meeting room. The Orleans Theatre once occupied this site and, adjacent to it, stood the Orleans Ballroom. These and many surrounding buildings were destroyed by fire in 1816, but the ball-

Police; dog.

room was rebuilt the following year. The ballroom was sometimes the scene of the famous – or infamous – quadroon balls. (A quadroon is a person who is one quarter black.) In fact, this was not the only site for the balls; they were held at various locations in the Quarter.

In the 19th century, these balls were held to introduce young and beautiful quadroons to affluent Creole gentlemen. The young women were escorted to the balls by their mothers, each of whom hoped that her daughter would become the mistress of a wealthy Creole. When a satisfactory arrangement was worked out, the mistress's mother could be assured that her daughter would be supported and taken care of, for many Creole men maintained two separate households – one for his wife and their children, the other for his quadroon mistress and family.

The Creole wives knew what the situation was and were not entirely happy about it. They would sometimes don disguises and attend the balls in order to find out what might be going on. (A great deal of voodooing went on in New Orleans at this time, and many a duel was fought over a beautiful young woman whose skin was the color of *café au lait*.)

Reams have been written about the quadroon balls, and there are varying accounts of the nature of these soirées. According to some historians they were glittering and glamorous; other reports testify they were nothing more than brawls. In any case, the particular ballroom in question was purchased in 1873 by the Catholic Sisters of the Holy Family, an order of black nuns, and from being a place of "brawls" it became a convent and school. In 1964, the Sisters moved to the suburbs and a part of this structure was incorporated into the Bourbon Orleans Hotel.

Among the well-nurtured legends of New Orleans is one concerning the ghost of a naked quadroon slave girl said to float around the rooftops in this area on cold winter nights. She is sup-

posed to have been a quadroon whose lover was an elite Creole. When she demanded that he marry her, he said he would – but only if she would demonstrate her love by spending the night on the roof naked. Of course, it was the middle of winter and she froze to death.

Trivia question: Who was America's first Princess of Monaco? No, not the actress Grace Kelly. The first was a woman named Alice Heine, whose great-grandmother – the Widow Miltenberger – built the houses at **900-906-910 Royal** in 1838 for her three sons. Ms Heine, born in 1910, became a duchess when she married the Duc de Richelieu, and a princess when she became the wife of Prince Louis of Monaco. The Princess Monaco café, whose pretty courtyard is a fine place in which to while away some time, is named in honor of this lady.

Across the street, at 915 Royal, is a well-known landmark, the **Cornstalk Fence**, behind which sits the Cornstalk Hotel. Of ornate design involving corn-

stalks, ears of corn and morning glories, the cast-iron fence was shipped from Philadelphia sometime after 1834. The fence has a twin in the Garden District, surrounding the stunning house known as Colonel Short's Villa.

Another of the Quarter's house museums is the **Gallier House**, at 1118–32 Royal. It was built in 1857 by the well-known architect James Gallier, Jr as a home for him and his family. Gallier's father, James Gallier, Sr, was also a famous architect whose work can be seen all over town. The senior Gallier was an Irishman whose real name was Gallagher; he Gallicized it after he arrived in New Orleans. Open for tours, the house is beautifully furnished and well-researched. It's a fine example of how the well-heeled Creoles of the 19th century lived.

Sometimes it seems as if every nook and cranny of New Orleans is inhabited by one or more ghosts. A host of them is said to hang out at 1140 Royal, in what is known as the **Haunted House**. According to local lore, in 1831 this was the residence of Madame Delphine LaLaurie, a socialite who entertained lavishly. But her guests gossiped about the condition of the lady's slaves; they were emaciated, and appeared to be terrified. A neighbor reported seeing Madame LaLaurie beating a small slave girl, who later fell from the roof. Madame LaLaurie was hauled into court, but was merely fined.

In 1834, when a fire broke out in the house, neighbors broke down doors and discovered in a smoke-filled room seven chained and starving slaves gasping for breath. A newspaper account implied that Madame LaLaurie set the fire, and an angry mob gathered in front of her home. The LaLauries escaped in a carriage, after which the mob destroyed the house. In 1837, the building was bought and restored, and is now a private residence. It is not open to the public, but some people insist they can hear hideous shrieks emanating from the house on dark, stormy nights.

Left, it's a dog's life. **Right**, the corner of St Peter and Royal has "starred" in movies.

BOURBON STREET

An initial stroll along Bourbon Street might lead one to believe it was named for the intoxicant. New Orleans' best-known thoroughfare – locals just call it "the Street" – has more bars than you can shake a swizzle stick at. All kinds of bars – jazz, piano, gay, straight, sleek, sleazy, historic, topless, bottomless, and oyster.

Many who come here, especially during particularly festive occasions such as Mardi Gras and the Sugar Bowl, feel obligated to try to drink Bourbon Street dry. When people let their hair down on Bourbon, they let it way down. (Beware. There are unsavory folk here who have creative ways of relieving the inebriated of their valuables.)

Actually, the name of the thoroughfare was carefully chosen by the unscrupulous John Law when the colony was founded. The Duke of Bourbon was a major investor in Law's Mississippi Company, and it was thought polite to to give the street his name. Law was nothing if not wise to political expediencies.

Bourbon Street is famed even more for its music than for its proliferation of watering holes. You can hear the street before you set foot on it. Bourbon has far and away a greater concentration of music clubs than anywhere else in town and possibly in the world.

Bourbon Street blues: Within a six-block stretch you can hear hard rock, rhythm and blues, Dixieland, honky-tonk piano, Irish music, gutbucket (low-down mean blues), Cajun and zydeco, can-cans, karaoke, and occasionally a bagpiper in full regalia pumping out *Scotland, the Brave*.

It isn't even necessary to go inside to be entertained. Doors of the clubs are flung wide all year round, and the music pours out and floods the streets. Almost any place that serves mixed drinks has "go-cups," so you can take your libation along as you stroll.

Mingling with the music are the sounds of the sidewalk tap dancers, young black kids who dance for dimes and, they hope, dollars. Break dancers are also out to entertain sightseers, spinning and gyrating on blankets they've spread out in the middle of the street.

Barkers, like those at carnival sideshows, stand outside the various clubs and keep up a running spiel, advising passers-by of the wonders to be seen inside. When doors are left open to let in a breath of "fresh" air, the topless/bottomless wonders can sometimes be glimpsed. Outside is the continuous din of merrymakers roaming up and down the street and in and out of bars.

During Mardi Gras, things, shall we say, intensify. There are so many people jamming the streets on Fat Tuesday that it's almost impossible to move. Every balcony on Bourbon is crowded with people, most of them not entirely sober, who toss beads and other trinkets to the shrieking throngs. Incidentally, regardless of what you've been told, there is no

ordinance or even tradition that *requires* women to bare their breasts on a Bourbon Street balcony during Mardi Gras. The law does prohibit the throwing of souvenirs from balconies, but it isn't enforced.

Midnight of Mardi Gras night presents one of the most incredible sights imaginable. Every square inch of street and balcony is covered with revelers who wish to continue reveling. But at midnight Mardi Gras is officially over and Ash Wednesday begins. At Canal Street, police mounted on horses begin slowly working their way down Bourbon, repeating through bullhorns, "Mardi Gras is over." No one wants to go home, and it takes a long time to clear the street. The devout go to church, but there are countless parties that last till dawn or later.

The **Old Absinthe House**, at 238 Bourbon, is an old, well-established institute of higher imbibing. It was built in 1806 as a commercial-cum-residential structure, and is typical of an *entresol* house. *Entresol* is a French word meaning mezzanine, and in this context it meant a half story between the upper and lower floors. Used for storage, it was lit by the arched fanlights on the lower floor windows. As for absinthe – that's a whole new story, which can be read on *page 59* of this book.

The **Inn on Bourbon** sits on a historic site at Bourbon and Toulouse streets. A plaque on the building notes that the French Opera House stood here for more than half a century, until it burned down in 1919. New Orleans was the first city in America in which opera was performed (though not on this site). The Creoles were much enamored of opera, and performances in the 1,800-seat theater were SRO affairs.

Attendance at the opera was one of the rites of a young woman's "coming out" in polite society. Lavish parties were sometimes held in the theater following a performance, and were attended by anyone of importance in the "ruling class." Notice that the curb

curves inward here; this was to accommodate the horse-drawn carriages that pulled up to let off ladies and gentlemen in their fancy dress.

It's true that the main fame of Bourbon is due to its music and bars, but the street is a mixed bag. Sophisticated **Galatoire's**, one of the city's old-line French Creole restaurants, has been on Bourbon since its founding around the turn of the century. Around noon on any given day (except Monday when the restaurant is closed), a quiet, well-dressed crowd queues up in front for lunch, for reservations are not acceptable. (Neither are credit cards.) Their garb is in sharp contrast to the short-shorts and T-shirts worn by casual Quarterites and sightseers.

In the next block are the smart green awnings of the Royal Sonesta, one of the city's fine hotels. Its balconied rooms are much coveted during Mardi Gras, at least for those who don't want to sleep. In the 500 block, tucked in among the girlie shows and gay revues, **No cover...**

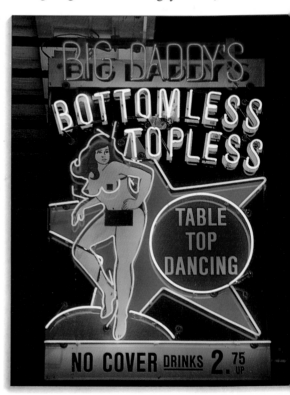

is the local branch of **Ripley's Believe It Or Not**. Across the street, the fabulous Chris Owens does classy Vegas-style shows in her own club.

Just off Bourbon, on St Louis Street, is the **Hermann-Grima House**. One of several house museums in the Quarter, this one is an American-style townhouse that dates from 1831. It was built for a man named Hermann, who later sold it to a Grima; hence the name. The mansion itself is handsome, but of particular note are the restored outbuildings that surround pretty ornamental gardens. There is a fascinating 19th-century kitchen, where, during the winter months, Creole cooking demonstrations (and tastings) take place.

Speaking of food, **Antoine's**, one of the city's most famous restaurants, is located on St Louis Street, between Bourbon and Royal streets. In 1840, Antoine Alciatore founded this restaurant (though in a different location), and it's still operated by his descendants. Antoine's is housed in a lovely old building dating from 1868 that's lavishly garnished with pale green ironwork. If you dine here you'll be given a souvenir pamphlet that lists, among other things, the scores of celebs and royals who've enjoyed an evening in the restaurant.

Below Jackson Square, in the lower Quarter, Bourbon Street is predominantly residential – and much quieter. At Bourbon and St Philip streets, the musty old **Lafitte's Blacksmith Shop** is a favorite neighborhood bar. The little cottage looks as if it's about to collapse. Ownership records date back as far as 1772, but it may be even older.

The legend persists that this building housed a blacksmith shop that was a front for local heroes Jean and Pierre Lafitte's smuggling and slave trading activities. (New Orleanians love their legends.) What is certain is that the construction of the cottage, known locally as brick-between-posts, is of the kind used in the earliest buildings erected in the city.

.any way
ou look at it.

THE UPPER AND LOWER QUARTER

One way to distinguish between an out-of-towner and a resident is whether they say "outer" or "lower," "inner" or "upper" when speaking about the French Quarter. Locals refer to the lower Quarter and the upper Quarter, because directions, as usual, follow the flow of the river. The lower Quarter is the area from Jackson Square to Esplanade Avenue, which is vaguely "east" on a map; the upper Quarter lies between Canal Street and Jackson Square. The description is used here because this chapter skips across the remaining French Quarter streets faster than a tap-dancer's toes.

Holding title to the "oldest" or "first in this country" is dear to the hearts of New Orleanians. Local historians still argue over which is the oldest structure in the Vieux Carré. It is undoubtedly true that the sole building to survive the 1788 fire intact is the **Old Ursuline Convent** at 1114 Chartres Street. It is the only remaining example in the city of pure French Creole architecture and one of the oldest buildings in the Mississippi Valley. As such, it is of national importance.

The large structure, with its portico, pediment, and dormer windows, was designed in 1745 by Ignance François Broutin, who was at the time Louisiana's Engineer-in-Chief. The building was completed in 1749–53. The Ursuline nuns who arrived here from France in 1727 occupied a nearby building, and moved into this one upon its completion. In this, Louisiana's first nunnery, the sisters conducted the first Catholic school, the first Indian school, the first Negro school, and the first orphanage. The Louisiana State Legislature convened in this building from 1831 till 1834, the convent having been moved to an uptown location. It now contains the archives of the Archdiocese of New Orleans and is not presently open to the public. The other candidate for "oldest"

is Madame John's Legacy, described later in this chapter.

Across the street from the convent, at 1113 Chartres, the **Beauregard-Keyes House** is a house museum which is open to the public. Many New Orleans houses have aliases; this one is also known as the Le Carpentier House. Of course, therein lies a tale. The porticoed Greek Revival raised cottage was built in 1826 for Joseph Le Carpentier, a New Orleans auctioneer. After the War Between the States, when it was a boarding house, General P.G.T. Beauregard – the man who ordered the first shot at Fort Sumter, which began the war – rented rooms here for a brief period. In the 1940s, the house was bought by novelist Frances Parkinson Keyes, who lived and wrote here till her death in 1970. The writer used the slave quarters as her studio; the many books she wrote about the city and the region include *Dinner at Antoine's* and *Steamboat Gothic*. Southern belles in antebellum costume conduct tours of the house and the

lovely walled garden adjacent to it.

Returning for a moment to Joseph Le Carpentier: he was the grandfather of world chess champion Paul Charles Morphy. Morphy was born in New Orleans in 1837 and learned to play chess by the time he was 10. At age 21, he was acknowledged as the greatest player in the world. He had a mind like the proverbial steel trap and could perform amazing feats, such as playing simultaneous games while blindfolded. He retired when he was 22, and it is said that his phenomenal mind became enfeebled. He died at age 48 as the result of a freak accident and is buried in St Louis Cemetery No. 1.

An only-in-New Orleans phenomenon is the Historic New Orleans **Voodoo Museum**, at 724 Dumaine Street between Royal and Bourbon. Though rather small and dimly lit, it's filled with all manner of voodoo doings, including dolls, potions, and *gris-gris*. There's a large portrait of Marie Laveau, the famous 19th-century Voodoo Queen,

and, in a back room, a voodoo altar. The museum folk conduct guided voodoo tours of the city, as well as a night-time visit to observe a voodoo ritual.

Some historians insist that the house known as **Madame John's Legacy**, at 632 Dumaine Street, predates the convent and should be crowned "oldest in New Orleans." A beautifully restored West Indies-style structure, typical of the homes built by the early planters, it has a sloping roof, dormer windows, and a broad gallery with slender wooden colonettes. The present house was built in 1788–79, immediately after the great fire, for Don Manuel Lanzos. However, the furor is due to the fact that an earlier house stood on this site. In 1725, it was built for Jean Pascal, a sailor who was killed during the Natchez Massacre of 1729. Pascal's widow lived here until 1777. Defenders of its "oldest" title say that the house was only partially destroyed by the fire, and when it was rebuilt much of the earlier structure was utilized. (Such

Preservation Hall is located in a former stable.

things are of grave importance to Southern historians.) Madame John's Legacy was given its unusual name after a fictional character in *'Tite Poulette*, a short story written in the 19th century by George Washington Cable. The house was restored and is furnished with Louisiana antiques by the Louisiana State Museum, its present owner.

The **Musée Conti Wax Museum** at 917 Conti Street, is New Orleans' answer to London's Madame Tussaud's. It traces the history of the city through a series of tableaux, beginning with the story of pioneer explorer La Salle. The wax figures, dressed in period costumes, are amazingly lifelike and presented with great pizzazz. The eyes of the voodoo dancers in the Marie Laveau scene are alarmingly realistic. All the city's heroes and villains are here, including General Andrew Jackson, pirate/hero Jean Lafitte, slave-beater Delphine LaLaurie – even Napoleon Bonaparte, depicted sitting in a bathtub while discussing the Louisiana Pur-

chase. A recent addition to the cast of waxed characters is New Orleans native and legendary clarinetist Pete Fountain. There is also a **Chamber of Horrors**, appropriately lit and properly ghoulish; and, a bit inexplicably, a figure of the singer Michael Jackson.

The 700 block of St Peter Street has two establishments worth mentioning. Grungy, world-famous **Preservation Hall**, at No. 726 in a former stable, presents some of the best traditional jazz in the world, every night. Its neighbor, **Pat O'Brien's**, is another well-known bar. Pat's is in an historic structure constructed around a stunning courtyard. It was built in 1791 and occupied by the first Spanish Theatre in the US. Louis Tabary's troupe of actors and musicians, refugees from the West Indies, also performed in this theater. On May 22, 1796, *Sylvain*, by Andre E. M. Gretry, one of the luminaries of 18th-century opera, was staged here

J.N.B. dePouilly, who designed many 19th-century New Orleans homes

Waxing historical: discovering the Mississippi for France.

and tombs, was the architect of the house at 514 Chartres, now occupied by the **New Orleans Pharmacy Museum**. It was built for druggist Louis J. Dufilho, who was America's first licensed pharmacist. DePouilly worked on this house at the same time as another of his projects, the fabulous St Louis Hotel, was under construction across the street. A pharmacy museum since the 1930s, it contains many strange and wondrous things: ancient prescriptions and sinister-looking medical implements, *gris-gris* potions, exotic herbs, and a handsome rose-colored Italian marble soda fountain from 1850.

There are lots of colorful apothecary jars and containers for such essentials as leeches. This is a fabulous, musty old place in which to poke around, and you can step into the pretty courtyard to catch a breath of fresh air.

Today, the **Napoleon House**, a few doors over at 500 Chartres, is one of the most popular bars in town. Another atmospheric place, this one with memorabilia of the Little Corporal everywhere in evidence, it was built in 1814 as the private home of New Orleans Mayor Nicholas Girod. Although constructed more than 10 years after America gained control of the city, the house is an excellent example of how the French architectural influence continued here.

As for its name, the story goes that Girod was a great admirer of Bonaparte and organized a syndicate whose purpose was to rescue the former emperor from exile on St Helena and bring him to New Orleans. Napoleon had many adoring fans here. The third floor of the mayor's house is said to have been added as apartments for the expected exile (the banquet room is called l'Apartement de l'Empereur).

According to some sources, a schooner was dispatched under the command of the swashbuckling Dominique You, one of Lafitte's men. Napoleon died before the rescue attempt could be accomplished. Legends aside, this house is one of the best places in the upper or lower Quarter, or anywhere in town for that matter, to linger over a Pimm's Cup or a cappuccino.

Much of the lower Quarter contains residential property, for, far from being just a tourist attraction, the French Quarter is home to around 7,000 inhabitants. Appearances can be deceptive: behind shuttered, inconspicuous facades are houses of grand proportions, many attached to spacious courtyards that vie for elegance with gardens in the Garden District. Other properties are charming, if shabby, hovels.

Quarterites are a mixed bunch: architects, poets, aristocrats, and waitresses are neighbors in the Vieux Carré. The living is easy. Cars are not only unnecessary but a liability. Everything (bar a movie theater) can be found in the area, at almost any hour. Quarterites tend to stay up late and, if they have the money, retire from working early. Once bitten, they will rarely live anywhere other than the French Quarter.

Left, convenience shopping. Right, a shining light.

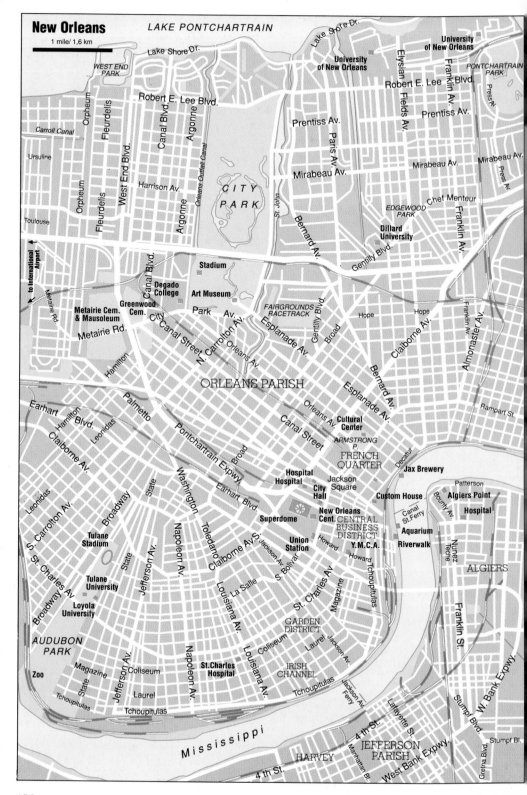

New Orleans

1 mile/ 1,6 km

LAKE PONTCHARTRAIN

Lake Shore Dr.

Lake Shore Dr.

WEST END PARK

Carroll Canal

Ursuline

Orpheum

Fleurdelis

Robert E. Lee Blvd.

Canal Blvd.

Argonne

West End Blvd.

Harrison Av.

Toulouse

Fleurdelis

Orpheum

to International Airport

Metairie Rd.

Metairie Cem. & Mausoleum

Greenwood Cem.

Metairie Rd.

Hamilton

Canal Blvd.

City

Degado College

Art Museum

Stadium

Park   Av.

Canal Street N.

Canal Street

Carrollton Av.

Orleans Av.

CITY PARK

Orleans Outfall Canal

St. John

Paris Av.

Bernard Av.

Prentiss Av.

Mirabeau Av.

Gentilly Blvd.

Esplanade Av.

Gentilly Blvd.

Broad

University of New Orleans

Robert E. Lee Blvd.

Prentiss Av.

Mirabeau Av.

Elysian Fields Av.

Franklin Av.

University of New Orleans

PONTCHARTRAIN PARK

Press Av.

Mirabeau Av.

Press Av.

Chef Menteur

EDGEWOOD PARK

Dillard University

FAIRGROUNDS RACETRACK

Hope

Hope

Claiborne Av.

Franklin Av.

Bernard Av.

Esplanade Av.

Almonaster Av.

Franklin Av.

Rampart St.

ORLEANS PARISH

Earhart

Hamilton

Blvd.

Leonidas

Palmetto

Claiborne Av.

Leonidas

S. Carrollton Av.

Broadway

State

Leonidas

Broadway

S. St. Charles Av

AUDUBON PARK

Zoo

Magazine

State

Tchoupitulas

Jefferson Av.

Coliseum

Laurel

Tchoupitulas

Pontchartrain Expwy.

Broad

Washington

Earhart   Blvd.

Toledano

Napoleon Av.

Tulane Stadium

Tulane University

Loyola University

Napoleon Av.

St.Charles Hospital

Claiborne Av.

Jackson Av.

Louisiana Av.

La Salle

Louisiana Av.

Coliseum

Laurel

Napoleon Av.

Canal Street

Orleans Av.

Cultural Center

ARMSTRONG P

Hospital
Hospital

City Hall

Superdome

Union Station

S. Claiborne Av.

S. Bolivar

Jackson Av.

Jackson Av.

Jackson Av. Ferry

Tchoupitulas

IRISH CHANNEL

GARDEN DISTRICT

St. Charles Av.

Magazine

Laurel

Coliseum

Jackson Av.

FRENCH QUARTER

Decatur

Jackson Square

Jax Brewery

Custom House

New Orleans Cent.

CENTRAL BUSINESS DISTRICT

Y.M.C.A.

Howard

Howard

Aquarium

Riverwalk

Canal St.Ferry

Patterson

Bourny Av.

Algiers Point

Hospital

Nunez

Yeche

ALGIERS

Franklin St.

W. Bank Expwy.

Stumpf Blvd.

Stumpf Bl.

Grefna Blvd.

Mississippi

HARVEY

4 th St.

4 th St.

JEFFERSON PARISH

Manhattan Bl.

Lafayette St.

West Bank Expwy.

Greater New Orleans is a well-kept secret. The French Quarter so dominates most people's perception that the rest of the city recedes into the background. A pity for visitors; a bonus, perhaps, for New Orleanians, who recognize a *lagniappe* when they see one. A *lagniappe* (pronounced lan-yap) is common parlance for a treat, a little reward, a pleasant "something extra." From the attractions and universities Uptown to the 19th-century charm of Algiers to the art galleries of the Warehouse District: these are bonuses to a visit to New Orleans. None are far away. Most can be reached without a car. All are less crowded than the French Quarter and often less expensive, too.

New Orleans' above-ground cemeteries are spread throughout the city. So are live oak trees, the most famous being the Dueling Oaks in City Park, the site of many a swashbuckling dare. Audubon Park, designed by Frederick Law Olmsted, the man who created New York's Central Park, has antebellum embellishments, plus several white alligators. Plantations, strung along the Mississippi like pale pearls on a necklace, can be visited in a day or a stay stretched to a week.

But New Orleans is not just 19th-century elegance. The Central Business District is home to the soaring Superdome, where 76,000 thoroughly modern football fans cheer the Sugar Bowl to victory every year, caring not a fig for cast-iron filigree, Andrew Jackson, or the "Wah." The New Orleans Convention Center ranks third in the US in terms of convenient exhibit space.

The gateway to Greater New Orleans is Canal Street, one of the widest thoroughfares in the country. Canal Street is the dividing line between uptown and downtown, or, locally, upriver and downriver. (New Orleanians also refer to "riverside" or "lakeside" when explaining directions.) Uptown is also a geographical location, an elegant neighborhood which contains the campuses of Tulane and Loyola universities.

Most Mardi Gras parades take place along Canal Street, and with it massive attendant paraphernalia. The largest parades, Endymion and Bacchus, feature a combined total of 75 floats and 60 marching bands. Their 2,300 members throw around 2½ million doubloons to avid spectators. In fact, the "Greatest Free Show on Earth" generates nearly half a billion dollars annually for the city of New Orleans. Which isn't a bad *lagniappe*, when you think about it.

Preceding pages: Mark Twain's favorite river; floating through space.

CITIES OF THE DEAD

Visitors should tour the graveyards in the company of an organized group.

Visitors to New Orleans may not be dying to tour the local cemeteries, but the city's unique burial grounds are certainly among the top sightseeing attractions. In contrast to the lush green lawns, landscaping, and headstones of graveyards in most other US cities, the old cemeteries in New Orleans are notable for their above-ground tombs and mausoleums.

Called **Cities of the Dead**, they look like small towns with tiny windowless houses and buildings whose front doors are stark white marble slabs. The tombs are lined up, row after row, with brick or stone walkways laid out in front. The oldest are stepped-top tombs of handmade brick, with inscriptions that have long since faded. Some of the tombs are small and very simple, others are toy-like versions of court houses, banks, and grand Garden District mansions, and still others are elaborate monuments featuring gleaming white marble statuary. Many are surrounded by ornate cast-iron fences and garnished with frilly grilles. The largest and most spectacular tombs are those of the city's many benevolent societies.

There were essentially two reasons for the custom of above-ground burials in New Orleans. The first had to do with Mother Nature, and the second had to do with the mother countries, France and Spain. With regard to the former, much of the city is four to five feet below sea level, and graves that were dug in the ground rapidly filled with water. (The 20th-century drainage system now makes underground burials possible.) In addition to that practical consideration, New Orleans French and Spanish Creoles were always fond of emulating fashions in Europe, where above-ground burials were customary.

In the 19th century, many of the grand tombs were graced with *immortelles*, which were ornamental wreaths made of wire, beads, and glass. They were usually imported from France, where they were quite the rage. In 1883, Mark Twain wrote sarcastically of this artificial ornamentation: "The *immortelle* requires no attention; you just hang it up, and there you are; just leave it alone, it will take care of your grief for you and keep it in mind better than you can; stands weather first rate, and lasts like boiler iron."

It is not recorded whether Twain influenced the demise of the *immortelle*, but the ornament is no longer used as a decoration on tombs.

All Saints Day (November 1) is a day of remembrance and a religious as well as a bank holiday in New Orleans. For several weeks prior to that day, New Orleanians are busy cleaning, repairing, and freshening up their family tombs. Early in the morning of All Saints Day, people begin arriving at cemeteries all

over the city, and thousands of chrysanthemums are placed on the tombs. The flowers are often elaborately fashioned in the shape of crosses and wreaths. By evening there are throngs of people in the cemeteries, and there is a surprisingly festive atmosphere.

The city's first officially designated cemetery no longer exists. It was laid out in around 1725 on St Peter Street between Burgundy and Rampart streets, and was in use for about 70 years. The great fire of 1788 destroyed virtually all of the city, and an ensuing epidemic of yellow fever took hundreds of lives. City officials closed the cemetery, and in 1789, **St Louis Cemetery No. 1**, the oldest extant graveyard, was established. (Interestingly, the Royal Edict for the new cemetery decreed that the old St Peter Cemetery must eventually be used for housing sites.)

This new cemetery was laid out back of town in a swampy area bordered by the present Basin, Treme, St Louis, and Conti streets. It was established during the Spanish colonial period, and the Spaniards followed a centuries-old custom of building a wall around the graveyard. The wall vaults, which are about 12 foot high and 9 foot wide, are called "ovens" because of their resemblance to bakers' ovens. They were used for multiple burials, often by indigent families who were unable to afford individual, private tombs.

Visitors are often curious to know how so many people could be buried in a single vault. The answer is, a year and a day after a body is interred the tomb is opened, the remains are swept to the back of the vault, and the remainder of the casket is taken out, thus creating room for another permanent resident. Most private tombs have two vaults, one above the other, and a lower receptacle in which bodies are placed after removal from the vault.

As a rule, the tombs in St Louis No. 1 are not quite as ornate as those in the later cemeteries, but this site is the final resting place for many prominent early

Fallen angel; Tiffany window in Tilton grave.

Orleanians. Among them are **Etienne de Bore**, who was the city's first mayor and the first to granulate sugar successfully. Others include Paul Morphy, a 19th-century world chess champion; Myra Clark Gaines, whose 65-year lawsuit over land ownership was one of the longest and most complicated of the 19th century; **Blaise Cenas**, the first US Postmaster in New Orleans; the two wives of William C. C. Claiborne, the first American Governor of Louisiana, whose tombs bear remarkably similar inscriptions; **Bernard de Marigny**, a fabulously wealthy Creole for whom the suburb Faubourg Marigny is named; and **Marie Laveau**, the city's most infamous voodoo queen, whose tomb is usually adorned with voodoo charms and brick-dust crosses. (Another Marie Laveau may be buried in St Louis Cemetery No. 2.)

Some of the more elaborate tombs are those of the Italian Mutual Benevolent Society and the French Society and the five-tiered structure of the Portuguese Benevolent Association. At the rear of the cemetery there used to be a Protestant section, but in the 1830s, due to an extension of Treme Street, most of the graves were emptied and the remains moved. Only a small, rather desolate part of the Protestant burial ground can still be seen today.

St Louis Cemetery No. 2, bounded by Iberville, Conti, St Louis, and Bienville streets, was consecrated in 1823. As well as containing the tombs of 19th-century New Orleans mayors **Pitot** and **Girod**, and **pirate captain Dominique You**, who fought with Andrew Jackson in the Battle of New Orleans, the cemetery boasts tombs designed by J.N.B. dePouilly.

When the French architect arrived here in the 1830s, having graduated from the Ecole des Beaux Arts, he brought with him sketches of Père Lachaise cemetery in Paris. The sketchbook still exists, and the influence of the well-known French cemetery can clearly be seen in the dePouilly-

St Louis Cemetery No. 1.

designed tombs still in New Orleans.

The worldwide popularity of the Greek Revival style was, quite literally, carried right to the grave. It was during this period that such flourishes as Ionic, Corinthian, and Doric columns, pediments, and other such ornamentation began to turn up in the New Orleans cemeteries. The best dePouilly designs in St Louis No. 2 are the society tomb of the **Orleans Cazadores** and those of the **Peniston-Duplantier**, **Miltenberger** and **Grailhe** families. DePouilly's final resting place is in a wall vault located between St Louis and Conti streets.

St Louis Cemetery No. 3, the newest and largest of the St Louis cemeteries, is on Esplanade Avenue near the entrance to City Park. It opened for business, so to speak, in 1854. The entrance is through a broad and very ornate iron gate, and the paved roads are wide enough for cars. The mortal remains of many priests and nuns are enshrined here, and there are several "society"

tombs: the Young Men's Benevolent Association's; the United Slavonian Benevolent Society's, and the unmistakably Greek, very ornate mausoleum of the Hellenic Orthodox Community.

The largest and most photographed of the city's many cemeteries is **Metairie Cemetery**, at Metairie Road and Pontchartrain Boulevard. The cemetery covers 150 acres and contains more than 7,000 graves. It was established in 1872 on the site of the old Metairie Race Course, and the plan for the cemetery follows the oval shape of the racetrack. Unlike other New Orleans cemeteries, this one is notable not only for the spectacular tombs and mausoleums but also for the lovely landscaping and pretty trees.

The oldest tomb in the cemetery is that of the **Duverje** family of Algiers. Erected in the Algiers cemetery in about 1848, it was dismantled and moved to Metairie in 1916. There are a number of extremely flashy mausoleums in Metairie, notably the pyramid-shaped **Brunswig mausoleum**, which features a large marble sphinx, and the gaudy Romanesque Revival tomb of Salvatore Pizzati, an immigrant who amassed a fortune when he began to import tropical fruit. The marble-winged angels clasping each other atop the **Aldige tomb** commemorate the wife and daughter who drowned at sea. Architect **James Gallier**, Sr also perished at sea, and he lies beneath a handsome monument that bears a touching inscription written by his son.

Four statues, representing Faith, Hope, Charity, and Memory, surround the base of a 60-foot shaft on the **Moriarity tomb**. An equestrian statue of Confederate General Albert Sidney Johnston tops the tomb of the **Army of Tennessee**. The body of Jefferson Davis, who died in New Orleans in 1889, was interred for four years in the tomb of the **Army of Northern Virginia**. The remains of the Confederate president were later removed to Richmond, Virginia.

Left, knockin' on heaven's door. Right, Metairie cemetery.

184

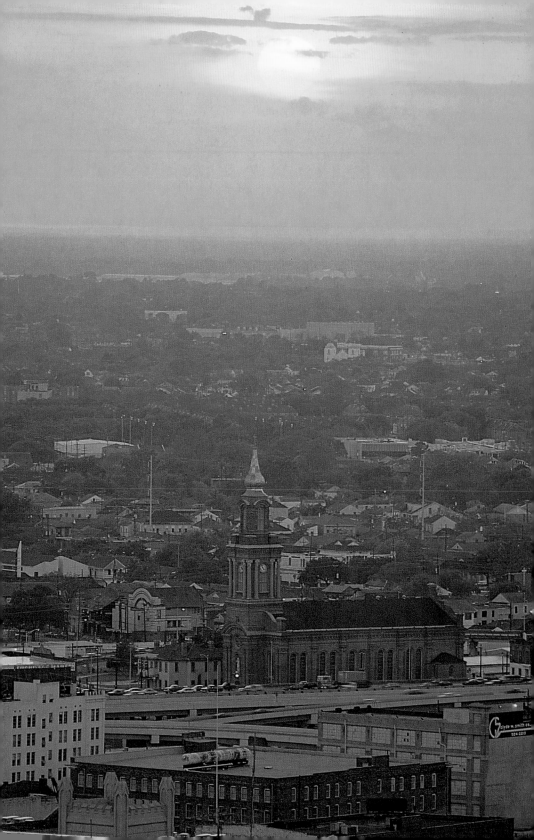

CANAL STREET TO THE WAREHOUSE DISTRICT

Canal Street, one of the widest shopping streets in America, leads all the way from the Mississippi River to City Park Avenue near City Park. A broad, tree-lined street with tall, graceful lamp-posts, it serves as a gateway to the river, a signpost towards the Central Business District, and the dividing line between uptown and downtown.

Bronze plaques in the base of each lamp-post commemorate the four governments whose flags have flown over the city: France, Spain, the Confederate States of America, and the United States. As a holdover from the early days, street names change when crossing Canal from the French Quarter.

At the foot of Canal Street – that is, the riverside end of the street – the **World Trade Center** rises 33 stories above the city. A glass elevator eases up the side of the building to the enclosed observation deck on the 31st floor, an excellent place to get a 360-degree lay of the land. In addition to coin-operated telescopes there are strategically placed blown-up photographs with descriptive labels. With the Mississippi River curving around to the rear, the spires of St Louis Cathedral and the sloping roofs of the French Quarter are to the right; Lake Pontchartrain is a long, blue ribbon in the far distance straight ahead; and the Warehouse District, the Garden District, and Uptown are to the left.

Directly behind the World Trade Center, lying alongside the river, is **Plaza de Espana**, a broad open expanse of colorful tiles whose centerpiece is a splendid fountain that bubbles up to 50 foot. One of four "foreign plazas" in the area, **Spanish Plaza**, as it is better known, was a Bicentennial gift to the city from Spain in 1976. A large bronze equestrian statue of Bernard Galvez, an early Spanish governor of Louisiana, stands at the entrance to the plaza. The **Canal Street Wharf** and the **Poydras**

Street Wharf along Spanish Plaza are departure points for the frilly sightseeing riverboats that go out to play on the Mississippi.

The ferry that crosses the Mississippi to Algiers Point (taking both pedestrians and vehicles) also puts in at the Canal Street Wharf. On Lundi Gras (literally, Fat Monday – the night before the Fat Tuesday of Mardi Gras), the city tosses a huge, free-to-the-public masked ball in Spanish Plaza, replete with music, fireworks, and frivolity. The mayor is on hand to kick off this final 24 hours of Mardi Gras and to welcome Rex, who arrives by barge to make his first Carnival appearance. The Krewe of Proteus, one of the oldest of the Carnival organizations, parades down to the plaza.

The front doors of **Riverwalk**, a festival marketplace, open onto Spanish Plaza. This multimillion-dollar complex occupies one of the sites of the 1984 World's Fair, and is similar to other recently developed riverfront

schemes in New York and Baltimore. As its name might suggest, Riverwalk runs smack along the river. The long, split-level collection of shops, restaurants, and fast-food outlets extends upriver from Spanish Plaza all the way to the New Orleans Convention Center. The Hilton Hotel on Poydras Street is adjacent to Riverwalk, so close as to be virtually a part of it. There is another entrance to Riverwalk at Julia Street, which is one of the main drags of the Warehouse District.

Paralleling Riverwalk, Convention Center Boulevard runs, interestingly, to the **New Orleans Convention Center**. Also sitting on one of the 1984 World's Fair sites, the NOCC is one of the largest such centers in the world. It has 700,000 square feet of contiguous exhibit space and is booked up right into the first decade of the 21st century. This building is big enough to swallow up all 27 floats of the Krewe of Bacchus, which mounts one of the most spectacular parades of Mardi Gras. The 700-member krewe parades through the streets the Sunday night before Mardi Gras and winds up in the Convention Center for its annual bash.

The madness called Mardi Gras begins to reach fever pitch the Friday night before Fat Tuesday. During the weekend and on through Fat Tuesday there are parades every day and every night. The downtown parades all march along Canal Street. Thousands of people line the parade routes, and by the big day as many as a million people throng the adjoining areas. Offices are closed, and Canal Street becomes one of the main venues for what is called the "greatest free show on earth." Mardi Gras in New Orleans is the biggest bash in all of North America.

At the upper end of Convention Center Boulevard and Riverwalk, in the area surrounding Julia Street, is the revitalized **Warehouse District**. From the 1830s until around the Civil War, Julia Row – the block of Julia Street between St Charles Avenue and Camp

Piazza d'Italia.

Street – was one of the most fashionable addresses in town. The 13 brick townhouses on the uptown side of Julia Street were known as the "13 Sisters." Around the turn of this century this area began to deteriorate. For many long years it was distinguished only by old abandoned warehouses and factories. Fortunately, **Julia Row** has been restored, and all has come to life again, with restaurants and sleek bars springing up as a result. The **Preservation Resource Center**, whose offices are in Julia Row, was one of the driving forces behind the restoration project. In addition to its displays of the city's historic structures the Center occasionally conducts guided architectural tours.

SoHo of the South: This area is the leading center for visual arts in New Orleans. Since 1984 more than 20 art galleries have opened here, leading to the formation of the prestigious Warehouse District Arts Association. The area's status was confirmed in late 1990, with the revamping of a 19th-

century four-story brick warehouse on Camp Street: the **Contemporary Arts Center**. Ten local artists assisted the architect, Stephen Bingler, with the renovation plans for the center, which, as well as showcasing local artists, provides a venue for drama, dance, and performance art shows.

There's a flourishing style scene around the center, the nearby galleries and local watering holes, which escalates in the fall with the beginning of "the season." Gallery owners from other parts of the US have gravitated to the area, with an eagerness that has led to one magazine describing the Warehouse District as "the SoHo of the South" (after the district in New York).

All this activity is not simply window dressing. An art columnist for the *Times-Picayune*, Roger Green, identifed a local artistic movement, which he called "Visionary Imagists," in which artists and sculptors "give expression to fantastic visions, rendered meticulously and tending towards moraliza-

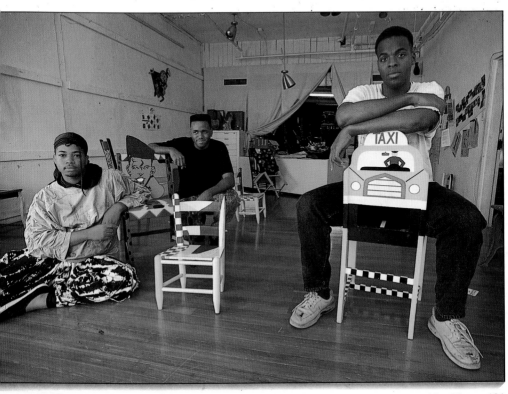

tion, often cloaked in absurd humor."

Two museums of note can be found in this vicinity. The **Louisiana Children's Museum** on Julia Street is a first-class facility, offering hands-on exhibits that are both educational and fun for the little ones. And on Camp Street, housed in a rather brooding Romanesque building, the **Confederate Museum** contains memorabilia pertaining to the Civil War, including personal effects of Jefferson Davis, president of the Confederate States of America, and a campaign chest that belonged to General Robert E. Lee.

New Orleans has other foreign plazas as well as Spanish Plaza, and they're all grouped near to each other. An unflattering statue of Sir Winston Churchill stands in **British Place**, a circle of green grass near the front entrance to the Hilton Hotel. On Poydras Street near Tchoupitoulas Street, **Piazza d'Italia**, featuring a fountain shaped like Italy, pays tribute to the more than 200,000 Italians who live in the city. This is the scene of much festivity during the annual Columbus Day celebration. Piazza d'Italia "starred" in the opening scene of the film *The Big Easy*. **Place de France** boasts a small but quite bright gold-plated statue of Joan of Arc.

The huge modern structure anchored on Canal Street across from the Canal Street Wharf is the $40 million **Aquarium of the Americas**, which opened in 1990. The one million-gallon aquarium houses over 10,000 fish, reptiles, birds, and foliage indigenous to North, Central, and South America. Major exhibits are the Caribbean Reef Environment; the Amazon Rainforest Habitat; the Mississippi River and Delta Habitat; and the Gulf of Mexico Exhibit. The aquarium is part of landscaped, 16-acre **Woldenberg Riverfront Park**, which stretches along the Mississippi from Canal Street to Jackson Square in the French Quarter, with possible plans for an extension.

Across Canal Street from the Rivergate, **Canal Place** is a classy in-

The Aquarium holds one million gallons of water.

door mall whose tenants include the likes of Saks Fifth Avenue, Godiva Chocolatiers, and FAO Schwarz. Built around a stunning atrium, the mall connects Canal Street with Iberville Street in the French Quarter. On the third level there is a food court and four first-run cinemas. Sitting on top of the mall is the upscale Westin Canal Place Hotel. Glass elevators purr up to its posh marbled lobby on the 11th floor.

Occupying the entire next block, away from the river, is the grey-granite **US Customhouse**. This behemoth is on the site of Fort St Louis, which guarded the 18th-century French city. Work began on the Customhouse in 1848 but was halted by the unpleasantness known in these parts as the War of Northern Aggression. New Orleans fell to the Union forces in 1862, and this building was headquarters for General Benjamin "Spoons" Butler. The general earned his spurious nickname as a result of his alleged penchant for pilfering fine Southern silver.

The building was then called Federal Prison No. 6, and at one time imprisoned 2,000 Confederate soldiers. Construction of the building was not completed until 1881, long after the war ended. It still has a rather unfinished look due to the empty niches on the exterior walls. The niches were meant to hold statues but for reasons unknown they were never put in place.

Despite its austere exterior, the Customhouse is worth a visit to see the **Great Marble Hall**. Hailed by the American Institute of Architects as one of the finest examples of Greek Revival architecture in this country, the marbled hall measures 95 feet by 125 feet and is 54 feet high. Fourteen Corinthian columns, each 41 feet high and 4 feet in diameter, support a dramatic skylight. On the riverside wall a huge marble bas-relief depicts the Great Seal of the State of Louisiana flanked by General Andrew Jackson and Jean Baptiste le Moyne, Sieur de Bienville, who founded the city of New Orleans.

iverwalk ccupies a te of the 984 World's air.

THE CENTRAL BUSINESS DISTRICT

In the earliest days a vast plantation owned by the Jesuits extended upriver from what is now the French Quarter. In 1763, the Jesuits were expelled from Louisiana (the order was subsequently re-established here); their land was confiscated and sold at public auction. This area comprises much of today's Central Business District (which locals call the CBD), which is roughly bordered by the Mississippi River, Canal Street, Loyola Avenue, and Howard Avenue. It also includes the Riverwalk complex and the Warehouse District, discussed in the preceding chapter.

The Jesuits' land passed on to Bernard Gravier and his wife, Marie. Following a cataclysmic fire in 1788 that virtually decimated the original French Creole city, the Graviers began to parcel the former plantation into lots, developing it into the city's first *faubourg* (suburb). The *magazins*, or warehouses, along the river led to the name Magazine Street; Camp Street was named for the camp of huts in which the slaves lived; and Poydras Street and Girod Street were named for investors in this real estate venture. The suburb was first called Ville Gravier, but after the death of his wife, Gravier changed the name to Faubourg Ste. Marie in tribute.

After the Louisiana Purchase, Anglo-Americans began to pour into New Orleans. Snubbed by the Creoles, they settled in **Faubourg Ste. Marie** and in time the suburb became known as the American Section. By the 1830s, New Orleans was an officially divided city with separate city governments for the Creoles and the Americans.

Dividing the American Section from the French Quarter was a wide stretch of land along which a canal was to have been built. The plan for the canal was never actually implemented, and the land designated for it became a neutral ground on which the Americans and the Creoles sometimes skirmished. The median down the center of Canal Street – and in fact, all medians – is still known to New Orleanians as the "**neutral ground**."

Within the boundaries of the CBD are "progressive" glass-and-concrete skyscrapers and quaint cast-iron buildings. This area is home to the sprawling Superdome, the high-tech, high-rise convention hotels and several important monuments. At Canal and Carondelet streets the historic **St Charles streetcar** takes on passengers for its Uptown ramble through the Garden District and beyond.

The white, three-story Greek Revival building at 824 Canal Street was designed by James Gallier, Sr as a home for the Mercer family. It now houses the exclusive **Boston Club**, an elite private club that was founded in 1841. Around the corner from the Boston Club, at 132 Baronne Street, is the Jesuit **Church of the Immaculate Conception**. The ex-

Preceding pages: blues on a summer night. **Left**, the Superdome. **Right**, the Orpheum Theatre.

otic Spanish-Moorish building, with its twin onion domes and horseshoe arches, is a CBD standout. Built in 1930, it is an exact replica of a church that stood on this site in 1857. The early church fell into a state of disrepair and had to be demolished.

The interior of the more recent church is no less dramatic than the exterior. Much of it – notably the cast-iron pews and bronze gilt altar – was retained from the 19th-century church. The statue of the Virgin Mary was to have stood in the royal chapel at Tuileries, but that plan was swept away along with the royal family during the Revolution of 1848. Much later, the New Orleans congregation bought the statue in France for the sum of $5,000.

A pleasant shortcut from Baronne Street to University Place is through the plush scarlet-carpeted lobby of the Fairmont Hotel. **University Place** is so named because this was the original home of Tulane University. Founded in 1834, the university moved Uptown in 1894. The **Orpheum Theatre** is almost directly across the street from the Fairmont. Built in 1918 and boasting an elaborate Beaux Arts facade, the theater has been home to the New Orleans Symphony Orchestra. In its early days it was one of the major stops on the Orpheum vaudeville circuit; top performers, from Harry Houdini to Bob Hope, played the theater.

Touring companies and other top-name entertainers are booked into the **Saenger Theatre** at the corner of Canal and Rampart streets. Its surroundings are tacky, but this theater has a lovely Italian Renaissance auditorium, replete with statuary and "stars" that twinkle in the midnight-blue ceiling when the lights are lowered.

Rampart Street, the lakeside border of the French Quarter, has for many years been in a disgraceful state of repair. The stretch between St Peter and Canal streets is fairly safe during daylight hours, but visitors should avoid walking alone on any section of Ram- **Shades.**

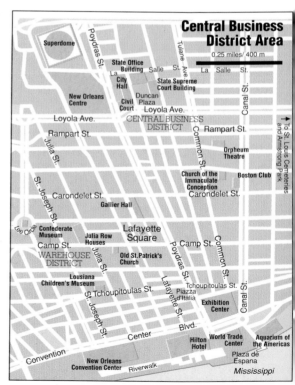

part Street after dark. **Armstrong Park**, whose entrance is at St Ann Street, is dangerous. This is a particular shame, since an entertainment complex sits within the park. The New Orleans Ballet performs in the **Theatre for the Performing Arts**, and many Carnival balls and concerts are held in its **Municipal Auditorium**.

Old Congo Square, which many historians believe was the actual birthplace of jazz, lies in front of Municipal Auditorium. Now called **Beauregard Square**, this was the place where 18th- and 19th-century slaves gathered each Sunday afternoon to chant and dance to the accompaniment of tam-tams. The etiology of jazz aside, these days it's only really safe to venture into Armstrong Park with the large crowds that attend various arts performances or who mill around the auditorium after a Carnival parade.

During the day it is safe to stop in **Our Lady of Guadalupe Church** (400 N. Rampart St). This small, unpretentious

ome believe ızz began ere.

church dates from 1826, when this area was on the fringes of the city. Originally called the Mortuary Chapel, it was built near the cemeteries as a "burying chapel" for victims of yellow fever and cholera. To the right of the entrance is a statue of St Expedite. According to a local legend, a crate arrived at the church marked "expedite," and the statue inside was duly mounted. That may be true, but St Expedite also figures prominently in voodoo culture.

Basin Street, of song and legend, parallels Rampart Street. This, too, is an extremely unsavory, unsafe thoroughfare. St Louis Cemetery No. 1, the city's oldest extant cemetery, is on Basin Street behind Our Lady of Guadalupe Church. (The cemetery is covered on pages 182–83.)

A notorious housing project occupies the site of Storyville, the city's old red-light district, which was itself notorious. In the mid-19th century New Orleans, never exactly a tame town, seems to have been awash with "lewd and las-

civious women." An outraged city alderman introduced a bill that set down boundaries within which prostitution could be practiced. The bill passed, and in 1897, **Storyville** was established. Storyville was bounded by Iberville, St Louis, North Robertson, and Basin streets, and within that area some classy establishments flourished, along with tough bordellos. Lulu White's Mahogany Hall and Josie Arlington's place were among the fancier "sporting houses."

Jazz musicians entertained in the parlors, and on the street corners ragtag groups called "spasm bands" held forth. Storyville thrived for 20 years, before being closed in 1917 by order of the United States Navy. Absolutely nothing remains of the red-light district, and visitors are strongly advised not to go exploring here.

For one block, between Canal Street and Tulane Avenue (which is an extension of Common Street), Basin Street is called **Elk Place** – so-named for the

Elks Club that used to be located here. The **statue** at Canal and Basin streets is of **Simon Bolivar**. In the tree-shaded neutral ground of Elk Place the sidewalk is carved with all of the historic events and dates in the city's history.

Upriver of Elk Place, Basin Street becomes Loyola Avenue. At the corner of Tulane and Loyola avenues is the main branch of the New Orleans Public Library. Charity Hospital and the medical schools of Louisiana State University and Tulane University are nearby on Tulane Avenue.

Heavily trafficked Loyola Avenue zips smartly along, whizzing past **Duncan Plaza** and the **Civic Center**. The landscaped green lawn of the plaza rolls out before **City Hall**, the **State Office Building**, and the **State Supreme Court Building**. A few blocks farther along on Loyola Avenue is **Union Passenger Terminal**, where interstate buses and Amtrak trains pull in. Although they are very busy during the day, neither the terminal nor Duncan

Super exhibition center.

Plaza is the place to dawdle after dark.

Poydras Street is another of the CBD's main drags. Like Canal Street, it is a wide boulevard whose foot stands near the Mississippi. If the streets of the CBD didn't fan out to follow the river's curves, Poydras would parallel Canal Street. The street is notable for its plethora of towering, streamlined office buildings. Not far from the Civic Center, the stupendous **Superdome** hunkers like a giant spaceship on Poydras Street. The Dome is home to the New Orleans Saints football team and host of the annual Sugar Bowl college football game. More Super Bowl games have been played here than in any other city.

In addition to sports events, the Dome has been the arena of everything from Rolling Stones concerts to the 1988 Republican National Convention. It opened in 1975, cost upwards of $180 million, and is touted as the largest facility of its kind in the world. The statistics are mind-boggling. It encompasses a total land area of 52 acres – the dome alone covers more than 9 acres – and has on-premises parking for 5,000 cars and 250 buses. It rises to a height of 27 stories; the diameter of the dome is 680 feet. There's much, much more that can be learned on one of the daily guided tours.

The Superdome, New Orleans Centre, the Hyatt Regency Hotel, and Poydras Plaza form a veritable community along Poydras Street. The newest and most stylish kid on the block is the pretty pink **New Orleans Centre**, which is a high-rise complex of offices and shops. Macy's and Lord & Taylor are the best-known of its many stores. **Poydras Plaza**, of which the Hyatt Regency is a part, also contains offices and shops, and has been a fixture on this street for many years.

At St Charles Avenue, Poydras Street forms the lower border of Lafayette Square, the city's second oldest square. Gallier Hall on St Charles Avenue faces the square, adding a distinguished air.

New Orleans Centre.

In the 19th century, when the city was divided into separate municipalities, this area served the Americans in the same way that Place d'Armes (now Jackson Square) served the Creoles. Gallier Hall was their city hall, Lafayette Square was a social center, and St Patrick's Cathedral (on Camp Street across the square) was the Irish American answer to the French St Louis Cathedral.

Gallier Hall is the most splendid Greek Revival building still on its feet in New Orleans. It was designed by noted New Orleans architect James Gallier, Sr and constructed between 1845 and 1850. Ionic columns support an elaborate pediment on which there are sculptured figures representing Justice, Liberty, and Commerce. Gallier Hall remained the seat of city government until the present City Hall was completed in 1957. Here, on April 29, 1862, not long after Admiral Farragut shouted the famous words, "Damn the torpedoes, full speed ahead!" Union forces took possession of the city.

In the parlor of Gallier Hall the bodies of Jefferson Davis, P.G.T. Beauregard, and city mayors have lain in state. Since 1958 the building has been administered by the New Orleans Cultural Center Commission. The building contains offices and is not open to the public. A highlight of Mardi Gras takes place when the Rex parade pauses and the King of Carnival, resplendent on his royal float, exchanges toasts with the mayor at Gallier Hall.

Lafayette Square dates back to 1788, when it was laid out as part of Faubourg Ste. Marie. Centerpiece of the landscaped square is a tall bronze statue of Henry Clay, who served in the US Senate in the 19th century and frequently visited New Orleans. The statue was originally erected in 1860 at Canal and St Charles; it was moved to Lafayette Square in 1901. A statue of John McDonogh, a benefactor for whom several of the city's public schools are named, stands on a gar-

Gallier Hall; Lee Circle.

landed pedestal facing St Charles Avenue. The square is a beehive of activity during business hours, but it is not at all safe after the sun goes down.

To the Irish Catholics who came to New Orleans it seemed that in St Louis Cathedral, God spoke only in French. They first built a small wooden church on this site, and then laid plans for a grand cathedral. Charles and James Dakin were the original architects for **St Patrick's Cathedral**, and they patterned the church after York Minster in England. There were structural problems in the marshy area, and James Gallier, Sr was called in to assist. (He bought pew No. 27 on the center aisle and worshipped here).

The cornerstone for St Patrick's Cathedral was laid in 1838, and completed in 1840. The interior is stunning, with a vaulted, ribbed ceiling and handsome stained-glass windows. Three huge murals behind the main altar were painted in 1841 by Leon Pomarede. The Transfiguration is flanked on the right by *Christ Walking on the Water* and on the left by St Patrick.

A few blocks up at Howard Avenue, several streets converge and traffic whips around the **statue** of **General Robert E. Lee** at **Lee Circle**. The Confederate general died in 1870, and his admirers here immediately began a fund-raising drive to establish a monument in his memory. At that time the city was still under Reconstruction rule, and that fact plus many difficulties in raising money delayed completion of the statue until 1884.

Dignitaries present at the unveiling included Jefferson Davis and P.G.T. Beauregard, the Fort Sumter Confederate general. The bronze statue of Lee stands on a 60-foot pedestal, with the general resolutely facing north. In a city where Eastern Avenue steadfastly runs north and south, this is about the only place in town where direction actually means anything. (A local joke has it that the nearby YMCA was built to remind Lee that the Yankees Might Come Again.)

My elephant
s over there,
fficer.

THE GARDEN DISTRICT

According to some people's accounts, by the 1800s New Orleans was the wealthiest city in the United States. Cotton, sugar, and timber had made local Americans (as opposed to Creoles) millionaires, and they built elegant, sometimes fanciful homes in an area upriver from the Vieux Carré. The 1830s ushered in what is known as the city's Golden Age, a period of boom-town prosperity that lasted until the Civil War. Even after the war, splendid homes continued to be built in this suddenly desirable part of New Orleans.

Growth was spurred by the opening in 1835 of the New Orleans and Carrollton Railroad along what is now **St Charles Avenue**. The **St Charles streetcar**, itself a National Historic Landmark, follows the route of the railroad and is the oldest continuously operating street railway system in the world. By the time the city of Lafayette was annexed by New Orleans in 1852, the Garden District, as the area became known, was already a very posh residential section of town.

The district is bordered by Magazine Street and Jackson, Louisiana, and St Charles avenues. It's possible to get a tempting taste of the area by driving along **Prytania Street**, the Garden District's main thoroughfare, which is lined with handsome homes. The best way to see the sights is with an organized tour. Or, you can take the St Charles streetcar, get off at Jackson Avenue, and simply wander around.

The most predominant – which is not to say the purest – architectural style in the Garden District is **Greek Revival**. By the early 19th century the enthusiasm for classic antiquity that began with the excavations in Pompeii, Herculaneum and Greece had reached the architectural equivalent of a crescendo. The Garden District is aslosh with Ionic, Doric, and Corinthian columns; Greek key motifs; ornamental molding, and fanciful details.

But other styles are also in evidence. With the Victorian Age came pointed Gothic arched windows with diamond-patterned lights; ornate **Italianate mansions** inspired by the Italian Renaissance; the mansard roofs and bull's-eye dormer windows of the Second Empire; and the fussy busyness of **Eastlake** and **Queen Anne**-style houses, with all kinds of spindlework, wooden beads, turrets, and trim. The lavish wrought- and cast-iron garnishes on the houses rival the most fanciful grillework in the French Quarter, and beveled and leaded glass embellish many of the houses' doors.

Among the famed architects who worked in New Orleans during the Golden Age were Jacques Nicholas Bussiere dePouilly, a graduate of the Ecole des Beaux Arts in Paris; James and Charles Dakin, whose work includes St Patrick's Cathedral on Camp Street; James Gallier, Sr; James Gallier,

Jr, and Henry Howard, who designed Italianate mansions in the Garden District, as well as Nottoway and Madewood, two restored plantations that can be seen west of New Orleans.

The area's status as a "center for gardens" was assured from the very beginning, when a break in the levee guarding the Mississippi broke, flooding several plantations, leaving them virtually bankrupt and depositing instead a fertile layer of silt. Another advantage was the district's position above the river, which provided a higher elevation and better drainage. Vegetation flourished. In contrast to the Creoles, whose homes were built around lush but hidden courtyards, the Americans surrounded their estates with landscaped lawns and gardens. The aptly named district of gardens is thick with magnolia trees, palm and banana trees, camellias, azaleas, and thousands of species of subtropical shrubs, plants, and flowers.

At Jackson and St Charles avenues, the snappy canopy of the **Pontchart-rain Hotel** (2031 St Charles Avenue) has long been one of the city's landmarks. The traditional, old-world hotel is one of the finest in the city and considered the best place to stay in the Garden District. Suites are named for the celebrities who made this their home while on the road – among them actors Richard Burton and Mary Martin.

The rather ghostly structure directly across the street from the Pontchartrain once housed the **Restaurant de la Tour Eiffel**. The building was designed and built for the restaurant that was for many years on the second level of the Eiffel Tower in Paris. Because of structural damage to the tower it was necessary that the restaurant be removed. It was meticulously disassembled, then shipped across the Atlantic, and ultimately reconstructed on this site. It opened with much hoopla in 1986, and enjoyed a couple of years of popularity before going bankrupt. Some locals speculate that New Orleanians will not support any restaurant that isn't at street

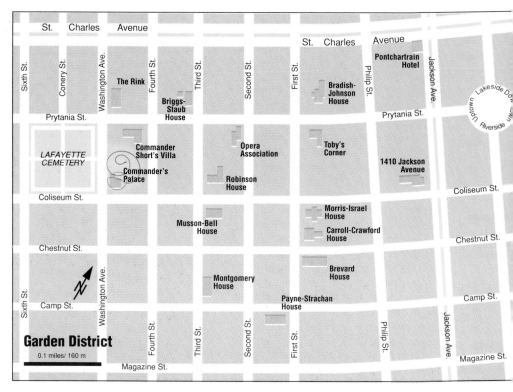

level, for this is not a "high-rise" town.

At **1410 Jackson Avenue** (corner of Coliseum Street), the huge plantation-style house with Greek Revival flourishes and belvedere was built in 1856 for a prosperous cotton factor named Henry Sullivan Buckner. The house is now occupied by the Soule Business College, the most established business school in the South.

The oldest house in the Garden District is believed to be **Toby's Corner** (also called the Toby-Westfeldt House) at 2340 Prytania Street. The rather simple (though hardly small) Greek Revival-raised cottage was built around 1838 for Thomas Toby, a Pennsylvania businessman. "Raised cottage," of which there are many examples in New Orleans, refers to a style of house in which the living quarters are on the upper level as protection from flooding. The lower floor, which is the marshland equivalent of a cellar, is usually used for storing non-valuable items.

Across the street from Toby's Cor-

ner, at 2343 Prytania Street, is the lavish **Bradish Johnson House**. Designed by New Orleans architect James Freret, who studied at the Ecole des Beaux Arts, this Second-Empire house dates from 1872. Since 1929 it has been the Louise S. McGehee School, a posh private school for girls.

Wrapped in elaborate, identical ironwork, the **Morris-Israel House** at 1331 First Street and the **Carroll-Crawford House** at 1315 First Street are Italianate mansions designed by William Jamison and built in 1869. At 1239 First Street, the rose motif in the cast-iron fence is carried over into the galleries of the stately **Brevard House**.

Cast-iron railings were rarely purely decorative. The houses in the Garden District had almost from the beginning been forced to surround themselves with fences (albeit wooden). This was to protect carefully tended lawns from the cattle which escaped on their way to the slaughterhouses by the river.

The imposing **Payne-Strachan**

he Bultman ouse as the inspiration for e set of uddenly, ast Summer.

House at 1134 First Street was built in the mid-1800s. In 1889, Jefferson Davis, former president of the Confederate States of America, fell ill while traveling through New Orleans en route to Beauvoir, his home in Mississippi. Unable to continue the trip, he was brought here to the home of his friend Jacob Payne, where he died.

By the time most of these existing houses were built, the layout for gardens in the Garden District had become more romantic and less rigid. Grounds surrounding the earliest houses had tended to be formal, their symmetrical lines following the European tradition for precise, highly stylized lawns. It was only later that planting began to be adapted for local purposes. Trees began to be placed well away from windows, to allow access to cooling breezes, and emphasis began to be placed on southern exposures, to ensure a warm spot to sit during the chilly winter months.

Surrounded by a white fence, the splendid two-story Italianate mansion

at 1415 Third Street is the **Robinson House**. Believed to have been the first house in New Orleans to have indoor plumbing, it was built in 1864–65, during the Civil War, for a Virginian named Walter Robinson.

Another handsome Italianate house is the **Musson-Bell House**, 1331 Third Street. It was built in 1853 for Michel Musson, a New Orleans Postmaster who was an uncle of French Impressionist painter Edgar Degas.

The interesting bracket-style **Montgomery House** at 1213 Third Street is the only one of its kind in the Garden District. It was built in 1868, after the Civil War, when most of New Orleans and the South were suffering under Reconstruction.

Note, while walking around the neighborhood, that several of the homes have covered front porches, ceilings painted a vivid sky blue. This is no accident. It's said that the underpinnings are deliberately painted this shade, in order to fool the local bee population. Rumor has it that hornets and other insects will not nest in the corners of sky-blue ceilings because they mistake it for the sky itself. Whether this is true or not is uncertain, but certainly it is a pleasing color.

Dating from 1849 and attributed to architect James Gallier, Jr, the **Briggs-Staub House**, 2605 Prytania, is a fanciful Gothic Revival house – the only such house in the Garden District. Nearby is an identical little guest house.

In the next block, at 2504 Prytania Street, the grand Greek Revival mansion with the octagonal turret houses headquarters for the **Women's Guild of the New Orleans Opera Association**. Groups of 20 or more can arrange for a tour of this lovely house.

Colonel Short's Villa, 1448 Fourth Street is a knockout in the Italianate style. Henry Howard designed it in 1859, the same year he concocted Nottoway Plantation upriver in White Castle. It was built for a merchant, Col. Robert Henry Short. The cast-iron corn-

Mile High Pie at the Pontchartrain Hotel.

stalk-and-morning-glories fence is almost identical to the one at 915 Royal Street in the French Quarter.

The delightful turreted Victorian mansion at 1403 Washington Avenue is home to the Brennan family's famed **Commander's Palace** restaurant. The ubiquitous New Orleans jazz brunches originated at Commander's, and are still considered the best in town.

Directly across the street from Commander's is **Lafayette Cemetery**, bordered by Washington Avenue, Coliseum, Prytania, and Sixth streets. It was established in 1833 as the burial ground for the City of Lafayette. Through the iron gates you can see the white aboveground tombs that are typical of New Orleans graveyards, but unfortunately, it is not safe to wander around alone. At 2727 Prytania, the small, multilevel shopping mall called **The Rink** was built in the late 1800s as the Crescent City Skating Rink.

Farther on, the well-known, 19th-century writer George Washington Cable lived in the raised cottage at **1313 Eighth Street**. Mark Twain was among the literary luminaries who were visitors in Cable's Garden District house.

Not far away, at 1525 Louisiana Avenue, is the elegant, three-story **Bultman House**. Architect William Freret built it in 1857 as his private residence. Nearly a century later the Bultman house was the inspiration for the set of Tennessee Williams' *Suddenly, Last Summer*. **Magazine Street** borders both the Garden District and the Irish Channel. This street is lined with Creole cottages and once-grand Victorian mansions that now house antique shops which offer pleasant browsing.

A Guide to New Orleans Architecture, published by the local chapter of the American Institute of Architects, is an illustrated paperback in which many Garden District homes are described. Except where noted, these are private residences, and are not open to the public except during Spring Fiesta when certain home owners allow tours.

NOTABLE NEIGHBORHOODS

From the foot of Canal Street, the ferry that carries both pedestrians and vehicles glides across the Mississippi River to **Algiers** on the West Bank. It's a delightful journey, lasting only a few minutes, but crossing Ol' Man River is a treat at any time, and this ride is even free. Although Algiers is incorporated into the city of New Orleans, the area has the appearance and ambience of a small turn-of-the-century town.

You somehow have the feeling that Algiers is peering over the levee at the skyscrapers of the Central Business District and wondering what life might be like in the 20th century. This little district is also called **Algiers Point**, the name by which the great bend in the river is known to the ship captains who must navigate around the difficult turn. (The West Bank is also accessible via the Crescent City Connection, formerly called the Greater New Orleans Mississippi River Bridge.)

Algiers dates from 1719, when Jean Baptiste le Moyne, Sieur de Bienville, was granted the West Bank tract. When African slaves were brought to this area in the early 18th century they were held in pens before being taken across the river and put on the auction block in New Orleans. The name Algiers perhaps comes from the African slave-trading center.

The Duverje Plantation served as the courthouse from 1866 until the Great Algiers Fire of 1895 destroyed it and some 200 other buildings. The present **Algiers Court House**, whose ornate crenellated turrets are clearly visible across the river in the French Quarter, was built in 1896 on the site of the plantation. Located on Morgan Street directly in front of the ferry landing, this is a marvelous Moorish-style structure whose interior features tall, dark, and handsome wooden doors, high ceilings, and a musty, somewhat anachronistic ambience. From the second floor balcony there is a splendid view across the river. If you visit weekdays between 8.30 a.m. and 2 p.m. you can have a look at the stately courtroom.

The main historical points of interest are in a small section bounded by **Opelousas Avenue**, **Belleville** and **Morgan** streets and the river. This is an easily walkable area, but it is not advisable to stroll around here after dark. To be sure, much of Algiers is in a sad state of repair, but the **Algiers Point Historic Renovation Project** is hard at work to remedy the situation. There are some delightful old restored homes sitting cheek by jowl with ramshackle shanties. Because of the 1895 fire, most of the homes date from around the turn of the century and reflect the ornate Victorian style.

The next street over from Morgan is Delaronde, the first block of which is dominated by the modern Louisiana Power and Light Building. But the next two blocks are lined with frilly ginger-

Preceding pages: the hazardous river bend at Algiers Point. **Left,** Irish dancing in the Irish Channel. **Right,** the West Bank lies across from the French Quarter.

bread row houses. The handsome Greek Revival **Seger-Rees House** at 405 Delaronde Street, built in 1849, mercifully survived the great fire.

Another survivor is the tiny Gothic **Mt Olivet Episcopal Church** at Pelican Avenue and Olivier Street. The church was built around 1854, and is the oldest remaining church in Algiers. A block away, at 705 Pelican Street, is the plantation-style **Vallette-Barrett House**, dating from around 1850. Next to it on the corner (725 Pelican Street), the **Algiers Point Public Library** is a small but eye-popping Italian Renaissance Revival building erected in 1910.

Olivier and Verret are two other streets that boast attractive buildings. Verret Street is also home to the grand French Gothic-style **Holy Name of Mary Church**, which was built in 1929 on the site of an older church. The stained glass and details are from the earlier, 1870 church.

Opelousas Avenue is a broad, pretty boulevard with fine old trees and a con-glomeration of handsome mansions and nondescript shotgun houses. ("Shotgun houses" are so-called because the floor plan develops in a straight line from front to rear, and a shot discharged in the front room would travel through every room in the house). The fiery red-brick **Firehouse** was built in 1925, and is still the place to call should a fire break out in town. The very fussy Byzantine-style building next to the station is a **Baptist Church**. And the Spanish Revival building with the red-tiled roof and bell tower is the **Martin Behrman School**, built in the 1930s.

At Opelousas and Brooklyn avenues there is a complex of buildings comprising the **Compass Marine Company**. The compound, built around a grassy lawn, looks for all the world like a tiny town within a small town. Within it are several **historic buildings** that have been moved from other areas, restored, and which now house offices. Of particular note is the tiny accountants' office, painted bright purple, which was

Leader of the band.

built in 1896 as the US Post Office in McDonoughville, Louisiana.

Two blocks from Opelousas Street, at 223 Newton Street, is the razzle-dazzle **Blaine Kern's Mardi Gras World**. (*See the short feature on page 223.*) This is the world's largest float building outfit and the place to watch Mardi Gras in the making. Think of it as Santa's Workshop, and take home a great souvenir photo of yourself and/or the kids with one of the gigantic figures.

Kern himself is captain of the Krewe of Alla, (which stands for **Al**giers, **La**ouisiana.) Mardi Gras memorabilia is on sale in the gift shop, and there is a short movie about Carnival shown in the little cinema.

UPTOWN AREA: The best way to get an overview of the Uptown sights is on the city's movable museum, the **St Charles streetcar**. It clangs and rumbles from **Canal Street** all the way up historic **St Charles Avenue**, turns with the bend of the river at **Carrollton Avenue**, and wheezes to a stop at **Palmer Park**.

There you can pay another fare and return to the CBD. A round-trip ride takes about an hour and a half; much longer, of course, if you get off to explore the Garden District, the University area, Audubon Park, and Audubon Zoo. A guided tour of the Uptown area is recommended for those interested in in-depth details.

The section of St Charles Avenue between Lee Circle and Jackson Avenue is not at the moment visually promising, lined as it is with fast-food chains and run-down houses. Known as the Lower Garden District, this area, like the Warehouse District, is, however, undergoing a renaissance as young, upwardly mobile folk buy and renovate these once-grand houses.

Above Jackson Avenue, things pick up considerably. Both sides of St Charles Avenue are adorned with handsome homes, many of them magnificent Greek Revival mansions. One such masterpiece is the **Dabney-O'Meallie House** at 2265 St Charles Avenue. As

Algiers architecture.

the avenue stretches upriver the homes are newer and the styles more eclectic.

Some of the St Charles Avenue landmarks to look for are the two Gothic-style churches: the Episcopal **Christ Church Cathedral** (No. 2919), which dates from 1887, and **Rayne Memorial Methodist Church** (No. 3900), which was built in 1875. The imposing **Bultman Funeral Home** (No. 3338) is the place to get laid to rest; behind the funeral home on Louisiana Avenue is the stellar **Bultman House**, described in the Garden District chapter. At No. 3811, the pretty, verandahed **Columns Hotel**, 3811 St Charles Avenue, was built as a private home in 1884. This house has been the set for several films, including Louis Malle's *Pretty Baby*, starring Brooke Shields. The Victorian Lounge of the hotel is a popular watering hole for Uptowners.

The **Sully House** (No. 4010) is an elaborate Queen Anne structure, replete with gables, gingerbread trim and towers, designed by Thomas Sully as his personal residence. The stunning **Sacred Heart Academy** (No. 4521) is a prestigious girls' school that was built around the turn of the century and run by the Sisters of the Sacred Heart.

One of the most exotic houses in the city is the **W.P. Brown House** (No. 4717), a Richardsonian Romanesque mansion with dramatic Syrian arches. Surrounded by perfectly manicured lawns, this house was built about 1902 at a cost of a quarter of a million dollars. The **Milton H. Latter Memorial Library** (No. 5120) is a Beaux Arts mansion that dates from 1907. In the 1940s it was the home of silent screen star Marguerite Clark and in 1948 was donated to the city. It's a fine place to sit and read Gothic Southern novels.

There are people in New Orleans who will tell you that scenes from *Gone With The Wind* were filmed at **Tara**, the house located at 5705 St Charles Avenue. This isn't true. Scarlett O'Hara's famed fictional home was a movie set in Hollywood, but the plans for Tara *were* used in constructing this exact replica, which was completed about 1941. The **Wedding Cake House** (No. 5809) is an elaborate Colonial Revival concoction that looks very much like… a wedding cake. The whimsical **Castle House** (No. 6000) is similar in flavor to the Wedding Cake House.

Campuses belonging to Loyola University and Tulane University sprawl over a considerable area of turf. The two almost overlap on St Charles Avenue, but that frontage is only a tiny portion of each campus. Both are splendidly landscaped, with lush green lawns and a huge variety of palm trees, magnolias, and shrubs.

Loyola University, the largest Roman Catholic university in the South, dates from 1840 when the Jesuits established the College of the Immaculate Conception downtown. The school moved to its present location in 1911. The university covers five city blocks and has an enrollment in excess of 5,000 students. Owned and operated by the

The Columns Hotel was featured in the film *Pretty Baby*.

Jesuits, Loyola is especially famed for its Law School. Facing St Charles Avenue, adjacent to the main building, the large Gothic-Tudor **Holy Name Church**, built in 1918, serves as the parish church for this section of the city.

Neighboring **Tulane University** also began as a downtown school. It opened in 1834 as the Medical College of Louisiana (in 1847 the name was changed to the University of Louisiana), and was located at Common and University Place. The school was rechristened in memory of Paul Tulane, a wealthy New Orleans merchant who, on his death in 1883, left a bequest to the school. In 1894 the university moved to its present Uptown location. With an enrollment of more than 13,000 students, the school sprawls over 110 acres.

Tulane, like Loyola, has a well-respected Law School, as well as an internationally acclaimed medical school. **Tilton Library**'s excellent research facilities include the New Orleans Jazz Archives and the Middle American Research Institute, which has extensive collections of pre-Columbian art. The prestigious Sophie H. Newcomb College for Women, once a separate institution, is a part of the university.

Directly across St Charles Avenue from the campuses, the 340-acre **Audubon Park** is an urban oasis for which the word elegant is not inappropriate. The beauty of its oak trees rivals that of those in City Park. Not surprisingly, this being New Orleans, the park is on the site of a former plantation. In the 18th century, the park was part of an estate owned by Etienne de Bore and his son-in-law, Pierre Foucher. In 1795, de Bore discovered how to granulate sugar for commercial purposes, which not only revolutionized the sugar industry but provided a windfall for dentists everywhere. In 1871, a state agency bought part of the land for a public park, but nothing much happened until 1884.

Landscape architect Frederick Law Olmsted, who designed New York's Central Park, had a hand in planning

Loyola University moved Uptown in 1911.

Audubon Park. It was named for naturalist John James Audubon, who spent a few years in this area working on his famed series *Birds of America*. Exactly 100 years before the 1984 World's Fair, the World's Industrial and Cotton Centennial Exhibition was held on this site. It featured, among other things, a 31-acre exhibition center – an architectural ancestor of the Superdome – that sprawled over the site of the present 18-hole golf course.

In addition to the golf course, the park has a lovely **lagoon**, a 1½-mile jogging path with 18 exercise stations (the path lopes along beneath a leafy canopy of oaks), a **riding stable**, **tennis courts**, and a **swimming pool**. This is one of the best places in town for biking and hiking. There are also ample grounds for picnicking, lolling about, and doing absolutely nothing.

Behind the park is the wonderful **Audubon Zoo**. Wooden walkways provide scenic viewing of the more than 1,500 critters who roam about in natural-habitat settings. Among the major exhibits are the Louisiana Swamp Exhibit (which includes rare white alligators); the Australian Exhibit, with its kangaroos and wallabies; the Reptile Encounter, which needs no explanation; and the African Savannah, through which runs the Mombassa **miniature train**. The user-friendly Audubon also has a petting zoo and elephant and camel rides. At the Zootique gift shop you can buy souvenirs.

IRISH CHANNEL: No one quite agrees on the actual boundaries of the neighborhood known as the Irish Channel. It undoubtedly lies between Magazine Street and the Mississippi River, but the Uptown and downtown borders depend upon whom you ask. We side with those who say it extends from Howard Avenue up to Louisiana Avenue.

This area, like the Garden District, was once a part of the Livaudais Plantation and the City of Lafayette. However, because of its proximity to the wharves along the river, it has always

Wearing of the green in the Irish Channel.

been a tough, working-class neighborhood. The Irish immigrants who flooded into New Orleans in the 1840s settled around Adele Street, which is still the heart of the Channel. But about the same time there were also large numbers of Germans who moved into this neighborhood, but for some reason the Channel remained "Irish." The Irish and Germans have since left, and the neighborhood is now predominantly black and Cuban.

The spirit of revitalization that swept through the nearby Warehouse District is gradually seeping into the Channel. But unfortunately, the centerpiece of the neighborhood is the notorious **St Thomas Street Housing Project**, a federal housing project that is extremely dangerous. New Orleanians avoid this area and so should visitors.

he St harles treetcar runs om Canal treet to almer Park.

Just past the interstate underpass, at the point where Camp, Prytania, and Clio streets converge, is a small park called **Margaret Place**. The park's statue, unveiled in 1884, honors Margaret Gaffney Haughery, an Irish woman much loved for her charitable deeds. She owned a bakery from which she donated food to the poor and was well-known for her tireless efforts during yellow fever epidemics.

Three blocks up from Margaret Place, the landscaped triangular park between Camp and Coliseum streets is **Coliseum Place**. The original, somewhat grandiose plan for the city called for this area to be modeled after villages in ancient Greece, each of which had a coliseum. The streets in this area are named for Greek muses, but the much-heralded coliseum never materialized.

At 1729 Coliseum Street is the **Goodrich-Stanley House**. A young Welshman named John Rowlands was adopted by Henry Hope Stanley, and in 1857, when he was 16 years old, came to live in the South. He took his adoptive father's name, and 30 years later, as Sir Henry Morton Stanley, he trekked through Africa and found... "Dr Livingstone, I presume." The boyhood home of the African explorer, built in the 1830s at 904 Orange Street, was moved to this location recently.

There are two baroque churches of note in the Channel, both of them Roman Catholic churches constructed in the mid-19th century. **St Mary's Assumption** (2030 Constance Street) was built for the German congregation, and **St Alphonsus**, directly across the street, was built for the Irish. A third church, for the French congregation, no longer exists. Services are still held in St Mary's, but St Alphonsus is being renovated and transformed into a home for the elderly.

Despite the fact that there are few Irish in the Channel now, this neighborhood is the stomping ground for one of the city's three **St Patrick's Day parades**. The "headquarters" for the greening festivities is **Parasol's Bar** (2533 Constance Street), which has been going strong since 1950. Many Orleanians swear that the po-boy sandwiches at Parasol's are the best in town.

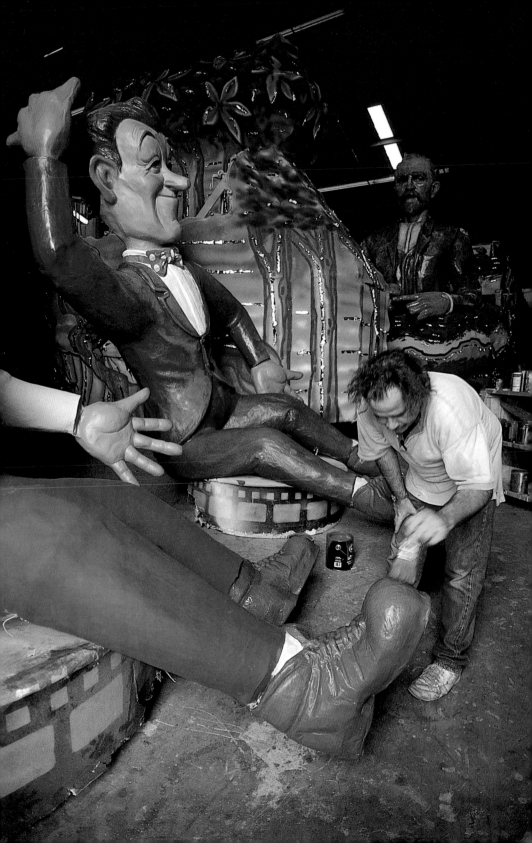

MARDI GRAS WORLD

For anyone unable to be in New Orleans during Carnival, a trip to Mardi Gras World in Algiers is the next best thing. Mardi Gras World is where many of the parade floats are designed, constructed and assembled, in a series of enormous warehouses on the banks of the Mississippi. Tours of the warehouses, called Carnival dens, are conducted daily throughout the year. The most pleasant way to reach Algiers is by hopping on the Canal Street ferry.

Mardi Gras World is the brainchild of entrepreneur Blaine Kern, who over the years has seen his team of designers and artists, sculptors and carpenters, electricians and others grow into the largest float-building firm in the world. Collectively this team represents over 750 years in the trade. Kern is an ebullient administrator, passionately interested in both Mardi Gras and the future of New Orleans. A native of Algiers, he grew up only four blocks away, raised by three maiden-aunt schoolteachers. Thirty years ago Kern was offered a job by Walt Disney, but chose to stay home, because "Louisiana feeds me well."

The first view of a Carnival den can be a shock. Gigantic heads rest on the floor and perch on top of shelves. Disembodied torsos lean against tables. Once assembled, a float can be as tall as a small department store; seeing pieces of Mardi Gras figures in isolation is like visiting a Salvador Dali movie set.

"Anything you want, we can make it for you," says Kern, expansively throwing open his arms to encompass some of the figures on display. "You want art? We'll give you Rodin, Degas, Botticelli's *Venus from the Sea*. Characters from *Planet of the Apes*? We've got 'em. You want a gorilla? We'll build you a gorilla. I once built a monster float that held 100 men. No problem."

Most of the Mardi Gras figures are hollow inside, coated with fiberglass or papier-mâché. The painted figures are mounted on bases that in turn are mounted on or pulled by tractors during the parades. Kern has his own hauling company for these purposes, having bought Russian tractors and special tires with latex in them, which provide better traction. For much of the year he employs around 60–70 people full-time; nearer to Carnival this rises to around 400 in New Orleans alone – there are Carnival dens scattered around the South, for he also makes floats for other celebrations like Macy's Thanksgiving Day parade in New York. But Kern's true love remains Mardi Gras.

His company makes the floats for 40 of the around 60 annual Carnival parades. With each parade displaying up to 40 floats, this festive occupation is hardly kids' stuff.

But prudence is Kern's motto. "See that Indian over there? Look again. It's really Charlton Heston. Clark Gable, Buster Keaton… Oh, look, over there's a typical thing. See Martha Washington? It's really Mamie Eisenhower, masquerading as Martha," he chortles. "Figures are so expensive to create that we reuse them year after year. We chop off their heads and start again."

These Mardi Gras figures move and wave their arms in the latest high-tech fashion. Some critics are less than fond of such modern innovations, seeing the introduction of Hollywood celebrities to parades and the staging of balls that are open to anyone, not just local society (both Kern credos), as eroding the traditions on which Mardi Gras was founded. Certainly these flamboyant, Disney-like floats are in contrast to the established floats, which repeat the same theme, and – in the aristocratic manner – tend to be understated and genteelly shabby.

But Kern is a popularist, proud to be a man of the people. "I'm doing what I like to do best in the world," he says. Mardi Gras is "the biggest private party ever held, and I would like as many people as possible to enjoy it."

Left,
painting the
clown red.

CITY PARK AND LAKE PONTCHARTRAIN

Conventional images of New Orleans play on the narrow streets and filigree balconies of the French Quarter or on steamboats chugging down the Mighty Mississippi. What local people already know, and what visitors are delighted to find out, is that the city boasts a romantically landscaped park – almost twice the size of New York's Central Park – in addition to well-equipped, well-stocked Lake Pontchartrain, whose shores contain some of the best seafood restaurants in town.

Occupying 1,500 lush, fertile acres, City Park is bordered on the north by **Robert E. Lee Boulevard**, on the east by **Bayou St John**, on the south by **City Park Avenue**, and on the west by **Orleans Avenue**. This is the fifth-largest urban park in the nation. The easiest way to reach City Park from the French Quarter is on Esplanade Avenue, which leads right to the entrance. The large **equestrian statue** standing smack in the middle of the street is of Confederate General Pierre Gustave Toutant Beauregard, a Creole who was one of the South's four-star generals.

Lying on the site of the old Louis Allard plantation, which accounts for its dreamy appearance, the park contains an art museum, botanical gardens, an amusement park, four golf courses, baseball diamonds, a soccer stadium, a riding stable, and lagoons for fishing and boating. It contains more than 2,000 stately live oak trees, dressed with frilly Spanish moss, which are among the loveliest in the South. Arched bridges over streams full of ducks complete the antebellum picture.

Lelong Avenue extends from the park entrance to the **New Orleans Museum of Art** (NOMA), a handsome white neoclassical building that has hosted international traveling exhibits such as "The Treasures of King Tutankhamun" and "The Search for Alexander." The museum's permanent collections include pre-Columbian, African, and local art; Fabergé treasures; and displays of early American furnishings.

One of the most stunning sights in the park are the enormous **Dueling Oaks**, located near the museum. The gnarled boughs of the leafy live oak trees sweep down and touch the ground. Hot-blooded Creoles are said to have fought duels beneath these trees, hence the name and the many legends that surround them.

The park is laced with broad paved streets. Behind the museum, Victory Avenue leads past the 10-acre **Botanical Garden**, with its lovely conservatory and parterre garden. Nearby are Storyland, a children's park replete with Mother Goose characters and storytelling, and the 39-court tennis center. The **Casino Building** – which has no casino – is the place to get a permit to fish within the park (the lagoons are well-stocked with bass and bream), and to enquire about **boat** and **bicycle**

rentals. Canoes and paddle boats are available for drifting out among the swans. There is also an inexpensive snack bar in the Casino. During the summer months, a miniature train runs from the Casino to the **amusement park**, whose rides include the magnificent turn-of-the-century **Last Carousel**. The **golf courses** and **riding stable** are in the northern section of the park.

Bayou St John forms the western border of the park and curves down to the south. Moss Street, which intersects Esplanade Avenue, drifts alongside the bayou. At 1440 Moss Street is the **Pitot House**, a West Indies-style house that was built in 1799. An excellent example of homes that were built by the early planters, the house is named for New Orleans mayor James Pitot, who bought it in 1810 and used it as a country home. It was restored by the Louisiana Landmarks Society and is now a museum.

Lakeshore rites: Cutting a wide swath across the northern border of New Orleans is sparkling **Lake Pontchartrain**.

Now the pleasure boating playground of New Orleanians, Lake Pontchartrain was once a major "highway" of the Choctaw Indians. When Pierre le Moyne, Sieur D'Iberville arrived in these watery parts in the late 18th century and launched the settlement of Louisiana, he named the lake after Count Pontchartrain, the French Minister of Marine.

The Choctaw had a much more appropriate name for it. They called it "Okwata," which means wide water. The shallow lake is 25 miles wide and 40 miles long; the toll causeway that crosses it, connecting New Orleans with St Tammany Parish, is one of the longest bridges in the world.

In the 19th century, Lake Pontchartrain played a prominent role in voodoo rituals. When the fear of voodoo prompted the authorities to ban slave gatherings in the city, voodoo cultists moved to this area for their strange and scarifying rites, which usually ended with frenzied splashes in the lake.

Lake Pontchartrain was named for the French Minister of Marine.

Things are considerably more peaceful around the lake today. During the warm weather months, New Orleanians flock to this area for **boating and fishing**. Just before sunset the lake has a lovely silvery cast, and the picture-postcard look is replete with trim sailboats drifting on the waters. The terraced concrete seawall steps right down to the lake, but, unfortunately, the polluted water is unsuitable for swimming. All along Lakeshore Drive are ample parking bays, as well as rest rooms, sandwich stands, and broad expanses of tree-shaded lawn for **picnicking**.

Accessible from downtown via Elysian Fields Avenue or Canal Boulevard (which is an extension of Canal Street), **Lakeshore Drive** breezes right along the lake for 5½ miles. The drive is anchored, roughly, to the east by the New Orleans Lakefront Airport (for private planes) and to the west by West End Park. Note that Lakeshore Drive is closed to traffic 10 p.m. until 6 a.m.

Just west of Lakefront Airport,

Lakeshore Drive skims past the campus of the **University of New Orleans** (UNO), which was established in 1958 on the site of an old World War II Naval Air Station. UNO is the state's second largest university, after Louisiana State University in Baton Rouge. The large modern structure hunkering to the left is the UNO **Lakefront Arena**, a 10,000-seat venue for top-name entertainers as well as sporting events.

Bayou St John flows alongside City Park, which lies to the south of Lakeshore Drive, and empties into Lake Pontchartrain. A small band of Frenchmen camped along the bayou as early as 1708, 10 years before the founding of New Orleans. On the banks of the bayou, near the intersection of Robert E. Lee Boulevard and Beauregard Avenue, are the remnants of **Fort St John**, also known as **Spanish Fort**. This was one of several outposts – all of them since demolished – built by the colonial French in the early 18th century.

Fort St John was meant to protect the

city from attack by way of Lake Pontchartrain. It was enlarged by the Spanish in 1779, restored by the Americans in 1808, and garrisoned during the War of 1812. In 1823, the Pontchartrain Hotel, an elaborate resort surrounded by botanical gardens, was built on this site and flourished until the 1920s. William Makepeace Thackeray and Oscar Wilde were among the hotel's guests. In truth, there is little to see here now except piles of ancient bricks, but the trees are lovely and the grounds are pleasant for picnicking.

Back on Lakeshore Drive, a few yards east of the intersection of Canal Boulevard and Lakeshore Drive is the **Mardi Gras Fountain**. Erected in 1962 by the New Orleans Levee Board, the fountain sprays to a height of 60 feet and is surrounded by plaques bearing the coat of arms of all the Carnival krewes. When it's fully operational (which is not all of the time due to maintenance costs), the fountain is illuminated in the Mardi Gras colors of purple, gold, and green. All around the fountain there are picnic grounds, pretty trees, and places to relax and enjoy a summer evening.

West End Park, the city's pleasure boating center, is awash with marinas, yacht clubs, and things of a nautical nature. Southern Yacht Club, established in 1849, is the nation's second oldest yacht club. It's a private club, but the drive to the entrance, along a broad boulevard with handsome trees, is well worth seeing. From West End Boulevard you can drive out and park on the yacht club's breakwater to enjoy a breathtaking view of the lake.

West End Park and the little fishing village of **Bucktown** just to the west are filled with excellent seafood restaurants. Most of them are quite informal, but what they may lack in decor is more than made up for in the high quality of food. New Orleanians, known for their notoriously picky palates, have been flocking to this area for ages.

West End Park is right at the border between Jefferson and Orleans parishes. Also straddling the parish borders is the beautiful plantation **Longue Vue House**. This classic estate, with its 8 acres of grounds, is modeled after the great country houses of England. The interior is filled with antiques and fine paintings, while the gardens are for a cooling stroll on a hot day.

Sprawling to the west of West End Park is **Metairie**, an old suburb of the city. The southern end of the **Lake Pontchartrain Causeway** is west of Bucktown in Metairie. Birdwatchers should note that beneath this bridge is a major nesting place for purple martins, which stop off here en route farther south. At sunset during July, an estimated 200,000 birds can be seen swooping around the bridge's underpinnings. The biggest show is right after sundown when the birds begin jockeying for a spot in which to rest for the night. There is a viewing area near the toll booth, and a group of New Orleanians is working to develop a bird sanctuary in the vicinity.

Left, firewater. Right, students at the University of New Orleans.

THE MIGHTY MISSISSIPPI

"The great Mississippi, the majestic, the magnificent Mississippi, rolling its mile-wide tide along, shining in the sun."
— Mark Twain, *Life on the Mississippi*

Noted for his withering sarcasm, sharp tongue, and caustic wit, Mark Twain waxed almost mushy when it came to his favorite river: "I still kept in mind a certain wonderful sunset which I witnessed when steamboating was new to me. A broad expanse of the river was turned to blood; in the middle distance the red hue brightened into gold... the dissolving lights drifted steadily, enriching its every passing moment with new marvels of coloring."

Many New Orleanians feel the same way, even though they may cross the river several times a day. Some use the little **Canal Street ferry**, which chugs between downtown and the West Bank in Algiers. Others use bridges, like the **Huey P. Long** bridge upriver near Harahan, or the heavily traveled **Crescent City Connection**, which links West Bank parishes with the Central Business District. Visitors and locals alike enjoy the **Moonwalk promenade**, the riverfront area of the French Quarter, where a saxophone solo may provide the soundtrack to Twain's drifting "dissolving lights." That Ol' Man just keeps on rolling along.

This great mile-wide tide – North America's longest river – begins in northern Minnesota as little streams so small you can step across them. It widens into miles as it washes through America's heartland, then narrows again as it sidles through New Orleans and surges down toward the Gulf of Mexico. By itself, the Mississippi River is about 2,350 miles long. Combined with its largest tributary, the Missouri River, which flows from the Rocky Mountains and into the Mississippi just north of St Louis, the river system is more than 3,700 miles long. In all the world, only the Nile and the Amazon are longer. The Ohio River gets into the swim of things at Cairo, Illinois; other rivers going with the flow include the Red, the Arkansas, the Tensas, and the Yazoo. The great river and its tributaries drain 1,245,000 square miles of the central part of the United States, including all or part of 31 states, and 13,000 square miles of Alberta and Saskatchewan in Canada.

In addition to bordering metropolises like Minneapolis/St Paul, St Louis, and New Orleans, the Mississippi flows through places with quaint names like Prairie du Chien in Wisconsin, where in a bygone era French fur traders bargained with the Winnebago Indians; Cave-In-Rock, Illinois, where an 18th-century man lured passing flatboaters into a big hole in a limestock rock and robbed them blind; Vicksburg, Mississippi, with its vast Civil War battlefield, where the Southerners withstood Gen-

*Preceding pages: the Mississippi River is 2,350 miles long; paddle power. **Left** and **right**, passenger boats sail up the river year round.*

eral Grant's siege for 47 days and nights; and, of course, Hannibal, the Missouri town that was the boyhood home of Mark Twain.

Father of waters: Legends abound about the Father of Waters, many of them having to do with steamboating. The first steamboat, the *New Orleans*, sailed into the Crescent City in 1811 and ushered in a whole new era. Forerunners of the phone and the fax, the steamboats brought news and gossip as well as goods to eager people on the river banks. In time they also brought entertainment. The 1830s saw the beginning of the showboat era, which roared through the 19th century and fizzled out in the early 20th.

What wonderful images the word showboat conjures up! Floating palaces, they were called, with huge paddle wheels stirring up frothy Mississippi surf; salons decked out with gilt, scarlet velvet, and bright white paneling; plunkety-de-plunking banjos, fancy dance-hall girls, flamboyant magicians,

and silly vaudeville slapstick; cheroot-smoking river-boat gamblers in crisp white suits with slick tricks up their sleeves. Numerous films have depicted the excitement with which the showboats were greeted. The cry of "Steamboat's a-comin'" and the jubilant songs of the calliope attracted folks down to the river to see the show.

One of the great legends of the Mississippi, celebrated in song, is of the Great Steamboat Race of 1870, between the *Natchez* and the *Robert E. Lee*. Cheered on by crowds along the levee all the way from New Orleans to St Louis, the two steamboats raced upriver at the dizzying pace of 17 miles an hour. (The *R. E. Lee* won by more than six hours.)

Fortunately, for those of us who live in a fast-paced age of frenzied high-speed travel, sightseeing boats in river cities up and down the Mississippi take passengers back in time for an outing at a leisurely 19th-century pace. New Orleans, St Louis, and Louisville are but three of the cities that boast great white paddle streamers, embellished with gingerbread gee-gaws, big crimson paddles, and all the trimmings.

The steamboat *Natchez* in New Orleans is a 1,600-passenger four-decker that hosts, quite possibly, the world's most enthusiastic calliope concerts to alert the whole wide world that she's here. The five-deck side-wheeler *President*, which plys the river's northern waters, is a great white sight to behold.

New Orleans is also home port for the only two remaining overnight excursion boats in America. The *Delta Queen* and her larger, newer sibling, the *Mississippi Queen*, ease up and down river the year round, making trips that last from three to 12 nights. The two boats (no, they're not ships) are done up with teakwood trim, Tiffany stained glass, and every imaginable steamboat accouterment. Of the two, the *Delta Queen*, which is a National Historic Landmark, is cozier and somehow more evocative of the steamboat era.

Ol' Man River...

The *Mississippi Queen*, the largest steamboat ever built, is outfitted with modern "conveniences," such as a gym, sauna, and swimming pool. (With five bountiful meals a day, such accessories seem more necessities than luxuries.) Both boats do all manner of "theme" cruises, on which the focus ranges from Fall Foliage to Mardi Gras to the Kentucky Derby, and an enthusiastic entertainment staff choreographs a whole raft of crowd-pleasers. (The cruise crowd, incidentally, consists predominantly of retirees who have the time and the wherewithal to enjoy the voyage, which is both leisurely and costly.)

The steamboat agenda includes everything from bingo, raffles, and lectures to a zany Floozie Parade, talent contests, and ear-shattering cabarets. (One of the great challenges of the riverboat ride is finding a place for a bit of peace and quiet.) A "riverlorean" presents talks about port cities and life on the water, and there's an observation deck affording great views.

..keeps on ollin' along.

Between New Orleans and **Baton Rouge**, the view is mostly of belching chemical and industrial plants; upriver of the Louisiana capital things improve considerably. Along the way, the steamboat slides by high yellow-gold bluffs; navy-blue oxbow lakes left behind when the Mississippi grew fickle and changed its course; **elegant plantation mansions** glimpsed beyond alleyways of **moss-draped oak trees**; patchworks of green in the tall grass prairies; and a profusion of colorful flowers, trees, and shrubs.

The annual re-enactment of the race between the *Natchez* and the *Robert E. Lee* is a popular event, usually sold out far in advance. A cannon roars, balloons fly skyward, and Dixieland music blares as the two boats steam upriver for the 11-day excursion. Along the way, the crews of both boats compete in foot races and other games for the benefit of those on board.

Another popular voyage calls at Natchez during that town's annual

Spring Pilgrimage. Shore excursions take you on tours of grand old mansions, where hoop-skirted **Southern belles** tell romantic tales having to do with saving the house and the silver from the cussed Yankee invaders. (Walker Percy was once asked why there were so many good Southern writers. He replied, "Because we lost the war.")

Whatever the theme or destination, the steamboats depart from New Orleans in grand fashion amid a flurry of parasols, antebellum gowns, and a calliope whistling "Dixie" at about a zillion decibels.

Hot news on the river is the revival, after more than a century, of **river-boat gambling**. Floating casinos already ply the Mississippi River in several states, and blueprints are well in hand for several, grand multimillion-dollar gambling boats. High-rolling out of the Crescent City is a tradition that certainly visitors – and many locals – welcome, revitalizing the river banks and carrying on a tradition for which New Orleans is famed.

Meandering: Over the millennia, the river has changed its course many times. From Minnesota to Louisiana, there are lakes and marshes left behind as mementoes of the Mississippi. It is somberly predicted that the Ol' Man is itching to change course again, this time to divert through the Atchafalaya River – and bypass New Orleans entirely. The social and economic consequences of such a cataclysmic shift are unthinkable. The 15-mile-long Port of New Orleans is one of the largest ports in the world, in terms of tonnage. Imagine the havoc it would wreak if the river just drifted away.

For the present, anyway, there is comfort and a sense of vast eternity in these words of Mark Twain: "League after league, it still pours its chocolate tide along, between its solid forest walls... and so the day goes, the night comes, and again the day – and still the same – majestic, unchanging sameness of serenity, repose, tranquility."

PLANTATION COUNTRY

The Southern plantation, with its vast acres of cotton fields and hundreds of slaves, ruled by a kindly ol' marse or a mean-eyed monster, is the stuff of novelists and scriptwriters. Descriptions are always similar: a massive white-columned mansion shaded by moss-draped trees and sweetened with the scent of honeysuckle. Sweet (or sultry) young belles with milk-white skin, a three-inch waistline, and teasing eyes, gotten up in miles of hoops and tons of crinoline. Handsome, though sometimes a mite sinister, cavaliers with stunning tans and bright white teeth, dashing off to the "wah" or wherever they must go in order to fight for love or honor, or preferably both.

New Orleans is surrounded by such plantations, some with wistful names like **Rosedown** and **Destrehan**, some old and crumbling, some dolled up and fit for overnight guests. All, however, offer the requisite degree of romance and a few even add in a mystery or two.

Although scholars still argue about the causes and social structure of the plantation system, they are agreed on certain characteristics and the physical layout of the homes. Whether a result of demographics or economics, and whether large or small, the plantation was essentially a colony, a village-like complex with a "big house," small slave cabins, and outbuildings for the blacksmith's shop, milkhouse, barn, doctor's and dentist's offices, store, and other necessities. For obvious reasons, plantations were usually situated on or near a waterway; they were dependent on the cities for marketing their products, and also for purchasing supplies that could not be grown, sewn, or manufactured on the grounds.

Distances between plantations were not far by contemporary standards; however, a 10 to 15-mile jaunt by horse-and-buggy over rough dirt roads did take all day. Each plantation had accommodation for guests, who might stay for days or even weeks at a time. In Creole south Louisiana homes, there was always a separate quarter, called the *garçonnière*, where young unmarried men of the house lived, and where visiting gentlemen callers stayed.

As for crops, King Cotton is the most celebrated in legend. Other products included rice, indigo, hemp, tobacco, sorghum, corn, peanuts, potatoes, and sugar – not necessarily in that order of importance. The first sugar plantation appeared in south Louisiana in 1742, and by 1849 there were more than 1,500 sugar mills in the state.

In Louisiana, there are only a handful of plantations whose original outbuildings still remain. One is the **Cottage Plantation** in West Feliciana Parish, about 115 miles north of New Orleans. Nestled in 400 acres, punctuated by majestic live oak trees dressed in Spanish moss, the main house, with its broad gallery and dormer windows, was built

in 1795; construction of the other buildings continued until 1850. The main house is appropriately elegant, the outbuildings properly rustic and weathered. Following his triumph in the Battle of New Orleans, General Andrew Jackson was a house guest of the original owner. Today, the Cottage is one of several Louisiana plantation homes that accept overnight guests for bed-and-breakfast accommodation.

The well-known naturalist John James Audubon lived in West Feliciana while working on his *Birds of America* series. During his stay, Audubon tutored the young daughter of the owner of **Oakley Plantation**, a three-story mansion that is now part of the beautifully landscaped, 100-acre Audubon State Commemorative Area. In this region, also, is one of the state's most impressive homes, **Rosedown Plantation House and Gardens**. Built in 1835, the restored mansion retains its original furnishings, and the 28-acre gardens feature centuries-old camellias and azaleas. All the aforementioned plantations and a number of others, are clustered around the little town of **St Francisville** and are open to the public.

Visitors to New Orleans often take a day trip to the area west of town, which boasts several plantation homes worthy of note. The closest one, on the Great River Road about 8 miles west of the New Orleans International Airport, is said to be the oldest intact plantation in the lower Mississippi Valley. **Destrehan**, notable primarily for its age and architectural style – it is neither elaborate nor of awesome size – was built by a freeman of color in about 1787. The house is typical of those constructed by the early planters; a later owner added the Greek Revival features.

Although the term "Great River Road" conjures up wonderful images the road is, unfortunately, neither great nor in river's view. Actually, since there are two banks of the river, there are two roads that meander alongside the Mississippi between New Orleans and Ba-

Southern hospitality.

ton Rouge; farther along, the route is known variously as highways 1, 18, 75, 405, and 942 – to name but a few. Worse, the drive is lined with sprawling chemical and industrial plants.

The plantation known as **San Francisco** sits in the shadow of a giant oil refinery. (To be fair, it should be noted that the oil company restored and maintains the house.) Some visitors express disappointment at the site and relatively small size of San Francisco, but it is a unique home that is well worth seeing. An elaborate "Steamboat Gothic" house (Francis Parkinson Keyes used it as the setting for her novel of that title), it was built in 1856 by Edmond Bozonier Marmillion. The cost of construction prompted Marmillion's son to christen the house San Frusquin, a French slang term meaning "one's all" – or, loosely, "without a penny in my pocket." Gussied up with elaborate exterior ornamentation, the house is noted for its stunning ceiling frescoes and intricate millwork.

Several of these old plantation homes have served as sets for movies and television shows. Bette Davis and Olivia De Havilland starred in the Gothic thriller *Hush, Hush Sweet Charlotte*, which was filmed at **Houmas House**. The mansion actually comprises two houses. A two-story house built in the late 1700s is connected by a carriageway to the handsome white Greek Revival home that was completed in 1840. Tastefully furnished with antiques, the house boasts a graceful spiral staircase that swirls up to the third floor. The front lawn rolls up to the levee, from which there is a fine view of the Mississippi River.

No Louisiana plantation house has appeared in more movies than **Ashland-Belle Hélène**. Clark Gable, Rex Harrison, Clint Eastwood, Ava Gardner, Cybill Shepherd, Maureen O'Hara, and Don Johnson are among the actors who have starred in films shot here. Like the other plantation homes, Ashland-Belle Hélène is on the Na-

Beauregard House.

tional Register of Historic Places; however, unlike the others, it is not restored. Visiting here one gets a real sense of how Scarlett must have felt when she returned to Tara after The War.

The South's largest plantation home is on the West Bank, across the river from those described above. **Nottoway** is, quite simply, a knockout. It wants a bit of freshening up, but one cannot help but be impressed by its grandeur. (The nearby town of White Castle was named for this mansion.) Henry Howard designed the house, which was completed in 1859 – just two years before the War of Northern Aggression. When Union gunboats prowled the Mississippi and aimed to destroy the house, a Yankee soldier who had once been a house guest at Nottoway asked that it be spared. Nottoway's statistics are splendid: the house contains 53,000 square feet of space, 64 rooms, 200 windows, and 22 columns. It bears some resemblance to a gigantic wedding cake. There is an excellent restaurant here;

the river rolls by across the road; the grounds are lush and lovely, with handsome trees and statuary; and 13 rooms are let to overnight guests.

Perhaps the most photographed of the Louisiana plantations and a movie backdrop in its own right is **Oak Alley**. The home is set well back from the road beyond a stately avenue of 28 live oak trees. In fact, the grounds and the exterior of the house are grander than the interior. No one knows who planted the trees, but they are said to date from the late 17th century. According to legend, the plantation, which was built in 1837, was called Bon Séjour by its original owner, but awestruck steamboat passengers on the river referred to it as Oak Alley, and so it has long been known.

Madewood, whose architect was Henry Howard of Nottoway fame, is one of the best-restored and well-maintained plantations near New Orleans. Cicely Tyson's *A Woman Called Moses* was filmed here, and the house is open for bed-and-breakfast guests. Painted a pristine white, the elegant Greek Revival mansion dates from 1846, when it was built for Colonel Thomas Pugh. The Colonel's family is buried in Madewood's small picturesque cemetery. Madewood's 21-foot-high ceiling rooms are decorated with American and European antiques, and there are several outbuildings scattered through the grounds that reflect different styles of Louisiana architecture.

The Great River Road and its offshoot roads play host to a number of larger and smaller plantations, most all of which were built in order to escape the ferocity of the close, dripping heat. Other plantations in the New Orleans/ Baton Rouge area include **Tezcuco**, **Felicity**, **Belle Alliance**, **Magnolia Mound**, and **The Myrtles**, said to be built on the site of ancient Indian burial grounds and sometimes referred to as "America's most haunted house."

Details of plantations and tours are listed in the Travel Tips section.

Left, garden at Rosedown. **Right**, a gentleman always wears a hat.

It's not uncommon to take a drive on the outskirts of New Orleans and end up in a swamp. The road, once paved, will peter out gradually. Houses will be replaced by shacks, river banks by marsh, and canoes (the Cajun word is *pirous*) will appear just as frequently as cars.

The Mississippi River has had seven different deltas over the past 5,000 years. Before it was controlled through the use of flood walls, the river meandered in different directions, following its natural course. When levees streamlined the flow of the water, the result was a series of abandoned river channels, the well-known **bayous** of southern Louisiana. It is these bayous, and the smaller **sloughs** (shallow dead-end bayous) that make up most of the state's swamps and provide refuge for local and migrating wildlife.

For many people the idea of a swamp is a forbidding one, with images culled from Hollywood movies: mosquito-infested lagoons, escaped convicts seeking refuge, moss hanging from cypress trees like sinister gray fingers waiting to ensnare hapless tourists. And man-eating alligators, of course.

Several commercial companies operating out of New Orleans offer a range of trips to local swamps, from kids' tours to bus tours to tours that also take in Cajun country, or even a plantation or two. Some takers hope for a glimpse of "Wookie," the **Louisiana swamp monster**, who, like Nessie of Scotland's Loch Ness, galvanizes interest and a little tourist profit.

One of the most fascinating tours is that organized and conducted by Dr Paul Wagner, a wetland ecologist and environmental consultant, who has studied Louisiana's swamps for more than 30 years. His tour covers the backwaters of **Honey Island**, one of the

A Louisiana white alligator.

wildest and most pristine river swamps in America, located on the far side of Lake Pontchartrain about an hour's drive from the city.

Dr Wagner and his wife Sue began taking groups of interested people out in their small boat in 1982. What began as a part-time hobby has graduated into a full-blown family profession, with tours twice a day throughout the year, except for major holidays. Sue's sister organizes the mini-bus pickups from New Orlean's downtown hotels.

The emphasis of Dr Wagner's trips is on the ecological makeup of the swamp, a subject in which he is passionately interested. Honey Island is the second biggest swamp in Louisiana, 35 to 40 miles long by about 7 or 8 miles wide. It's part of the flood plain of the Pearl River, which forms the boundary between the states of Louisiana and Mississippi. It is much less altered than Florida's Everglades, which has been chopped into small parcels for lumber, drained for agriculture, polluted by ur-

ban runoff, and ditched for mosquito control. So far Honey Island (named for the honeybees which once nested there) has escaped this fate. Nearly 70,000 acres form a permanently protected wildlife area, where **feral hogs**, **otters** and even **black bears** roam. Dr Wagner assisted the Walt Disney company in their design for a "model swamp" and the result can be seen in the wetlands section of the "Magic Kingdom" exhibition at Disney World. It is based on Honey Island.

The old-fashioned landing dock for the Wagners' trip is fringed by **palmetto** and **tupelo trees.** In a cage on the verandah of the company's headquarters, a wooden cabin, is an orphaned baby **nutria** (water raccoon), waiting to be returned to the wild. There are no mosquitoes; because the swamps are flowing waters, they can't breed. There are more mosquitoes in downtown New Orleans than here, since city ponds are likely to be still waters.

The din of a thousand **bird-voiced**

Honey Island swamp.

tree frogs almost drowns out Dr Wagner's commentary on what we are likely to encounter. "We almost always see **mallard** and **wood ducks**, **wading ducks**, some **blue herons**, and maybe a **bobcat** or two," he says. "If we're lucky we might see some alligator **snappin' turtles**. Cajuns calls these turtles *'cowens,'* and they're the oldest creatures in the entire swamp."

There is a murmur of approval from those waiting to catch the boat, but really, everyone wants to hear about the **alligators**. Dr Wagner complies. "When it's warm, we usually see about eight or 10 of them. They're big things, running from about 10 to 14 feet, and they can weigh up to a thousand pounds each." But he also goes on to explain that each swamp tour is different, that we are there for nature's convenience rather than vice versa, and although we may see some of the swamp's more exciting inhabitants there's no money-back guarantee – not even of seeing alligators, especially the man-eating kind. Normally alligators don't mess with people. They eat fish and frogs, turtles and snakes, sometimes even dogs." He pauses for effect. "And Yankee girls. Yankee girls have sweet meat, and the 'gators really go for them."

In fact, alligators do have a very sweet tooth. On some trips Dr Wagner employs an old trapper's trick of throwing marshmallows into the water, to entice them closer to the boat. Marshmallows are used because their stark, white color shows up clearly in the murky swamp. This high-profile color is also the reason Louisiana's famous white alligators are so rare. These part-albino creatures are eaten, not only by known predators, but by other alligators as well.

We chug towards an area known as **Maple Slough** (pronounced *slew*). **Cypress trees** line the banks, their bulbous, twisted trunks rising to meet the drooping **Spanish moss**. "Most of the trees in the swamp have a swollen buttress," Dr Wagner explains. "That's caused by the flooding making the wood swell. This is a good indication of the height of the water fluctuation." A few of the trees are between 400 and 500 years old. All the plants and animals are adept at coping with different water levels, from flooding to the dry season.

We pass an abandoned **trapper's shack**, once the home of Cajuns who caught and sold the furs of local animals. Virtually no Cajuns trap around Honey Island anymore, although a few still make a tolerable living farther out in the bayous. Dr Wagner is himself half-Cajun and half-German ("a real bad combination"), with a knowledge of the local waters so extensive as to have found an even more isolated trapper's cabin which was used as a location in the film *Down By Law*.

A loud cry interrupts our journey. A bird swoops on the skyline, dips near the water, then flies off. The sun is too dazzling for proper identification, but we think it is a **bald eagle**, that rarely sighted national symbol of the United

ajun
apper's
hack.
ollowing
ages:
eandering
rough the
ayous.

States. We do see legions of ducks. Apparently between 4 and 5 million ducks spend the winter in Louisiana every year.

Dr Wagner tries to teach us to recognize different forms of wildlife. "A swamp is like a zoo, but no animal is gonna sit out there and wave at you,'' he says. "You gotta spot them." An anonymous gray heap turns out to be the dome of a **beaver lodge**. A stick begins to move; it is a tiny **water snake**.

Some time ago, pirates used the swamp to store their booty. Other, more recent, outlaws gravitated towards Honey Island, too. "For a long time the swamp was considered a kind of no-man's land. Neither Louisiana nor Mississippi claimed it; neither state wanted it. The feeling was 'don't go in there, you'll never come out again.' Lots of people still feel that way," he says with a rueful smile.

At night, apparently, the swamp is alive with **owls**, **deer**, **raccoons** and a host of spooky night creatures, and a tour is for visitors made of stern stuff. This is the time that Wookie, the sea monster, supposedly makes his appearance. Dr Wagner has never seen him, but once, when fishing, he did hear gigantic footsteps and disturbing rustling in the undergrowth. It may or may have not been Wookie, but "I sure didn't hang around to find out."

We turn into a quiet lagoon. Dr Wagner cuts the motor and we float in silence on the **lime-green duckweed**, listening to the cacophony of daytime sounds. It is these quiet backwaters that contain the highest concentration of wildlife. The scene is of dripping trees and broken logs. A **diamondback water snake** slithers into the marshy depths. The area is very dense – and wild. "You know, people come here with the darnest preconceptions," Dr Wagner says quietly, getting ready to turn the boat back towards the landing. "I once asked a Yankee woman what she thought of the swamp. She said it was okay, but it was so unkept."

TRAVEL TIPS

GETTING THERE

Unless otherwise stated, all telephone numbers are preceded by the area code (504).

BY AIR

New Orleans has two airports, the largest being **New Orleans International Airport** (also called **Moisant Field**). It is located about 15 miles west of the city and is served by AeroMexico, American, Continental, Delta, Lacsa, Northwest, Piedmont, Sasha, Southwest, Taca, TWA, United, and USAir. **Lakefront Airport** in the eastern part of town is used by small local private and corporate planes.

BY SEA

Celebrated in song and legend, the mighty Mississippi River is the scenic route to the city. The venerable *Delta Queen* and her younger, larger sister, the *Mississippi Queen*, both make the trip downriver from Cincinnati, Pittsburgh, St Louis, and other northerly ports. Both boats are outfitted in nostalgic 19th-century style, and the sentimental journeys feature plenty of banjos, mint juleps and Dixieland bands. A wide variety of theme cruises are offered, including the annual Great Steamboat Race from New Orleans to St Louis in which the siblings recreate the famed 19th-century race between the *Natchez* and the *Robert E. Lee*. The Delta Queen Steamboat Company, which celebrated its centennial in 1990, also offers attractive packages that include hotel stopovers in port cities. It should be noted that steamboating down the Mississippi is neither swift nor inexpensive.

Details from a travel agent or the Delta Queen Steamboat Company, 30 Robin Street Wharf, New Orleans, LA 70130, tel: (toll-free) 1-800-543-1949.

BY RAIL

New Orleans is served by Amtrak trains that connect the city with Los Angeles, Chicago, New York, and Washington, DC. **Union Passenger Terminal** in the Central Business District is the arrival and departure point. Information is available through Amtrak, tel: (toll-free) 1-800-USA RAIL.

BY ROAD

Union Passenger Terminal is also the station for the buses that connect the city with points all across the continental US. Details from **Greyhound/Trailways**, tel: (toll-free) 1-800-237 8211.

For those arriving by car, the major east-west artery is **Interstate 10 (I-10)**, which strings across the southern US from Florida to California and through downtown New Orleans. **Interstate 55 (I-55)** is a north-south highway that connects with I-10 just west of the city. Other major routes into town are **US 90** and **US 61**.

To drive in Louisiana, you must have a current driving license (an international license is not required), a vehicle registration document, and proof of automobile insurance. Non-citizens must also have a valid passport.

TRAVEL ESSENTIALS

VISA & PASSPORTS

A valid passport is required for citizens of Great Britain and Canada who are visiting the US for up to 90 days and who have a return ticket. Citizens of all other countries must have a valid passport, a visa, and a return or ongoing ticket. Regulations at city gateways vary regarding transit stops, and a visa may be required for re-entry after a visit outside the US. Vaccinations are not required for entry into the US.

MONEY MATTERS

American visitors: Most, though not all, hotels, restaurants, and shops accept major credit cards (American Express, Diners Club, MasterCard, Visa, and En Route). It is inadvisable to carry large amounts of cash while wandering around the city; much better, in fact, to withdraw small sums of money from local banks or ATMs (automatic teller machines) every couple of days. Travelers checks are widely accepted, although you may have to provide proof of identification when cashing the checks at banks. (This is not required by most stores.)

Overseas visitors: The best rates of exchange for travelers checks are in banks, which are open Monday–Friday 9 a.m.–3 or 4 p.m. Be sure to take your passport along. Foreign exchange offices include **Whitney Bank** (228 St Charles Ave and several branch locations, including one at 5the lobby level at **New Orleans International Airport**; tel: 586-7272).

HEALTH TIPS

American medical services are extremely expensive. Always travel with full and comprehensive travel insurance, to cover any emergencies. Summers in New Orleans are very hot; visitors with sensitive skin should bring along a good sunscreen to guard against the sun.

WHAT TO WEAR

Street wear is quite casual, especially in the French Quarter where the summertime scene features short shorts, halters, tee-shirts, and sandals. Attire in all but the finest restaurants is informal, although some have restrictions against shorts and cutoffs. Several of the more elegant restaurants require that gentlemen wear ties and jackets. It is extremely hot and sticky in the summer, and while cottons do not pack as well as synthetics, they are considerably cooler and more comfortable. Summer nights are also hot and sultry, but air conditioners are often turned up full blast and a light sweater or jacket may be in order.

Winter weather is unpredictable; it's best to bring clothing that can be layered. A good bet is an all-weather coat that has a zip-out wool or pile lining. Even when the temperature hovers around 40° Fahrenheit the extremely high humidity makes it seem much colder. The wind can be bitterly cold. Comfortable walking shoes are essential for maneuvering along the French Quarter's cracked sidewalks and flagstone passageways. Shoes with non-skid soles are recommended for river-boat rides; you may also want to tuck in a scarf to guard against the river's breezes.

WHAT TO BRING

Whatever time of year you come bring sunglasses and an umbrella; believe it or not, there'll be times when you'll need both on the same day. Bring a camera and film and a small tote bag for carrying brochures, maps, and such. In the summertime bring insect repellent to ward off mosquitoes and a good sunscreen to protect your skin.

ANIMAL QUARANTINE

All importations are subject to health, quarantine, agriculture, wildlife, and customs requirements and prohibitions. Pets taken out of the US and returned are subject to the same requirements as those entering for the first time. Heartless though it may be, pets excluded from entry into the US must either be exported or destroyed. While awaiting disposition, the pet will be detained at the owner's expense at the port of arrival. The US Public Health Service requires that pets – particularly dogs, cats, and turtles – brought into this country be examined at the first port of entry for possible evidence of disease that can be transmitted to a human. Animals and birds (both domestic and wild) must be free from contagious, infectious, communicable diseases.

The Animal Welfare Act requires that all birds and animals must be imported under humane, healthful conditions. Every imported package or container of pets must be plainly marked, labeled, or tagged on the outside with the names and addresses of the shipper and consignee, along with an accurate invoice statement specifying the number of each species contained in the shipment. Since hours of service and availability of Customs inspectors vary from port to port, visitors who plan to bring animals or birds into the country are strongly advised to check with their anticipated port of arrival prior to importing a pet or other animal. For additional information, contact:

US Public Health Service
Centers for Disease Control
Division of Quarantine
Atlanta, Georgia 30333
Tel: (404) 329-2574

Animal and Plant Health Inspection Service
US Department of Agriculture
Hyattsville, Maryland 20782
Tel: (301) 436-7786

CUSTOMS FORMALITIES

Aboard ship or on the airplane you will be given a Customs declaration form. Fill out the identification part (upper portion) of the form and upon arrival present it to the Immigration and Customs Inspector. Visitors arriving by land borders must identify themselves during their oral declaration. All articles brought into the US, including gifts for other persons, must be declared to US Customs at the time you enter. If all the articles you have to declare are entitled to free entry under the exemptions allowed, you need not fill in the reverse side of the declaration form. Instead, you orally declare articles brought with you to the Customs Inspector. (If an inspector deems it necessary, you may be required to make a written declaration and list articles brought with you).

Visitors to the US are allowed to bring into the country items of a personal nature, plus 200 cigarettes or 100 cigars or 3 pounds (1.3 kg) of smoking tobacco (or proportionate amounts of each) and vehicles (e.g., automobiles, trailers, airplanes, motorcycles, and boats) for personal use if imported in connection with your arrival. Adult nonresidents may also bring in one liter (33.8 fl. oz.) of alcoholic beverage. The state of Louisiana has a lengthy list of restrictions on liquor imported from other states. In addition to the above restrictions, articles up to US $50 in total value for use as bona fide gifts to other persons may be brought in free of duty and tax, if you will be in the US for at least 72 hours and have not claimed this gift exemption in the past six months. You may include in this exemption up to 100 cigars. There is

no limit on the amount of money (US or foreign currency), travelers checks, money orders, or negotiable instruments in bearer form that you may bring into or take out of the US. However, a report must be filed with US Customs at the time you arrive or depart with an amount that exceeds $10,000 or the equivalent in foreign currency. A form will be provided for this purpose.

Don't even fantasize about bringing in illegal drugs.

If you require medicine that contains habit-forming drugs, carry only the quantity normally needed and properly identified. You should also have a prescription or written statement from your personal physician stating that the medicine is necessary for your physical well-being.

Some items must meet certain requirements, require a license or permit, or may be prohibited entry. Among these are fruit, plants and endangered species of plants, vegetables and their products; firearms and ammunition if not intended for legitimate hunting or lawful sporting purposes; hazardous articles (fireworks, dangerous toys, toxic or poisonous substances); lottery tickets; meats, poultry and products (e.g., sausage and pâté); pets; pornographic articles and publications; switchblade knives; certain trademarked items (cameras, watches, perfumes, musical instruments, jewelry, and metal flatware); vehicles and motorcycles not equipped to comply with US safety or clean air emission standards; wildlife and endangered species, including any part or product (e.g., articles from reptile skins, whalebone, or ivory, mounted specimens and trophies, feathers or skins of wild birds).

PORTER SERVICES

Porters (called Skycaps) are readily available in the baggage claim area at New Orleans International Airport. Armed with your baggage receipt and a description of your suitcases, a porter will retrieve your luggage from the carousel and deliver it to the ground transportation area. Porters are also available to assist with luggage at Union Passenger Terminal. All of the larger hotels have bellmen, but in many of the small, family-run guest houses you may be on your own in getting your luggage from lobby to guestroom.

RESERVATIONS

Those who plan to visit during Mardi Gras or other special events (e.g., the Jazz Fest or Sugar Bowl) should make hotel and even restaurant reservations about a year in advance. The busiest months are between September and May. During the summer, many hotels offer special incentives (i.e., slashed prices and attractive packages) to encourage visitors to come to the city. During slow periods such as the summer months, it is often possible to stroll in and be seated in a top-of-the-line restaurant without a reservation; an impossibility during the more popular months of the year.

EXTENSION TO STAY

For recorded instructions regarding visas, contact the Immigration and Naturalization Service in New Orleans, tel: (504) 589-6533. Applications must be made to the INS Southern Regional Service Center, P.O. Box 568808, Dallas, TX 75356-8808.

ON DEPARTURE

Your hotel or guest house can make arrangements for taxi or shuttle transportation to the airport. If you opt for the most economical (and slowest) route to the airport, you can catch an express bus at the corner of Tulane Avenue and Elk Place.

GETTING ACQUAINTED

GOVERNMENT & ECONOMY

New Orleans is governed by a mayor and a seven-member city council, all of whom are elected for a period of four years. Like many US oil-producing states, Louisiana in recent years suffered heavy losses in revenue; however, since 1988 there has been a slow but steady recovery. The state of Louisiana handles over 60 percent of US offshore oil production, and New Orleans serves as the offshore administrative oil center. The Port of New Orleans and port-related activities represent a key industry for the New Orleans region. The New Orleans port area is the largest in the US in terms of total cargo tonnage handled. The port and maritime activities in the six-parish metropolitan New Orleans region has an economic impact in excess of $3 billion.

Tourism is a $2 billion industry in New Orleans; Mardi Gras alone brings close to $500 million annually. With more than one million square feet of convention space and 25,000 hotel rooms, the city is ranked number six in the nation for conventions. As the largest city within 350 miles, New Orleans is a regional center for surrounding states. The addition of such shopping malls as the Jackson Brewery Corporation developments, Riverwalk, Canal Place, and the New Orleans Centre has established the city as a major shopping center in the region.

GEOGRAPHY & POPULATION

The largest city in the state of Louisiana, New Orleans sits smack on the Mississippi River, about 110 miles inland from the Gulf of Mexico. The land upon which the city sits, between the river and Lake Pontchartrain, was carved into the shape of a half moon ages ago by the mighty river, hence the Crescent City sobriquet. In the early 18th century, the city was known as the Isle of Orleans because it was accessible only by boat. Nowadays, of course, the swamps, lakes, marshlands, and the Mississippi are crisscrossed by bridges.

The Greater New Orleans metropolitan area comprises of four parishes (which in all other US states are called counties): Orleans, Jefferson, St Bernard, and St Tammany. The four-parish area has a population of some 1,200,000; Orleans Parish, or New Orleans proper, has a population of just under 600,000. In the Greater New Orleans area, 62 percent of the population consists of whites, and 35 percent consists of blacks.

TIME ZONES

New Orleans is in the Central Time Zone, one hour behind New York time and six hours behind Greenwich Mean Time. Daylight Savings Time is in effect from May until late October.

CLIMATE

The sultry, subtropical City That Care Forgot has an annual average temperature of 70° Fahrenheit (20° Celsius). Warm weather, and a profusion of blossoms, usually arrives in mid-March and often lingers through October. Early spring or fall, when the city is all decked out with flowers and greenery, is an ideal time to visit; by mid-May things begin to heat up.

The hottest months are June, July, and August, and they are very hot indeed. The mercury shoots up above 90°F (32°C) and lingers there for weeks at a stretch. The air is thick with moisture and the high humidity makes things feel quite sticky. Thunderstorms, replete with lightning, are frequent, and vanish as quickly as they appear. It is not at all unusual for the sun to shine brightly throughout a summer shower.

Hurricane season begins in June and extends through November. New Orleans, being so far inland, has rarely been hit with the full force of a hurricane, but high winds and torrential rains are sometimes the city's taste of a coastal storm.

Winters are far less predictable than hot-sticky summers. December, for example, can be a balmy 85°F (30 °C) or a chilly 35°F (2°C). As a general rule, the only two really cold months are January and February. Although the temperature during those months rarely dips below 40°F (5°C), the extremely high humidity produces a bitterly cold chill.

CULTURE & CUSTOMS

New Orleans' famous **jazz funerals** are still alive and well. In fact, the 1990s will probably see more of these remembrance services than usual, as veteran musicians reach an age where the Pearly Gates are beckoning. What happens to this tradition after most of its honorees have departed is anyone's guess: one social chronicler feels that New Orleans' music fraternity has so generously embraced the talents of young, up-and-coming artists that the continuation of this tradition is ensured.

Because this is New Orleans, **brass march-ing bands** tend to pop up out of nowhere and parade around town. A marching band generally picks up second-liners along the way. A second-liner is a parade follower; the term comes from jazz funerals, in which the "second line" follows the musicians, singing, dancing, and pumping parasols in the air in a joyous celebration of the release of the soul of the departed. Second-lining is as much a tradition as Mardi Gras and good food.

With more than 75 **fairs and festivals** held in New Orleans each year, and many more state-wide, a party is never hard to find. Among the less publicized events are the Greek Festival (May), the French Market Tomato Festival (June), and the Swamp Festival (October, held in Audubon Zoo). These smaller festivals are attended primarily by New Orleanians, and have a delightful, low-key feel about them which larger events can fail to achieve.

Festivals held elsewhere in Louisiana tend to center on Cajun culture, on food, or on both at the same time. Dates vary from year to year and it's best to inquire locally, or at the Tourist Office in New Orleans, for more precise information.

These are wholesome, outdoor events where the entire family gathers to participate in the *fais do-do* and to eat rib-tickling, down-home food. *Fais do-do* is a country dance: the phrase "do-do" is a juvenile variation on the French word "*dormir*," or "to sleep."

Some of the most interesting **country fairs** include the Cajun Heritage Festival (November), in a town called Cut Off; the Gumbo Festival in Bridge City (October); and the Annual World's Championship Crawfish Etouffée Cookoff in Eunice, Louisiana, held in March.

TIPPING

Restaurants in New Orleans do not include a service charge in the bill, and it is customary to leave a 15 to 20 percent tip if the service has been satisfactory. Airport and bus terminal porters are tipped per bag, as are hotel bellmen. Leave a tip based on the number of nights stayed for the hotel maid. The hotel doorman who calls a cab for you is also tipped a small sum. Cab drivers expect a 10 to 15 percent tip.

New Orleanians have peculiar ways of pronouncing certain words and there are a number of local shibboleths. For example, the quickest way to brand yourself an outsider is to say "New Orleens." The name of the city is drawled: "N'Awlins." However, the proper local pronunciation of Orleans Street and Orleans Parish is... Orleens.

In order to blend in with the locals, note the following pronunciations of streets: Burgundy (BurGUNdy); Chartres (Charters); Iberville (Eye-berville); and Tchoupitoulas (Chop-ah-too-lus). Terpsichore, more's the pity, is Terp-si-core here.

WEIGHTS & MEASURES

The US is one of the few industrialized nations that has not converted to the metric system. The basic unit of length is the yard; the basic unit of weight is the pound; and the basic unit for liquid measure is the gallon.

Here are some conversions:
1 oz = 28.50 gm
1 lb (16 ozs) = 453.592 gm
1 oz = 28.400 ml
1 pint = 0.568 liter
1 quart = 1.137l liter
1 gallon = 4.546l liter
1 inch = 2.54 cm
1 ft (12 inches) = 0.3048 m
1 yard (3 ft) = 0.9144 m
1 mile (1,760 yds) = 1.6093 km
1 gm = 0.035 oz
1 kg = 2.205 lb
1 mm = 0.0394 inch
1 cm = 0.3937 inch
1 meter = 3.28 ft
1 km = 0.62138 mile
1 liter = 1.056 quarts

ELECTRICITY

The standard for the United States is 110 volts, 60 cycles. Foreign visitors may need a transformer and/or adaptor for electrical appliances. These can be bought in hardware shops. US sockets only accept plugs with two flat pins.

BUSINESS HOURS

Offices, as a rule, are open weekdays from 8 or 8.30 a.m. until 5 or 5.30 p.m. Some are open on Saturday until noon. Banking hours are weekdays from 9 a.m. until 3 or 4 p.m. In general, shops in the Central Business District are open Monday to Saturday from 9.30 or 10 a.m. until 5.30 or 6 p.m. , but many of the mall shops stay open later, until 9 or 10 p.m. Opening and closing hours of French Quarter shops are whimsical, depending upon how business is doing; many are open on Sundays.

Opening hours for museums and art galleries vary greatly, depending on the premises and the season. It's best to check in advance the exact hours of those you wish to visit, but some of these, too, are open on Sundays.

HOLIDAYS

Banks and most offices are closed **New Year's Day**; **Martin Luther King Day** (January); **Inauguration Day** (3rd Monday in January, every four years); **Mardi Gras Day** (February or March); **Presidents' Day** (February); **Good Friday**; **Memorial Day** (last Monday in May); **Independence Day** (July 4); **Labor Day** (first Monday in September); **Columbus Day** (second Monday in October); **All Saints' Day** (November 1); **Veterans' Day** (November 11); **Thanksgiving** (fourth Thursday in November); and **Christmas Day**.

FESTIVALS

The city's all-out party is **Mardi Gras**, which occurs annually in **February** or **March**. (Because it occurs 46 days before Easter, the date varies from year to year). Carnival season begins on Twelfth Night (January 6), gradually gathers steam, and ends with a big bash on Mardi Gras. The literal translation of Mardi Gras is Fat (or Shrove) Tuesday, which is the big day, but the last two weeks of Carnival are also known as Mardi Gras. During the last four days before Fat Tuesday there are parades every day and every night, and the streets of the Central Business District and the French Quarter are awash with fantastic floats, marching bands, and highly enthusiastic spectators. On the night of Lundi Gras (Fat Monday, the night before Fat Tuesday), the city hosts a huge free-to-the-public masked ball in Spanish Plaza, replete with live music and fireworks. Fat Tuesday is given over entirely to parades and about a million masked, costumed revelers. At midnight on Fat Tuesday the celebration officially ends and Ash Wednesday – the beginning of Lent – commences.

Second only to Mardi Gras is the **Jazz & Heritage Festival**, commonly called the **Jazz Fest**. A celebration of music, food, and crafts, it begins the last weekend in **April** and continues through the following weekend, the first weekend in **May**. The internationally acclaimed event brings thousands to the city, including top-name musicians from all over the world.

During the two weekends the main venue for the festivities is the Fair Grounds; in between there are all-night jam sessions in many bars and nightclubs around the city. In addition to Mardi Gras and the Jazz Fest, there are more than 75 other festivals, many of them involving a great deal of food.

The following is a listing of some of the other major annual festivals:

February
The **Black Heritage Festival** features plenty of jazz and gospel music, as well as a mock jazz funeral.

March
The **Tennessee Williams/New Orleans Literary Festival** is a weekend of plays, symposia, parties, and leisurely French Quarter walking tours.

Mid-March
St Patrick's Day: in a city that loves parades, there are at least two St Pat's parades each year.
On **St Joseph's Day** the city's many Italians decorate altars with food and celebrate with a parade that brings out the Mardi Gras Indians for their only appearance other than on Fat Tuesday.

Early April
The **French Quarter Festival** is a full weekend of food, music, and fireworks.

April
Spring Fiesta, which takes place the weekend after Easter, features a parade through the French Quarter and tours of private homes and courtyards.

June
The **Great French Market Tomato Festival** is another great excuse for food, music, and festivities.

Late June-Early July
La Fête focuses on food and food-related events at venues all over the city.

September
The **New Orleans Writers' Conference** brings together aspiring writers and nationally known editors, agents, and publishers.

Early October
Festa d'Italia, centered around the Piazza d'Italia in the Central Business District, is the Italian festival that honors founding father Christopher Columbus with food, music, and parades.

Late October
Halloween, rapidly becoming a major event, includes much masking and eye-popping costumes, as well as a Witches Run and tours of haunted houses.

December
A Creole Christmas lasts the whole month and features Christmas tree lightings, caroling, Christmas teas, parades, and "open house" at historic homes.

As Louisiana's music and food becomes more and more popular, some discerning visitors are frequenting the numbers of local fairs and festivals which are held throughout the year in the countryside outside New Orleans. These have names like the **Zachary Sausage Festival** (Zachary), the **Gonzales Jambalaya Festival** (Sorrento), the **Franklin Cajun Fest** (Franklin), the **Cajun French Music and Food Festival** (Lake Charles), and the **Festival International de Louisiane** (Lafayette).

The best way to find out about these local fairs is by consulting the *Louisiana Fairs and Festivals Guide*, a pamphlet available from the New Orleans or Louisiana Tourist Boards. Next to each event listing is a telephone number which can be called for more specific information.

Baptist Churches
First Baptist Church, 4301 St Charles Ave, tel: 895-8632.
Lakeview Baptist Church, 6100 Canal Blvd, tel: 482-3109.
St Charles Avenue Baptist Church, 7100 St Charles Ave, tel: 861-9514.

Catholic Churches
St Louis Cathedral, Jackson Square, tel: 525-9585.
St Patrick's Church, 724 Camp St, tel: 525-4413.
Our Lady of Guadalupe, 411 N. Rampart St, tel: 525-1551.
Holy Name of Jesus, Loyola Campus, 6367 St Charles Ave, tel: 865-2776.
Jesuit Church of Immaculate Conception, 130 Baronne St, tel: 529-1477.

Episcopal Churches
Christ Church Cathedral, 2919 St Charles Ave, tel: 895-6602.
Grace Episcopal Church, 3700 Canal St, tel: 482-5242.
St George's Episcopal Church, 4600 St Charles Ave, tel: 899-2811.

Lutheran Churches
Grace Lutheran Church, 5800 Canal Blvd, tel: 482-4994.
Zion Lutheran Church, 1924 St Charles Ave, tel: 524-1025.

Methodist Churches
First United Methodist Church, 3401 Canal St, tel: 488-0856.
Rayne Memorial United Methodist Church, 3900 St Charles Ave, tel: 899-3431.
Wesley United Methodist Church, 2517 Jackson Ave, tel: 524-8270.

Presbyterian Churches
Covenant Presbyterian Church, 4422 St Charles Ave, tel: 899-2481.
St Charles Ave Presbyterian Church, 1545 State St, tel: 897-0101.

COMMUNICATIONS

MEDIA

The city's only daily newspaper is the *Times-Picayune*. On Friday, the newspaper's "Lagniappe" tabloid section carries information about weekend entertainment, plus cultural and sporting events. *Gambit* is a weekly newspaper, available free in supermarkets and many bookstores, that covers local events, including entertainment and a calendar listing of who's playing where at the various music clubs.

The well-written, glossy *New Orleans* Magazine focuses once a month on local stories and carries calendar listings of events. *Vignette*, published twice annually and sold in many bookstores, is a beautifully illustrated magazine with features about local history, lore, and entertainment. *GO*, *Where*, *This Week in New Orleans*, and *Travel Host* are all tourist-oriented publications that are available free in most hotels.

The *New York Times* and other "foreign" papers can be purchased at Riverside News (Jackson Brewery, 620 Decatur St) and at Matassas Grocery (1001 Dauphine St).

Most major hotels have TVs which feature the Tourist Channel, which broadcasts packaged stories about the city's history, nightlife, restaurants, and attractions.

The local network affiliates are WWL (CBS, Channel 4); WVUE (ABC, Channel 8); and WDSU (NBC, Channel 6). Most of the major hotels and some of the guest houses have cable service.

POSTAL SERVICES

The Postal Answer Line (tel: 589-1360) provides 24-hour recorded information about all US Postal Service facilities in the city. The Answer Line can be accessed from a Touch Tone phone.

The main branch of the US Postal Service

is at 701 Loyola Avenue (tel: 589-1112). Windows are open Monday to Friday 9 a.m. to 4.30 p.m.; Saturday 8 a.m. to 1 p.m. Branch offices (which are closed on Saturday) include those at the World Trade Center (tel: 524-0033); the Vieux Carré (1022 Iberville St, tel: 524-0072); the Carrollton Station (3400 S. Carrollton Ave, tel: 484-6473); and the New Orleans International Aiport (tel: 589-1294).The French Quarter Postal Emporium (940 Royal St, tel: 525-6651) provides stamps, package-mailing, and other services at prices slightly higher than at the US Postal Service.

TELEPHONE, TELEX, FAX

Public pay telephones can be found on the streets, as well as in bars and in the lobbies of many office buildings. Listen for a dial tone, deposit coins, and dial the desired number. There is no charge for dialing 911, the emergency number.

Western Union has a toll-free number (800-325-6000) for sending mailgrams, telegrams, or cablegrams. Their toll-free number for telexes is 800-527-5184. There are several Western Union stations where you can pick up or send money or messages, among them 334 Carondelet St, 2131 Canal St, and 5500 Prytania St.

Kinko's Copies (762 St Charles Avenue, tel: 581-2541) offers 24-hour facsimile service. American Express (158 Baronne St, tel: 586-8201) also provides a fax service.

EMERGENCIES

SECURITY & CRIME

Pickpockets are busy at work while others play during major events such as Mardi Gras. It is unwise at any time to carry cash or to wear flashy, expensive jewelry. Always carry travelers checks. Don't leave money or valuables unattended in your hotel room; put them in your hotel's safety deposit box. Be sure to lock your car, with any luggage or valuables stashed out of sight. Avoid wandering alone on dark, deserted streets; stick to well-lit, heavily trafficked areas. Avoid wandering alone through Armstrong Park or New Orleans' above-ground cemeteries, even in daylight hours.

LOSS OF BELONGINGS

If you think you've left belongings on a bus or streetcar, contact the Regional Transit Authority Lost and Found, 101 Dauphine St, tel: 569-2625. Otherwise, contact the police tel: 821-2222.

MEDICAL SERVICES

Emergency **ambulance** services, dial 911. **Hospitals** with 24-hour emergency departments include Tulane Medical Center (1415 Tulane Ave, tel: 588-5711) and Touro Infirmary (1401 Foucher, tel: 897-8250).
Pharmacies with branch locations throughout the city are Walgreen's, K&B, and Eckerd's. In the Central Business District, there is a Walgreen's at 900 Canal St, (tel: 523-7201) and a K&B at Lee Circle (586-1234). The Eckerd's store at 3400 Canal St (tel: 488-6661) is open 24 hours.
The **AIDS Hotline** (929 Bourbon St, tel: 522-2437) provides counseling and assistance.

LEFT LUGGAGE

There are coin-operated lockers at Union Passenger Terminal.

GETTING AROUND

ORIENTATION

First-time visitors are usually a bit disoriented, as "north, south, east, and west" mean very little in the Crescent City. The meandering Mississippi wreaks havoc with such mundane designations. Directions are defined by the waterways: Riverside is toward the Mississippi; lakeside toward Lake Pontchartrain; downriver is downtown; and upriver is uptown. As an example, the landmark bar called the Napoleon House is located on the downtown, riverside corner of Chartres Street.

The heart and soul of the city is the **French Quarter**, which was the original colony founded by French Creoles in 1718. Laid out in a perfect grid, the Quarter encompasses about a square mile and is bordered by Esplanade Avenue, the Mississippi River, and Canal and North Rampart streets. Strung alongside the Mississippi, downriver of Esplanade Avenue, are the residential suburbs of **Faubourg Marigny**, **Bywater**, and **Arabi**. Six miles downriver lies **Chalmette Battlefield**, site of the 1815 Battle of New Orleans.

Bordering the upriver side of the Quarter, the **Central Business District (CBD)** lies between the Mississippi River, Poydras Street, Howard Avenue, and Loyola Avenue. As its name indicates, the CBD is the center of business activity. The **Warehouse District**, nestled in the CBD, is a rapidly developing residential and cultural center.

St Charles Avenue stretches upriver from the CBD to the **Garden District**, a district of stately and palatial mansions, splendid gardens, and a sprinkling of hotels, guest houses, and restaurants. Between the Garden District and the River is the **Irish Channel**, a run-down neighborhood that is struggling for revitalization. It lies roughly (word used advisedly) between Howard Avenue, Magazine Street, Louisiana Avenue, and the river.

The **Uptown** area, beyond the Garden District, includes Audubon Park and Audubon Zoo and the university section, home of Loyola and Tulane Universities. **Mid-City** is a predominantly residential area that stretches from the CBD and the Quarter to Lake Pontchartrain, City Park, and the Fair Grounds. Several notable restaurants are located in this area.

Lake Pontchartrain cuts a blue 40-mile swath across the northern border of the city. **West End Park**, at the western end of Lakeshore Drive, is home to yacht clubs, marinas, and outstanding seafood restaurants. On the north shore of Lake Pontchartrain are the piney woods and quiet towns of **St Tammany Parish**, one of the four parishes comprising the greater metropolitan area.

Due east of the French Quarter – on the **West Bank**, across the river – **Algiers** is a very old, predominantly residential section of town. To the west of the city proper is **Jefferson Parish**, a vast area once consisting of sugar plantations. **Metairie**, a very old suburb of New Orleans, occupies a large chunk of Jefferson Parish and is loaded with good seafood restaurants. **Kenner**, home of New Orleans' only international airport, is also in Jefferson Parish, as is Jefferson Downs Race Track.

RECOMMENDED MAPS

The Greater New Orleans Tourist & Convention Bureau publishes excellent self-guided walking and driving tour maps that are available free at the New Orleans Welcome Center, 529 St Ann Street. Rand McNally also puts out a map of the city which can be purchased in most bookstores.

AIRPORT – CITY

The fastest way to reach the downtown area from the airport is by **taxi**. The fare is under $25 for one or two people, plus a sum for each additional passenger. The trip takes 20 to 30 minutes. The 14-passenger vans of the **Airport Shuttle** cost around a third of this price per person, one way. The vans drop passengers off at all hotels and guest houses; the length of the trip depends on whether your hotel is one of the first or the last along the route. **Express buses** (very cheap) operate between the airport and Elk Place in the Central Business District. The trip takes from 45 minutes to more than an hour.

DOMESTIC TRAVEL

WATER TRANSPORT

A ferry, which carries both pedestrians and vehicles, operates every 20–30 minutes between the Canal Street Wharf and Algiers on the West Bank. There is no charge for the trip to Algiers, but there is a small fee for the return trip.

PUBLIC TRANSPORT

The Regional Transport Authority (RTA) operates the city's buses and streetcars. Exact fare is required in all cases. The Easy Rider shuttle loops through the Central Business District. Transfers cost a few cents extra, on top of the normal fare. The RTA (tel: 569-2700, 24 hours) puts out an excellent color-coded map of the bus and streetcar routes which is available free at the New Orleans Welcome Center in Jackson Square. The RTA also has a 24-hour information RideLine (tel: 569-2700); call anytime day or night for information about the transit system. One- and three-day VisiTour Passes, allowing unlimited rides on buses and streetcars, are available from hotels and shopping areas.

PRIVATE TRANSPORT

Those who plan to rent a car should be aware that driving, and especially parking, in the French Quarter is not an easy task. Streets are narrow and often congested; cars parked illegally are towed away swiftly by sullen, hard-nosed tow-truck drivers and it's an expensive to-do to retrieve them again. During Mardi Gras there is a $100 fine for blocking a parade route.

While a car is convenient to have for weekend excursions, it's far better to put it in a secured parking lot and forget about it till you're ready to drive out of town.

Most car rental agencies have outlets at the airport as well as in the Central Business District:

Avis, 2024 Canal St, tel: 523-4317 or 800-331-1212.

Budget, 1317 Canal St, tel: 467-2277 or 800-527-0700.
Dollar, 1208 Canal St, tel: 525-3300 or 800-421-6868.
Hertz, 901 Convention Center Blvd, tel: 568-1645 or 800-654-3131.
National, 324 S. Rampart, St tel: 525-0416 or 800-227-7368.

TAXIS

Compared to other American cities, taxis are reasonably priced. Some drivers are loquacious and charming, story-telling a mile a minute and occasionally knocking a dollar or two off the fare if they find you, the passenger, suitably entertaining. Other drivers barely speak English, and negotiate without a map or a clue as to which direction to follow. They often end up lost in their own city. Taxis cruise the Riverwalk and French Quarter areas fairly regularly; it's not usually a problem finding one unless it's raining or you're in a hurry.

The *Yellow Pages* carry a list of taxi firms where a cab can be booked by phone. Booking is often a hair-pulling, nail-biting experience, for the easy-going way of life for which the city is famous seems to be especially prominent in cab firms. Despite honey-drawled reassurances that taxis are on their way, cabs are often late or nonexistent. If you plan to take many long-distance journeys by taxi, it's best to strike up a relationship with a specific driver or firm early on, and ask for a business card in order to book for future trips.

ON FOOT

The French Quarter is easily (and best) explored on foot. The Garden District and much of the CBD are also easily walkable. Apart from those areas, New Orleans is not a "walking city."
Hitchhiking: Hitchhiking is illegal in the state of Louisiana.

COMPLAINTS

Streetcars and buses: Direct complaints about streetcars and buses to the Regional Transit Authority, 101 Dauphine St, tel: 569-2625. Direct complaints about taxis to the Taxicab Bureau, City Hall, tel: 586-4621.

WHERE TO STAY

A wide variety of accommodations available, ranging from small, antique-filled guest houses to high-tech convention hotels complete with restaurants, bars, and health clubs. Unless otherwise stated, all buildings are air-conditioned and have swimming pools; most boast lush, subtropical courtyards.

The greatest concentration of hotels is in the French Quarter and the CBD. Accommodations are fairly easy to find during June, July, and August. However, New Orleans is a major convention city, and between September and May hotels in the French Quarter and CBD may be booked.

For special events such as Mardi Gras and the Jazz Fest, reservations should be made up to a year in advance, and almost all hotels and guest houses require a three- to five-day minimum stay. Some even hike their prices. It is wise to check the cancellation policy at the time you reserve. Many hotels offer attractive package deals; be sure to ask a travel agent or the hotel when you call to book. Almost all properties accept major credit cards, but this, too, should be ascertained in advance.

In the following categories (Deluxe, Expensive, Moderate, and Inexpensive), several hotels have moderate rooms as well as deluxe suites. The chains (Hilton, Marriott, Sheraton) are rather expensive, but frequently offer discounted rates that are very attractive to visitors. The selection is further subdivided into hotels (which includes motels) and guest houses.

Although occasionally the difference between the two categories is blurred, hotels tend to be large, more formal establishments, part of a chain, or good for business travelers. Guest houses are smaller, often family-run, with fewer amenities, but cozier ambiance.

HOTELS, MOTELS

DELUXE

Hotel Inter-Continental, 444 St Charles Ave, tel: 525-5566 or 800-33-AGAIN. Elegant hotel in the heart of the CBD, has sunny, attractively decorated rooms and very sumptuous suites. Geared toward business travelers, it is equipped with the latest high-tech features, such as teleconferencing via satellite, which can be received through TV sets in individual rooms. Good locations for shoppers, business travelers, and sightseers.
Omni Royal Orleans, 621 St Louis St, tel: 529-5333 or 800-THE-OMNI. Stunning French Quarter property, with vast marbled halls, oriental rugs, exotic statuary, and crystal chandeliers. Rooms are average size, but some large, individually decorated suites have canopy beds and jacuzzis. The standout among its several restaurants is the Rib Room, popular with politicos and movers-and-shakers. Near Jackson Square.
Royal Sonesta, 300 Bourbon St, tel: 586-0300 or 800-343-7170. Serene, elegant French Quarter hotel on busy, noisy Bourbon Street. The hotel has a French country flavor. There are tiny dormer rooms, as well as spacious, luxuriously decorated rooms and suites, some with canopy beds, parquet floors, oriental rugs, and jacuzzis. Many rooms and suites have balconies overlooking Bourbon Street, that should be avoided by those who sleep lightly.
Westin Canal Place, 100 Iberville St, tel: 566-7066 or 800-228-3000. A glamorous luxury hotel located at a corner of the CBD and the French Quarter. Glass elevators sweep up through the Canal Place atrium to the 11th-floor lobby, which is resplendent with rose Carrara marble, period furnishings, oriental carpeting, and large windows with a commanding view of the river and the Quarter. Extensive use of marble, artwork, and antiques throughout the hotel.

EXPENSIVE

Fairmont Hotel, University Place, tel: 529-7111 or 800-527-4727. Venerable grand hotel centrally located in the CBD across Canal Street from the French Quarter. Most of the rooms are exceptionally large, and the suites are sumptuous. Eight US presidents, from

Coolidge to Ford, have stayed here, as well as kings, princes, and prime ministers. Home of the Sazerac Bar and Bailey's, an up-market 24-hour restaurant.

Le Meridien, 614 Canal St, tel: 525-6500 or 800-543-4300. Air France's contribution to the hotel scene is a sleek, modern, $65 million high-rise property in the CBD, across the street from the French Quarter. Many rooms are average-sized with monochromatic decor, but corner rooms are split-level with two-story windows that offer exciting views. There are also exquisite penthouse suites. A popular convention hotel with many high-tech features.

Marriott Hotel, 555 Canal St, tel: 581-1000 or 800-228-9290. Another sleek chain hotel in the CBD geared toward tour groups and conventioneers, the Marriott has an enormous, bustling lobby, rooms and suites in two towers, and several restaurants and lounges. It's on the French Quarter side of Canal Street.

Monteleone, 214 Royal St, tel: 523-3341 or 800-535-9595. The French Quarter's oldest hotel, still operated by the Monteleone family, celebrated its 100th anniversary in 1986. The elegant, 600-room hotel has a baroque facade, a large, bustling lobby with glittering chandeliers, and handsome rooms and suites. Ideal location for shopping as well as sightseeing.

New Orleans Airport Hilton & Conference Center, 901 Airline Hwy, tel: 469-5000 or 800-HILTONS. Completed in 1989, this $32 million, soundproof property is across the street from New Orleans International Airport. An ultramodern hotel, all of whose rooms are identical, it numbers among its guests former president Ronald Reagan. Reaching the city, i.e., the French Quarter and the CBD, takes 20 to 30 minutes.

New Orleans Hilton Riverside and Towers, 2 Poydras tel: 561-0500 or 800-HILTONS. Great location in the CBD, adjacent to Riverwalk and a short walk from the Convention Center, this is a large, splashy chain hotel that's awash with restaurants, bars, and lounges, including Pete Fountain's Club. The Rivercenter Tennis & Racquetball Club is one of the best such facilities in town. Rooms in the Riverside section afford unsurpassed views of the Mississippi River. George Bush stayed here while president of the United States.

New Orleans Sheraton, 500 Canal St, tel: 525-2500 or 800-325-3535. The local Sheraton link, in the CBD across the street from the Marriott, offers an attractive lobby with spiral staircase and contemporary rooms and suites. Service is excellent. There are several restaurants and lounges and music nightly in the lobby. A major convention hotel.

Pontchartrain Hotel, 2031 St Charles Ave, tel: 524-0581 or 800-777-1700. Elegant old-world hotel in the Garden District whose accommodations range from small, darkish rooms to some of the most exquisite suites in town. Several of the latter category are named for some the many celebrities (e.g., Mary Martin and Richard Burton) who made this their home-away-from-home over the years. It has neither pool nor health club, but is the location of the elegant Caribbean Room restaurant. It's situated right along the St Charles streetcar line, about 10 minutes from the CBD and French Quarter.

Windsor Court, 300 Gravier St, tel: 523-6000 or 800-262-2662. The city's most luxurious hotel, built around a $5 million private art collection, is thoroughly British in flavor. Located in the CBD near Canal Place and Riverwalk, it has a stunning lobby and elegantly appointed suites. Afternoon tea, served daily to the tune of chamber music, features scones, finger sandwiches, and chocolates, and is enormously popular. The main dining room is the superb Grill Room. Princess Anne is among the royals who have been guests here.

MODERATE

Dauphine Orleans, 415 Dauphine St, tel: 586-1800 or 800-521-6111 (LA); 800-521-7111 (US). In the French Quarter, close to the CBD, this is a rather simply furnished motel whose amenities include on-site parking, minibars and cable TV in each room, and complimentary Continental breakfast served in a cheerful, sunny breakfast room. A complimentary jitney scoots guests around different parts of the city.

De la Poste, 316 Chartres St, tel: 581-1200 or 800-448-4927. An up-market motel with splendid courtyard, located in the French Quarter three blocks from the CBD. Large, sunny, tastefully decorated rooms, but those on the front of the building are noisy. Carriage house suites on the courtyard are large bedsitting rooms with private patios. In 1990, a Brennan family restaurant opened on the premises.

Le Richelieu, 1234 Chartres St, tel: 529-2492 or 800-535-9653. A restored macaroni factory and 19th-century rowhouses comprise much of this elegant 88-room hotel in the residential lower Quarter, considered by many to be the best bargain in town. Large rooms are individually decorated, with balconies, brass ceiling fans, and small refrigerators. Paul McCartney stayed in one of the suites for several weeks while he was in the city cutting an album.

Provincial Hotel, 1024 Chartres St, tel: 581-4995 or 800-621-5295 (LA); 800-535-7922 (US). Also in the lower Quarter near the French Market, this hotel comprises four-balconied units built around five lush patios. Large rooms are furnished with antiques and period reproductions. Friendly staff; charming little restaurant. On-site parking.

INEXPENSIVE

Chateau Motor Hotel, 1001 Chartres St, tel: 524-9636. Small, tastefully furnished motel with a charming courtyard; located in the residential lower Quarter. Good choice for budget travelers.

GUEST HOUSES

DELUXE

Maison de Ville, 727 Toulouse St, tel: 561-5858 or 800-634-1600. A small European-style hotel in the heart of the French Quarter. Though exquisitely furnished with antiques, rooms in the main house and adjoining slave quarters are small and can be quite noisy (it's near Bourbon Street). Posh, spacious apartments, replete with full kitchens and many amenities, are nearby in the hotel's exclusive Audubon Cottages that surround a serene courtyard and pool. Complimentary Continental breakfast is served in-room on a silver tray in the main hotel and cottages.

Melrose Mansion, 937 Esplanade Ave, tel: 949-3705. Restored in 1990, this luxurious nine-room guest house on the fringe of the French Quarter is housed in a Victorian mansion. Rooms and suites, each individually decorated with period antiques, have hardwood floors, high ceilings, and old-

world charm. Because it isn't exactly in the center of things, there is a complimentary chauffeured limo for the use of guests. There are frequent soirées, replete with an astonishing array of foods, and a complimentary Continental breakfast is served poolside each morning. Expect to be pampered.

EXPENSIVE

Josephine Guest House, 1450 Josephine St, tel: 524-6361. In the Garden District, just a block off the St Charles streetcar line, this lovely white Italianate mansion contains an elaborate display of antique furnishings. There are six guest rooms, each individually decorated. Complimentary Continental breakfast (which includes homemade biscuits) is served on Wedgwood china. No pool or restaurant.

Soniat House, 1133 Chartres St, tel: 522-0570 or 800-544-8808. Built as a townhouse in 1830, this small, charming French Quarter guest house is a pleasant alternative to the splashy convention hotels. Furnished throughout with antiques, it's located in the quiet, predominantly residential lower Quarter. Although it has neither restaurant nor pool, it has many amenities one normally associates with a full-service hotel. A Continental breakfast, served in room on a silver tray, is included in the rate.

MODERATE

Cornstalk Hotel, 915 Royal St, tel: 523-1515. Housed in a Victorian Gothic mansion, this hotel boasts crystal chandeliers, canopy beds, four-posters, and other antiques. Some of the 14 rooms have fireplaces. Complimentary Continental breakfast. No pool or restaurant. Convenient to Jackson Square and other French Quarter sights.

Olivier House Hotel, 828 Toulouse St, tel: 525-8456. Small, friendly family-run guest house in the French Quarter, a block off Bourbon Street. The building was constructed in 1836 as a Creole townhouse. Some rooms are furnished in antiques, others are in contemporary decor. There are also some split-level suites with canopy beds and fireplaces. Popular with Europeans and casts of touring shows that play at the Saenger Center. No restaurant, but there are many nearby, and there *is* a swimming pool.

Terrell House, 1441 Magazine St, tel: 524-9859. A Greek Revival mansion with filigreed iron galleries, the hotel contains a most impressive collection of antiques. Guest rooms are in the main mansion, the carriage house, and the old servants' quarters. Complimentary Continental breakfast and afternoon cocktails. No pool or restaurant.

Villa Convento, 616 Ursulines St, tel: 522-1793. A simply furnished, 24-room guest house, family owned and operated, located in a 19th-century townhouse in a secluded section of the French Quarter. Complimentary Continental breakfast is served in a pretty courtyard. No pool or restaurant.

INEXPENSIVE

French Quarter Maisonettes, 1130 Chartres St, tel: 514-9918. Secluded French Quarter location with seven simply furnished but spacious units. Lovely courtyard and helpful advice from owner/manager, but few amenities in sight. Located conveniently near the French Market.

St Charles Guest House, 1748 Prytania St, tel: 523-6556. Simple but charming guest house frequented by artists and visitors on a budget, which has friendly, helpful hosts. Small "backpacker" rooms are not air-conditioned, and you must share a bathroom. Amenities include complimentary breakfast and afternoon tea. In the lower Garden District, a block off the St Charles streetcar line. There is a pool, but no restaurant.

BED & BREAKFAST

There are two organizations in the city that arrange accommodations in private homes with friendly, knowledgeable hosts. Contact **New Orleans Bed & Breakfast**, P.O. Box 8128, New Orleans, LA 70182, tel: 504/822-5038 or **Bed & Breakfast, Inc.**, 1360 Moss St, Box 52257, New Orleans, LA 70152-2257, tel: 504/525-4640 or 800-228-9711.

CAMPGROUNDS

Jude Travel Park of New Orleans, 7400 Chef Menteur Hwy, tel: 241-0632 or 800-523-2196. Located in the eastern part of the city, with a shuttle bus to the French Quarter. 43 sites with full hook-ups, showers, restrooms, laundry, pool, and playground.

YOUTH HOSTELS

Marquette New Orleans International Hostel, 2253 Carondelet St, tel: 523-3014. Dormitory accommodations in an antebellum home; community kitchen, dining area, reading room, and patio. Located near the Garden District, a block from the St Charles streetcar line.

FOOD DIGEST

WHAT TO EAT

For New Orleanians, the act of dining out is virtually an art form. As is the case with many European countries – notably France and Italy – dining is done leisurely and is frequently the evening's only entertainment. New Orleans is noted the world over for Creole and Cajun cuisine. Creole dishes are exemplified by rich, creamy sauces, while Cajun cooking, often called the country version of Creole cuisine, tends to be red-hot and spicy, more robust. While there are still distinctions, the two culinary traditions have blended over the years into what is locally called New Orleans-style cuisine. The area has an embarrassment of riches from the sea, and seafood is showcased on virtually all Creole and Cajun menus. There are also a number of terms indigenous to the region, such as:

Andouill: (ahn-doo-ee): A hot Cajun sausage made with ham and garlic.

Bananas Foster: A delicious dessert concoction of bananas sauteed with sugar, butter and cinnamon, flambéed with brandy, and served over vanilla ice cream.

Barbecue shrimp: Another local favorite, baked in the shell and served in a butter-and-garlic sauce.

Beignet (bin-yea): The specialty of Café du Monde is a square doughnut, minus the hole, which is liberally sprinkled with powdered sugar.

Boudin (boo-dan): Also a red-hot Cajun sausage, this one involving spicy pork, rice, herbs, and onions.

Café au lait: Potent chickory coffee with an equal mixture of hot milk.

Cajun popcorn: Batter-fried shrimp or crawfish.

Chickory: A herb, the roots of which are ground and used to flavor coffee.

Crawfish: Tiny sea creatures that resemble lobsters, which are boiled and served on a platter, or appear in dishes such as *etouffées*. Often called "mud-bugs" because they live in the mud of freshwater streams. Enormously popular in New Orleans.

Dressed: A "dressed" sandwich means it has everything on it – the works.

Etouffée (Ay-too-fay): A rich, tomato-based sauce for crawfish or shrimp dishes.

Gumbo: A hearty soup made with rice, it comes in many varieties, including seafood and andouille.

Jambalaya: A cousin of Spanish paella, it's made with rice, tomatoes, seasonings, seafood, and sausage.

Muffuletta: Big thick sandwiches on a seeded roll with heaps of Italian sausage, cheeses, and olive salad.

Po-boy: Another sandwich, this one served between thick slices of French bread. You can get any number of different fillings, including oysters, roast beef and gravy, ham, alligator, or meat balls.

Praline (prah-leen): A very sweet candy patty made with sugar, water, butter, and pecans.

Red beans and rice: Traditionally served on Mondays, this hearty dish consists of kidney beans mixed with rice, seasonings, spices, and sausage.

WHERE TO EAT

New Orleans has more than 1,500 restaurants. The following is a small, highly selective sampling. Unless otherwise noted in the description with words like "casual" or "informal," men are requested to wear a jacket and tie in the restaurants listed.

DELUXE

Antoine's, 713 St Louis St, French Quarter, tel: 581-4422. Closed: Sunday. Reservations are essential during peak periods. Elegant, famed French Creole restaurant that celebrated its 150th anniversary in 1990, Antoine's is the oldest continuously operated family-run restaurant in America. Oysters Rockefeller and Pompano en Papillote originated here. Many of the dishes are sensational, especially its best-known dessert, Baked Alaska. Stroll around after dinner to see the many dining rooms, including the Rex Room, with its glittering display of Mardi Gras memorabilia, or the 50,000-bottle wine cellar.

Arnaud's, 813 Bienville St, French Quarter, tel: 523-0611. Reservations essential during peak periods. A large, handsome restaurant with mosaic tile floors and etched glass windows, Arnaud's has been a favorite since its opening in 1918. Specialties are French and Creole dishes. There's a delightful jazz brunch each Sunday.

Brennan's, 417 Royal St, tel: 525-9711. Reservations essential during peak periods. "Breakfast at Brennan's" is famed virtually the world over and justifiably so. Eggs Benedict, Eggs Houssarde, and Eggs Sardou are among the offerings. Lunch and dinner are also culinary delights. There are 12 elegant dining rooms and a splendid courtyard. Bananas Foster originated here, the traditional breakfast dessert.

Commander's Palace, 1403 Washington Ave, Garden District, tel: 899-8221. Reservations essential during peak periods. First-rate restaurant serving Creole and American dishes in a marvelous Victorian mansion. The Garden Room overlooks a glorious courtyard. The jazz brunch originated here, and it's the city's best. Commander's is the only restaurant that has a jazz brunch on both Saturday and Sunday. The bread pudding is delicious, but the dessert list also includes a diet-destroyer called the Celebration.

Galatoire's, 209 Bourbon St, French Quarter, tel: 525-2021. Closed: Monday. Reservations and credit cards not accepted. Long lines form outside this old-line French Creole restaurant, which has an extensive menu. It's an intimate, 140-seat restaurant, paneled with mirrors, ceiling fans whirring above. Sunday afternoons resemble a salon, with upscale New Orleanians table-hopping to chat with friends. The long wait can be avoided by arriving for lunch about 11:30 a.m. or around 1 or 2 p.m. in the afternoon.

EXPENSIVE

Andrea's, 3100 19th St, Metairie, tel: 834-8583. A rather elegant restaurant (though dress is casual) serving northern Italian and continental cuisine. The pasta is homemade, and there's a tempting antipasto display. Low calorie dishes are also featured on the menu. There's a festive Sunday brunch with lively Italian music.

Brigtsen's, 723 Dante St, Uptown, tel: 861-7610. Closed: Sunday and Monday. Open for dinner only; reservations required. Small, informal, and very popular, this restaurant has a changing menu that features a blending of Cajun and Creole specialties.

Caribbean Room, Pontchartrain Hotel, 2031 St Charles Ave, Garden District, tel: 524-0581. Reservations suggested. Luxurious hotel dining room serving innovative French Creole dishes with a focus on seafood. Mile-High Pie is the dessert extravaganza.

Grill Room, Windsor Court Hotel, 300 Gravier St, CBD, tel: 522-1992. Reservations suggested. An elegant hotel dining room with marbled floors and Austrian drapes. As the name might indicate, most of the specialties come from the grill: grilled salmon, grilled sirloin and grilled marinated rack of lamb are among the standouts. A harpist plays during Sunday brunch.

K-Paul's Louisiana Kitchen, 416 Chartres St, French Quarter, tel: 942-7200. Closed: Saturday and Sunday. Reservations not accepted. This is the bastion of world-famed Cajun chef Paul Prudhomme. It's a small, country-kitchen café, where casually dressed patrons consume his blackened redfish and other delectable creations. Expect queues of people outside from all over America waiting to be let in.

La Riviera, 4506 Shores Dr., Metairie, tel: 888-6238. Closed: Sunday. Northern Italian dishes, homemade pasta, and delicious desserts are served in attractively appointed dining rooms. Dress is upscale casual.

Mr B's Bistro, 201 Royal St, French Quarter, tel: 523-2078. Reservations recommended. A large, handsome room with etched glass and mahogany paneling, this Brennan family restaurant offers Creole and New American cuisine. Seafood, pasta, and steaks are featured. Desserts are exotic, especially those involving chocolate. Dress is casual but not funky.

Mosca's, 4137 US Highway 90 W, tel: 436-9942. Out of the way Italian restaurant worth traveling for. Try the oysters in bread crumbs or the superb roasted chicken.

Pelican Club, 615 Bienville St/312 Exchange Alley, tel: 523-1504. Open for lunch Monday–Friday, dinner nightly. Hushed, with romantic lighting and white-clothed tables, this sophisticated restaurant has entrances on Bienville St and Exchange Alley. Specials include seafood and pasta dishes, duck and poultry, and excellent steaks.

Rib Room, Omni Royal Orleans Hotel, 621 St Louis St, French Quarter, tel: 529-7045. Reservations suggested. Old-brick walls and a sizzling rotisserie create a cozy atmosphere. Beef, game, fowl, and seafood are featured. Huge windows overlook the Royal Street scene. Good oyster po-boys at lunch.

MODERATE

Alex Patout's, 221 Royal St, French Quarter, tel: 525-7788. Closed for lunch on weekends. Chef/Owner Alex comes from a long line of Cajun culinary artists in South Louisiana. His stylish restaurant showcases seafoods done up in exotic sauces and seasonings. At lunch and dinner there are good fixed-price menus. Jackets and reservations are suggested for dinner.

Bayona, 430 Dauphine St, French Quarter, tel: 525-4455. Small, chic, noisy, and enormously popular with the adoring fans of chef/owner Susan Spicer. The nouvelle cuisine is imaginative, with a Mediterranean flavor to it. Jackets are suggested, reservations a must.

Charlie's Steak House, 4510 Dryades St, Uptown, tel: 895-9705. Informal neighborhood eatery featuring thick, succulent steaks. An old-timer on the restaurant scene.

Chez Helene, 1540 N. Robertson St, Mid-City, tel: 947-1206. A casual down-home soul food restaurant with red-checked tablecloths, Chez Helene was the model for the television series *Frank's Place*. Red beans and rice, fried chicken, cornbread, and black-eyed peas are among the offerings.

Emeril's, 800 Tchoupitoulas St, Warehouse District, tel: 528-9393. Reservations required. Chef Emeril Lagasse, formerly of Commander's Palace, opened his own place in 1990, and it's been a hot ticket ever since. The cuisine is nouvelle, and virtually everything is homemade. Dress is upscale casual.

Gautreau's, 1728 Soniat St, Uptown, tel: 899-7397. Closed: Sunday and for lunch Saturday. Reservations suggested. Housed in a former pharmacy, this small, casual neighborhood eatery is a great local favorite, serving steaks, fish, and veal dishes.

Palace Café, 605 Canal St, CBD, tel: 523-1661. An addition to the Commander's Palace and Mr. B's family of famed restaurants, the Palace is New Orleans' version of a grand Parisian café. It showcases meat, fowl and seafood, plus sinfully delicious desserts. Reservations are not accepted.

Ralph & Kacoo's, 519 Toulouse St, French Quarter, tel: 522-5226. Seafood (and huge portions of it) is the specialty in this casual restaurant. A complimentary serving of mouth-watering hush puppies (potatoes) comes with each meal.

Tujaque's, 832 Decatur St, French Quarter, tel: 525-8676. The city's second oldest restaurant, in business since 1856, is in an atmospheric building across from the French Market. A six-course, fixed-price meal is served nightly; the entrée specialty is brisket of beef. Dress is casual.

Upperline, 1413 Upperline St, Uptown, tel: 581-9680. Closed: Monday nights. Reservations suggested. An intimate café with displays of Louisiana artists and taped New Orleans jazz as background, the Upperline serves New Orleans and continental dishes.

INEXPENSIVE

Acme Oyster House, 724 Iberville St, French Quarter, tel: 522-5973. A plain and simple venue that's been going strong since around the turn of the century, the Acme has a big marble oyster bar as well as table seating. Oysters are showcased, but there are sandwiches and salads as well.

Bozo's, 3117 21st, Metairie (across Causeway Blvd from Lakeside Mall), tel: 831 8666. A popular place for gumbo and seafood dishes, too.

Bruning's, West End Park, tel: 282 9395. Located right on Lake Pontchartrain, the view whets the appetite for the terrific selection of seafood.

Camellia Grill, 626 S. Carrollton Ave, Uptown, tel: 866-9573. Very popular diner whose customers are sometimes lined up outside the door. Virtually a New Orleans institution, the Camellia is famed for its burgers, waffles, chili, and homemade pastries.

Flagons, 3222 Magazine St, tel; 895-6471. New Orleans' definitive wine bar, with some 50 wines offered by the glass, which is also a good nouvelle-Creole bistro.

Gumbo Shop, 630 St Peter St, French Quarter, tel: 525-1486. An informal room with an adjoining patio, the Gumbo Shop offers traditional Creole fare. Their combination platter of red beans and rice, shrimp Creole, and jambalaya is a good introduction to the local cuisine.

La Madeleine, 547 St Ann St, French Quarter, tel: 568-9950. Open for breakfast, lunch, and light dinners, this is a small, very simple place in Jackson Square that's almost always packed solid. Salads, sandwiches, and quiches are served, but the main attraction is the breads and pastries. Breads are baked in a wood-burning oven, and the delicious aroma wafts out into the Square.

Miss Ruby's, 539 St Philip, French Quarter, tel: 523-3514. Lunch and dinner daily. A tiny and casual French Quarter institution, with red-and-white checked cloths and a neighborhood crowd. Plate lunches (chicken and dumplings, barbecue ribs, meatloaf, and such) are served, along with Cajun and Creole specialties.

Mother's, 401 Poydras St, CBD, tel: 523-9656. Closed: Sunday and Monday. Open at 5 a.m. for breakfast (homemade biscuits, ham and eggs, grits), this small, funky eatery has been a favorite for more than 50 years. Superb po-boys, Creole and Cajun dishes, and fried seafood are featured for both lunch and dinner.

Praline Connection, 542 Frenchmen St, Faubourg Marigny, tel: 943-3934. Open for breakfast, lunch and dinner; stays open late on weekends. Casual neighborhood restaurant featuring wonderful Southern cooking – cornbread, barbecue pork, turnip greens, blackeyed peas, fried chicken, and such. The name comes from the sweet-shop adjacent to the main dining room, where many delectations involving chocolate are served.

SANDWICHES, PASTRIES & ICE-CREAM SHOPS

Angelo Brocato's, 537 St Ann St, French Quarter, tel: 525-9767. This little ice-cream shop is right on Jackson Square. Delicious

Italian ice creams and pastries have been served here for more than 80 years.

Café du Monde, 813 Decatur St, French Quarter, tel: 581-2914. Almost always packed with locals and tourists, this casual 24-hour haven serves only coffee (regular and *café au lait*), orange juice, and *beignets*. A great spot for people-watching, it's right on Jackson Square and is the traditional last stop after a night on the town.

Café Maspero, 601 Decatur St, French Quarter, tel: 523-6250. There's almost always a long line of locals and tourists waiting to get in for the famous oversized sandwiches and thick-cut French fries. Very casual dress.

La Marquise, 625 Chartres St, French Quarter, tel: 524-0420. Closed: Wednesday. Wonderful French pastries are served here. There are two small rooms, as well as seating in a rear courtyard. Very casual.

Napoleon House, 500 Chartres St, French Quarter, tel: 524-9752. One of the most popular spots in town, the Napoleon House has peeling sepia walls, pictures of the Little Corporal, taped classical music, and wonderful muffulettas, as well as a salad bar, sandwiches, and desserts. There's also seating in a pretty courtyard that adjoins the bar.

DRINKING NOTES

New Orleans is a hard-drinking town; the only US city in which go-cups are ubiquitous. A go-cup is a paper or plastic container for drinks "to go." It's illegal, and punishable by a stiff fine, to carry a glass or open beer can on the streets; thus, virtually every drinking establishment in town provides go-cups for its customers. The legal drinking age in New Orleans is 21. Package liquor, beer, and wine can be purchased seven days a week, 24 hours a day, in grocery stores, pharmacies, and convenience stores.

There are several local alcoholic concoctions about which visitors should be aware. The ubiquitous Hurricane, which originated at Pat O'Brien's, is a potent libation made with dark rum and fruit juices. Definitely not for the faint of heart, the Sazerac, claimed to be the world's first cocktail, is bourbon and bitters served in a glass that's first swirled through the air to coat it with ersatz absinthe. (In the original drink the absinthe was actually absinthe; now it's illegal in this country,

the mix is a diluted substitute). The rich Ramos gin fizz involves gin, egg white, soda, cream, and orange flower water. The mint julep of song and legend is made with bourbon, quinine, and mint.

For a list of bars, dance halls and clubs where drinking has been known to take place, see the "Nightlife" section of Travel Tips.

THINGS TO DO

IN THE CITY

Aquarium of the Americas, Canal St at the River, tel: 861-2537. Open: daily 9 a.m.–6 p.m. Closed: Christmas and Mardi Gras. The aquarium is a $40 million facility with four major exhibits: The Mississippi River, which features a free-flowing bayou, moss-draped trees, and alligators; the Caribbean Reef, where you can walk through a transparent tunnel and look above at a coral reef, sharks and angel fish; the Gulf of Mexico, where one of the world's largest underwater windows provides a 180-degree view of sharks, tarpon, and sting rays; and the Amazon Rainforest, which replicates the humidity, aromas, and vegetation of a jungle. Touch tanks and hands-on exhibits help children (and grown-ups) get acquainted with sea critters. There is a café on the premises, as well as picnic areas in adjacent Woldenberg Park which overlooks the River.

Audubon Park and Audubon Zoo, 6500 Magazine St, tel: 861-2537. Open: Monday–Friday 9.30 a.m.–5 p.m; Saturday–Sunday 9.30 a.m.–6 p.m. Closes one hour earlier during summer months. The Park is a 375-acre urban oasis, lush with greenery and magnificent live oak trees splashed with Spanish moss. There is an 18-hole golf course, a stable for guided trail rides on horseback, a swimming pool, tennis courts, and the wonderful Audubon Zoo. More than 1,000 critters roam freely in the zoo's natural habitats such as the African Savannah, the

Louisiana Swamp Exhibit, the Asian Domain, and the Australian Exhibit. The feeding of the sea lions is a fun occasion for spectators as well as the sea creatures. Wooden walkways ramble throughout the 58 acres, and the Mombassa mini-train tools through the back part of the zoo. Monkey Hill was constructed so that children growing up in these flatlands might be able to grasp the meaning of the word "hill." At the Wisner Children's Zoo there are elephant and camel rides for children. Allow a full day to explore the zoo; you might want another one for the park itself.

Blaine Kern's Mardi Gras World, 233 Newton St, Algiers, tel: 362 8211. Open: daily 9.30 a.m.–4 p.m. Kern is the world's largest float-builder. His gigantic, fantastic concoctions roll through the streets of New Orleans during Mardi Gras. Visitors can watch Mardi Gras in the making in the huge "dens," or warehouses, as artists create the papier-mâché and fiberglass figures that delight the crowds. Kids (and grown-ups, too) get a kick out of having their pictures taken with some of the giant statues and other float ornamentation. If you're unable to be in New Orleans during Mardi Gras, you can get a tempting taste of it here. There's also a souvenir shop selling Carnival memorabilia.

Cemeteries: New Orleans' "Cities of the Dead" are among its most popular attractions. The tombs range from crumbling old-brick "step tombs" to ornate masterpieces adorned with fanciful ironwork and statuary. The oldest is St Louis Cemetery No. 1, located on the fringe of the French Quarter; the most photographed is Metairie Cemetery, which has far and away the most elaborate tombs and monuments. Regrettably, most of the cemeteries are in crime-ridden areas, and it is not advisable to visit them alone. See the section "Tour guides" for details of tours.

Chalmette Battlefield, 6 miles downriver of the city in Chalmette, LA; tel: 589-2636. Open: daily 9 a.m.–5 p.m. On January 8, 1815, crack British forces under the command of Major General Sir Edward Pakenham clashed on this site with General Andrew Jackson and his ragtag band of Creoles, Tennessee Volunteers, and some of Jean Lafitte's pirates. The hard-fought Battle of New Orleans, in which the Americans were victorious, was the last battle in the last war ever fought between Great Britain and the US. Chalmette is operated by the Jean Lafitte National Historical Park, and four times daily in the Visitors Center the Park Rangers give talks about the battlefield. They also provide free self-guided walking and driving tours of the park. In truth there is little for most people to see except the Chalmette Cemetery, which was established in 1864 and contains the graves of Union soldiers killed in the area during the Civil War, plus the Beauregard House, an unfurnished plantation home. History buffs will enjoy seeing the battlefield, however, and there are ample grounds for picnicking.

City Park, located at the northern end of Esplanade Ave. These 1,500 acres contain the New Orleans Museum of Art; gnarled live oak trees, some of which are 800 years old; Storyland, a children's playground with Mother Goose characters; 8 miles of lagoons decorated with ducks and swans; the Botanical Gardens, with statuary and fountains; four golf courses and a 100-tee, double-deck driving range; a 39-acre tennis center; an amusement park with a historic, turn-of-the-century carousel and other rides; and baseball and softball diamonds. The Casino is the place to rent bikes and boats; pick up a fishing permit; or just have a snack. The *P.G.T. Beauregard*, a vintage miniature train, is a fun ride through the busiest and most scenic parts of the park.

Faulkner House, 624 Pirate's Alley, French Quarter. Private home with bookstore on the ground floor. Nobel prize winning novelist William Faulkner wrote his first novel, *A Soldier's Pay*, while living in an apartment in this building.

First Skyscraper, 640 Royal St. Now an apartment building with commercial establishments on the ground floor, this weathered masonry building was erected in 1796 as a home for Dr Yves LeMonnier, whose initials are worked into the wrought-iron balcony. The curved wall overlooking St Peter Street follows the contours of the rooms; the third floor study is an architectural masterpiece. Also known as 'Sieur George after a character in a George Washington Cable short story, the house originally had three stories; according to legend the top floor was added later so that the "tallest building" title could be retained.

LaBranche Buildings, 700 block of Royal St and 600 block of St Peter St. This is the most photographed corner in the city and with good reason. The buildings have almost an embarrassment of lavish cast-iron riches in galleries and colonettes. The buildings dates from about 1840 and comprise 11 separate three-story brick row houses.

Louisiana Nature and Science Center, 11000 Lake Forest Blvd, tel: 246-9381. Open: Tuesday–Friday 9 a.m.–5 p.m; Saturday–Sunday noon–5 p.m. Closed: major holidays. If time doesn't permit a full day's excursion out of the city, this 86-acre nature reserve, only about 20 minutes from downtown, offers a fine in-town sample of the swamplands. A full-time naturalist is on hand to interpret the exhibits, and there are nature trails, a planetarium, and hands-on exhibits for children. The Center organizes special events such as backpacking trips, canoe trips, and moonlight hikes. Planetarium shows are Tuesday–Friday at 4 p.m; weekends 2 p.m. and 4 p.m.

Madame John's Legacy, 632 Dumaine St. Not open to the public. This beautifully restored West Indies-style house is typical of homes built by early planters in Louisiana. It was built in 1726, and some historians believe it survived the fire of 1788 with partial damage. Others contend that it was completely destroyed and rebuilt following the fire. That there is a debate at all is because if it did survive the fire intact, it would be the oldest structure still on its feet in the Lower Mississippi Valley – a title now claimed by the Old Ursuline Convent (*see below*). The name of this house comes from a short story, '*Tite Poulette*, by 19th-century New Orleans novelist George Washington Cable. The house plays a prominent role in the story, and is beautifully described therein.

Museums: *see listing on pages 280–82.*

New Orleans School of Cooking, Jackson Brewery, 620 Decatur St, tel: 525-2665. Proprietor Joe Cahn conducts demonstrations of south Louisiana-style cooking, with a different menu each day. It isn't a hands-on experience, but after the demonstration you do get to eat the results. There is also a retail store selling indigenous condiments and cookbooks.

Old Ursuline Convent, 1114 Chartres St. Not open to the public. This handsome old building dates from 1745 and is the only undisputed survivor of the great fire of 1788. A fine example of French Colonial architecture, it is the second building on this site, the first having been constructed in 1727. That same year the Sisters of Ursula arrived in New Orleans from Paris; they moved into this convent in 1749. It now contains archives of New Orleans archdiocese. Tours are conducted occasionally.

Pirate's Alley and Père Antoine's Alley. These twin flagstone passageways run parallel alongside St Louis Cathedral and the Cathedral Gardens, connecting Jackson Square with Royal Street.

Riverboat Cruises: *see page 280.*

Streetcars: Merely a means of transportation for many Uptowners, the St Charles streetcar is a delightful outing for visitors. It boards in the Central Business District at Canal and Carondelet, and jingles, rumbles, and clanks its way up St Charles Avenue, through the Garden District, and on past Audubon Park and the university section. The enormously popular Riverfront streetcar, which began rolling in 1988, breezes along the Mississippi, making 10 stops between Esplanade Avenue and the Robin Street Wharf (where the *Delta Queen* and *Mississippi Queen* dock) – five stops below Canal Street and five above Canal Street. It runs alongside the French Market, the Jax Brewery, the Aquarium, and Riverwalk, among other riverside sites.

Viewpoint, World Trade Center. Open: daily 9 a.m.–5 p.m. This observation deck on the 31st floor of the WTC affords a spectacular 360-degree view of the Crescent City. A glass elevator eases up the side of the building, and on the enclosed deck there are coin-operated telescopes. This is a superb place in which to get your bearings of the city.

Walking Tours: *see Guided Tours, p. 280.*

OUTSIDE THE CITY

There are two popular day excursions from New Orleans: Plantation country and the surrounding swamps. Both trips can easily be made in a day; in some cases half a day. The swamps and bayous can best be explored with a guided tour. In the case of the plantations, you can either rent a car and go it alone or take one of several tours to the area. (*See Tour Operators and Guided Tours on page 280*).

PLANTATION COUNTRY

A number of grand, restored plantation homes decorate the Great River Road that runs along the Mississippi between New Orleans and Baton Rouge. The lovely antebellum antique-filled homes are open to the public; several of them have been sets for movies and some are elegant bed-and-breakfast establishments. Most are open all year round (except major holidays), but close slightly earlier in the winter. Guided tours are usually provided, and all of the mansions are listed on the National Register of Historic Places. Some of the more outstanding are:

Destrehan, 9999 River Road, Destrehan, LA, tel: 764-9315. The oldest plantation house in the lower Mississippi Valley, Destrehan was built in 1787.

Houmas House, 40136 Highway 942 Burnside, Darrow, LA, tel: 522-2262. A large white Greek Revival mansion set in lush grounds and surrounded on three sides by massive columns, this house was the set for *Hush, Hush, Sweet Charlotte*, a Gothic thriller starring Bette Davis and Olivia De Havilland.

Madewood, 4250 Highway 308, Napoleonville, LA, tel: 369-7151. A 21-room Greek Revival mansion, Madewood is a stately place that manages to combine elegance and a homey atmosphere. It's a sumptuous bed-and-breakfast establishment; guests are served wine and cheeses in the parlor before adjourning to the formal dining room for a gourmet candlelit dinner. This was the setting for the Cicely Tyson film *A Woman Called Moses*.

Nottoway, LA Highway 1 and Mississippi River Road, White Castle, LA, tel: 545 2730. The South's largest plantation, this palatial Greek Revival/Italianate mansion, loaded with exquisite antiques, offers bed-and-breakfast to visitors. Randolph Hall, a dining room on the grounds, is open for lunch and dinner.

Rosedown, US Highway 61 at LA Highway 10, tel: 635-3332. Rosedown has been restored to museum quality, featuring many original furnishings and acres of formal gardens. The grounds contain flowering plants that are almost as old as the house itself, which was built in 1835.

Oak Alley, 3645 LA Highway 18, Vacherie, LA, tel: 265-2151. Oak Alley was named for the 28 live oak trees that form a stunning archway from the road to the house. An impressive white-columned Greek Revival mansion, it is somewhat less interesting on the inside than the other mansions.

San Francisco, Highway 44, Garyville, LA, tel: 535-2341. A bit smaller than the other plantation homes, San Francisco is a classic Steamboat Gothic house noted for elaborate millwork and pretty ceiling frescoes. Frances Parkinson Keyes based her novel, *Steamboat Gothic*, on this house, which does look like a colorful riverboat run aground.

SWAMP & RIVER CRUISES

Honey Island Swamp Tours, tel: 641-1769. Conducted by wetland ecologist Dr Paul Wagner, flatboat tours take in the scenery and swamp creatures of one of the nation's least altered wetlands. Price for the tour includes hotel pickup and return.

New Orleans Paddle Wheels, tel: 524-0814. The sleek, luxurious *Creole Queen* and her sister, the *Cajun Queen*, can be boarded for a variety of cruises. Join the *Creole Queen* for narrated harbor cruises, cruises to Chalmette Battlefield, and dinner/jazz cruises; the *Cajun Queen* paddles down into the bayous. Both river boats board at Riverwalk.

New Orleans Steamboat Co., tel: 586-8777 or 800-223-BOAT. The frilly *Natchez* (the city's only authentic stern-wheeler) does daily 2-hour harbor cruises, as well as dinner-plus-jazz evening cruises. Boarding is at the Toulouse Street Wharf behind the Jackson Brewery. The *Bayou Jean Lafitte*, which docks behind the Jackson Brewery, is a small, air-conditioned vessel that does narrated, 45-mile cruises to the bayous.

Voyageur, tel: 523-5555. A 200-passenger, air-conditioned vessel, boarded next to the ferry landing at the foot of Canal Street, the Voyageur does 5-hour narrated cruises into the swamps and bayous; sandwiches and drinks are available.

CAJUN COUNTRY

An hour and a half west of New Orleans is **Lafayette**, the unofficial capital of French Louisiana. For visitors who have the time, a visit to Acadiana – or **Cajun Country**, as it is most often called – is highly recommended.

This is the heart and soul of the Cajun "craze" that has swept virtually the whole world. The difference is, here it isn't a craze; it's a centuries-old tradition. If you happen to arrive while a festival is on – be prepared. The music is hot (zydeco features prominently); the food rib-tickling good and chances are you'll be dancing the *fais do-do* before the night is out. The Cajun slogan is, "*Laissez les bons temps rouler*," which means, "Let the good times roll." And roll they do.

TRAVEL PACKAGES

There are several companies that offer attractive packages for travelers who'd rather not go it alone in or out of the city:

American Express Vacations, Box 5014, Atlanta, GA 30302, tel: 800-241-1700; in GA 800-282-0800.

Domenico Tours, 751 Broadway, Bayonne, NJ, tel: 800-554-TOUR.

Maupintour, Box 807, Lawrence, KS, tel: 800-255-4266.

Tours by Andrea, 826 Perdido St, New Orleans, LA 70112, tel: 504/524-8521.

TOUR OPERATORS

Gray Line, tel: 587-0861 or 800-535-7787. City tours, plantation country tours, riverboat/city tours, and nightclub tours.

McGee's Landing, tel: 318-228-2384. An hour-and-half drive west of New Orleans, pontoon-boat tours take in parts of the exotic, 800,000-acre Atchafalaya Basin.

New Orleans Tours, tel: 482-1991 or 800-543-6332. City tours, plantation country tours, and combination riverboat/city tours.

Tours by Isabelle, tel: 367-3963. Multilingual guides in small minivans conduct city tours, bayou tours (which include a visit to a Cajun alligator hunter), plantation tours (with lunch at Nottoway included), and a Grand Tour (the bayou tour, including lunch and a visit to Oak Alley).

GUIDED TOURS

Save Our Cemeteries, tel: 588-9357. A local group conducts walking tours of St Louis Cemetery No. 1 each Sunday at 10 a.m. Interested parties should meet at the Royal Blend Coffeehouse, 623 Royal Street. Reservations are recommended for the 90-minute walk, and a security guard accompanies the group.

Friends of the Cabildo tel: 523-3939. Walking tours of the French Quarter are conducted Tuesday–Saturday at 9.30 a.m. and 1.30 p.m. (Sunday at 1.30 only). Meet in front of the Presbytère; the tour price includes admission to at least two Louisiana State Museum buildings.

Heritage Tours, tel: 949-9805. A noted authority on Southern writers conducts French Quarter walking tours to the homes and haunts of internationally known writers such as Tennessee Williams, William Faulkner, Sherwood Anderson, plus dozens of others.

Jean Lafitte National Historical Park, tel: 589-2636. Park Rangers conduct a variety of free tours, including the French Quarter and Garden District. Reservations are required for the Garden District tour, and you must purchase your own streetcar fare. Tours are conducted rain or shine (except Christmas, New Year's Day, and Mardi Gras), and begin at the Folk Life Center, 916–18 N. Peters St in the French Market.

Preservation Resource Center, tel: 581-7032. An organization actively involved in preserving historical districts of the city, the PRC occasionally conducts interesting and informative walking tours with a focus on architecture.

CULTURE PLUS

MUSEUMS

Beauregard-Keyes House, 1113 Chartres St. Open: Monday–Saturday 10 a.m.–3 p.m. Closed: Sunday. Costumed docents conduct tours of this graceful Greek Revival mansion. Built in 1826, it was for a brief time the home of Confederate General P.G.T. Beauregard, the man who ordered the first shot fired at Fort Sumter – the event that began the War Between the States.

Confederate Museum, 929 Camp St. Open: Monday–Saturday 10 a.m.–4 p.m. Closed: Monday. Memorabilia pertaining to the War Between the States. Collection includes uniforms, flags, weapons, personal effects of Confederate President Jefferson Davis and General Robert E. Lee.

Gallier House, 1118–23 Royal St. Open: Monday–Saturday 10 a.m.–4.30 p.m. (last tour starts at 3.45 p.m.). Closed: Sunday. Renowned architect James Gallier, Jr designed and built this house in 1857 as a home for himself and his family. One of the best researched house museums in the city, it is also exquisitely furnished with 19th-century antiques. An excellent example of how wealthy Creoles lived.

Germaine Wells Mardi Gras Museum, Arnaud's Restaurant, 813 Bienville St. Open: daily 11.30 a.m.–2.30 p.m. and 6–10 p.m. Daughter of the founder of Arnaud's Restaurant, the late Ms Wells reigned as queen over more than 20 Carnival balls. Displayed on the second floor of the restaurant are her regal gowns and other Carnival costumes and memorabilia.

Hermann-Grima House, 820 St Louis St. Open: Monday–Saturday 10 a.m.–4 p.m. (last tour starts at 3.30 p.m.). Closed: Sunday. An American-style townhouse dating from 1831, this house is occasionally "dressed" in period attire, such as for a 19th-century Creole funeral. It is especially noted for the outbuildings, where in the kitchens Creole cooking demonstrations take place between October and May.

Historic New Orleans Collection, 533 Royal St. Open: Tuesday–Saturday 10 a.m.–4.45 p.m. (last tour at 3.15 p.m.). This research center for state and local history is housed in a complex of historic buildings. Changing exhibits are located on the ground floor Williams Gallery. Guided tours of the premises are available.

Longue Vue House and Gardens, 7 Bamboo Rd. Open: Tuesday–Saturday 10 a.m.–4.30 p.m; Sunday 1–5 p.m. Closed: Monday. The former home of Sears heiress Edith Stern is a handsome estate set in eight acres of manicured lawns and formal gardens. The house contains the original furnishings, which include European and American antiques, exquisite tapestries, and porcelains.

Louisiana Children's Museum, 428 Julia St. Open: Tuesday–Sunday 9.30 a.m.–4.30 p.m. Excellent facility with fun and educational hands-on exhibits, such as a mini-market, TV studio, and a miniature port, where kids can help load cargo.

Louisiana State Museum, Jackson Square. Open: Wednesday–Sunday 10 a.m.–5 p.m. Four separate buildings make up this museum complex. The **Cabildo** and the **Presbytère**, both of which contain historical exhibits, are virtually identical 18th-century buildings that flank St Louis Cathedral on Jackson Square. The Cabildo was the government center in Colonial times; in 1803, transfer papers for the Louisiana Purchase were signed on the second floor of the building. The Presbytère, built originally as a home for priests serving the Cathedral, was never used as such; it now houses changing exhibits. The **1850 House**, 525 St Ann Street in the lower Pontalbas, gives visitors a glimpse of what apartment living was like for well-heeled 19th-century Creoles. The apartment is furnished with antiques such as canopied beds and quaint old dolls. The **Old US Mint**, 400 Esplanade Avenue, formerly a branch of the federal mint, now houses research facilities as well as two excellent only-in-New Orleans attractions: the Mardi Gras Exhibit contains glittering costumes, masks, scepters and other mementoes, and the Jazz Exhibit traces the history of jazz with displays of instruments, sheet music, and various memorabilia.

Musée Conti Wax Museum, 917 Conti St. Open: daily 10 a.m.–5.30 p.m. Well-executed, historically accurate wax museum featuring tableaux of famed New Orleans legends. The Haunted Dungeon waxes grim with depictions of Dracula, Frankenstein, the Wolf Man, and other horrifying folk.

New Orleans Museum of Art, Lelong Dr., City Park. Open: Tuesday–Sunday 10 a.m.–5 p.m. Closed: Monday. Housed in a handsome neoclassic building, the museum contains a permanent collection of artworks from the pre-Columbian era to the present: Italian paintings from the 13th through the 18th century; the arts of Africa and the Far East; Impressionists; American paintings and sculptures; and Imperial Treasures by Carl Faberge, including bejeweled Easter eggs that once belonged to the Russian royal family. The museum has hosted major traveling exhibits such as "The Search for Alexander" and "Treasures of King Tut."

New Orleans Pharmacy Museum, 514 Chartres St. Open: Tuesday–Sunday 10 a.m.–5 p.m. Closed: Monday. Musty, atmospheric old place that was built in 1823 for America's first licensed pharmacist. Displays include hand-blown apothecary jars, ancient medical utensils, and a handsome Italian marble soda fountain dating from the 1850s.

Pitot House, 1440 Moss St. Open: Wednesday–Saturday 10 a.m.–3 p.m. Built in the late-18th century, this is a fine West Indies-style house typical of those built by early planters. It's furnished with early American and Louisiana antiques.

Ripley's Believe It Or Not, 501 Bourbon St. Open: daily 10 a.m.–midnight. Multilevel museum with displays from Robert Ripley's Odditorium: two-headed animals, shrunken heads, the world's smallest, tallest, and such. There's also an exhibit of fabulous feathered costumes worn by the Mardi Gras Indians during Carnival.

Voodoo Museum, 724 Dumaine St. Open: Sunday–Thursday 10 a.m.–7 p.m; Friday–Saturday 10 a.m.–10 p.m. An only-in-New Orleans museum, with displays of voodoo *gris-gris* (voodoo charms, dolls, potions, and an altar. An apocryphal painting of 19th-century Voodoo Queen Marie Laveau is prominently displayed. The museum also conducts a variety of tours that take a closer look at the cult; one of them goes into the swamps for a "voodoo ritual." Interesting, if you don't take it too seriously.

ART GALLERIES

Until the late 1980s, the greatest concentration of art galleries was in the French Quarter. However, the revitalization of the Warehouse District has spawned a profusion of galleries, and the area has been called by some the "SoHo of the South." The **Contemporary Arts Center**, 900 Camp St, has long been the center for avant-garde visual arts, and it continues to be the focal point of the Warehouse District contemporary arts scene. Each fall the visual arts season kicks off with "Arts for Art's Sake," an evening of formal gallery openings followed by a gala celebration at the CAC.

Arthur Roger Gallery, 432 Julia St, Warehouse District. Extensive selection of contemporary paintings and sculpture by local and regional artists.

Bryant Galleries, 524 Royal St, French Quarter. Haitian, European, and American art, including sculptures, graphics, glass, and primitives.

Carol Robinson Gallery, 4537 Magazine St, Uptown. Contemporary paintings, sculpture, and graphics.

Dyansen Gallery, 433 Royal St, French Quarter. Collection includes a stunning selection of Erté sculptures, lithographs, seriographs, and gouaches.

Downtown Gallery, 420 Julia St, Warehouse District. Features contemporary works by local and regional artists.

Galerie Simonne Stern, 518 Julia St, Warehouse District. The works of Louisiana and regional artists, including paintings, drawings, sculpture, glass, and ceramics.

Gasperi Gallery, 320 Julia St, Warehouse District. A folk art gallery focusing on the works of local and regional artists.

Hanson Galleries, 229 Royal St, French Quarter. Internationally known contemporary artists are represented, including Peter Max and Leroy Neiman.

LeMieux Galleries, 332 Julia St, Warehouse District. Monthly exhibitions of aspiring and nationally known Louisiana artists working in various media.

Miriam Walmsley Gallery, 201 N. Peters, French Quarter. The works of local and regional artists, including paintings, drawings, sculptures, pottery, and crafts.

Nahan Galleries, 540 Royal St, French Quarter. Features top-quality contemporary paintings and sculptures by nationally known artists.

Rodrigue Gallery, 721 Royal St, French Quarter. Paintings and prints by internationally renowned Louisiana artist George Rodrigue.

St Charles Gallery, 541 Julia St, Warehouse District. Features Old Master drawings, 19th-century French and English paintings, fine watercolors, antique maps, and beautiful old prints.

Kurt E. Schon Ltd, 510 St Louis St. Traditional 19th-century English and French paintings, including Impressionists, Victorian, and salon works.

Tilden-Foley Gallery, 4119 Magazine St, Uptown. Contemporary paintings and sculptures, as well as 19th- and early 20th-century American paintings.

CONCERTS

Classical concerts are occasionally performed at several of the city's churches, notably **St Louis Cathedral** (Jackson Square, tel: 525-9585); **St Charles Avenue Presbyterian Church** (1545 State St, tel: 897-0101); and **Trinity Episcopal Church** (1329 Jackson Ave, tel: 522-0277). The universities, among them **Tulane** (tel: 865-5000), **Loyola** (tel: 861-2011), **Dillard** (tel: 283-8822), and the **University of New Orleans**, known as **UNO** (tel: 286-6000), also present concerts during the year.

To hear great modern music, visitors have but to stroll down **Bourbon Street**, stop by **Jackson Square**, or rest on **Moonwalk**. Street musicians – ranging from a lone saxophonist to a 10-piece Dixieland band – perform all over the French Quarter. There are also free jazz concerts in **Dutch Alley** in the French Market. Schedules are available at the Dutch Alley kiosk (foot of St Philip Street in the French Market.)

BALLET

The New Orleans City Ballet (tel: 522-0996) performs contemporary and classical dance at the **Theatre of the Performing Arts** in Armstrong Park. The company usually mounts four productions between September and May.

OPERA

The New Orleans Opera mounts four productions annually between October and March. Performances are at the Theatre of the Performing Arts in Armstrong Park. Tickets are available through the New Orleans Opera Association (tel: 529-2278).

THEATERS

Touring Broadway shows and top-name entertainers appear at the **Saenger Performing Arts Center** (143 N. Rampart St, Box Office tel: 524-2490).

Major rock concerts are often held in the **Louisiana Superdome** (Sugar Bowl Drive, Box Office tel: 587-3800). The **UNO Lakefront Arena** (6801 Franklin Ave, Box Office tel: 286-7222) is another popular venue for nationally known performers.

New Orleans has several first-rate community theaters. **Le Petit Théâtre du Vieux Carré** (616 St Peter St, tel: 522-208 L), the oldest community theater in the country, presents a season of plays and musicals between September and June; the **Children's Corner** presents plays geared for children aged three and up.

The **Contemporary Arts Center** (900 Camp St, tel: 522-0122) showcases new playwrights and mounts avant-garde productions. **Southern Rep** (1437 S. Carrollton Ave, tel: 861-2254) presents plays by Southern playwrights at various venues during the year. **Summer Lyric Theatre** (Tulane University, St Charles Ave, tel: 865-5269) offers musical productions throughout the summer season.

MOVIES

The great majority of movie theaters in the city are located in shopping malls throughout the metropolitan area. The New Orleans *Times-Picayune* carries daily listings of current features.

DIARY OF EVENTS

January 1: The Sugar Bowl Classic, played in the Superdome, is one of the nation's oldest college bowl games, and attracts thousands of ardent football fans. Under the umbrella of the Sugar Bowl Classic are tennis, basketball, and sailing match-ups.

February: Black Heritage Festival (*see Festivals, pages 263–64*)

February or March: Mardi Gras (*see Festivals*)

March: Tennessee Williams/New Orleans Literary Festival (*see Festivals*)
St Patrick's Day (*see Festivals*)
St Joseph's Day (*see Festivals*)

Early April: French Quarter Festival (*see Festivals*)

April: Spring Fiesta (*see Festivals*)

Mid-April: The Crescent City Classic, a popular 10K road race, begins in Jackson Square and ends with much hoopla at the Audubon Zoo.

Late April: The USF&G Golf Tournament, which takes place at the English Turn Country club, is a prestigious PGA golf tournament that attracts golfers from around the globe.

April/May: New Orleans Jazz & Heritage Festival (*see Festivals*)

May: The Zoo-To-Do, a major social event, is the largest nonmedical fund-raiser in the country.

June: The Great French Market Tomato Festival (*see Festivals*).

Late June–Early July: La Fête (*see Festivals*)

September: New Orleans Writers' Conference (*see Festivals*)

October: Festa d'Italia (*see Festivals*)

Late October: Halloween (*see Festivals*)

November 1: All Saints Day is a local memorial day when graveyard tombs are banked with flowers and New Orleanians flock to the cemeteries for candlelight vigils.

November: The Bayou Classic is an annual "shoot-out" between the Southern University and Grambling University football teams.

December: A Creole Christmas (*see Festivals*)

Christmas in the Oaks, when City Park's majestic trees are festooned with Christmas lights.

December 24: Bonfires on the Levee is an ages-old Christmas Eve tradition in the parishes to the west of the city, where gigantic bonfires on both sides of the Mississippi are torched to light the way for Papa Noel. As part of Creole Christmas there are river-boat excursions from Jackson Square to see the lightings.

December 31: The Countdown in Jackson Square is the New Orleans version of the New Year's Eve celebration in New York's Times Square.

ARCHITECTURE

New Orleans' distinctive architecture reflects the cultures, personalities, and nationalities that have been drawn to the city since its founding in the early 18th century. Here is a brief breakdown of styles:

EARLY BUILDINGS

Little remains of the original French city, as disastrous fires in 1788 and 1794 devastated Nouvelle Orleans. There is, however, one structure surviving from the French Colonial period, the **Old Ursuline Convent** at 1114 Chartres Street. While the rebuilt city reflects the domination of the Spaniards, the determination of French Creoles to continue French Colonial architectural traditions is apparent everywhere. The **Gird House**, at 500 Chartres, is a fine example of French Colonial detailing.

Two methods of construction used by the early Creoles were *colombage* and *brique-entre-poteaux*. In the former, heavy timbers, used as jambs and window frames, were constructed in the mortise and tenon mode, i.e., with holes cut in the wood to receive projecting parts. For stability and insulation, bricks were used as infill between the frames, or posts – *brique-entre-poteaux* (brick-between-posts). An additional insulation technique was called *bousillage*, which was a mixture of mud, moss, and animal hair.

Following the fires, the Spanish government imposed rigid regulations on all structures. Buildings of *colombage* had to be covered with inch-thick cement, and roofs were to be flat and covered with either brick or tile. New Orleans began, visually, to change from a French to a Spanish city.

SPANISH COLONIAL

Some of the finest examples of Spanish Colonial architecture are located on Jackson Square. The **Cabildo** and the **Presbytère**, both of which date from 1795, were built over earlier colonial structures destroyed by the fires. Each building has broad sweeping arcades, wide arches over second-level windows, and some of the finest wrought-iron from the Spanish period. The pediment of the Cabildo is by Italian sculptor Pietro Cardelli; its mansard roof, with rows of delicately curved dormers, was added in 1847. The present **St Louis Cathedral** dates from 1851, the third church to be erected on the site. The stained-glass windows in the front of the church were a gift from the Spanish government.

CREOLE COTTAGES

Creole cottages, built flush with the *banquette* (i.e., the sidewalk), are square-shaped, hall-less houses usually containing four rooms of equal size with two small rooms flanking a recessed "cabinet gallery" in the rear. Other distinguishing characteristics of

Creole cottages are gable sides and parapet; steep sloping roof with dormers on the front and back pitch; four openings across the front, either square-headed or arched; transoms divided by rectangular or curvilinear muntins; and an abat-vent, or overhang, supported by iron bearers.

Examples of a brick-between-posts house can be seen in the beautifully restored Creole cottage at **1436 Pauger**, in Faubourg-Mariny, which dates from 1819, and also the house at **820 Elysian Fields** (*circa* 1820). Across the street from 1436 Pauger, there is a one-and-a-half story Creole cottage at **1445 Pauger**, dating from 1826, which has a lovely arched transom over the entrance; pilasters on the surround; a dormer with arched lights and pediments; and short double-hung windows – the latter are alterations that were done at a later stage. **Jean Lafitte's Blacksmith Shop** at 941 Bourbon Street – now a neighborhood bar – is also an example of brick-between-posts construction. No one knows when, or by whom this "blacksmith shop" was built, but existing ownership records date back to 1772. It is probably very much like the early Creole cottages of the original French town.

In the French Quarter, **St Peter Street**, between Bourbon and Dauphine streets, is a solid block of Creole cottages decked out in a variety of fashions – simple Greek Revival lintels, jigsaw brackets, showy gingerbread trim, and ornamental parapets. **Burgundy Street** nearby also has row after row of decorative early cottages.

"RAISED" PLANTATION HOMES

"Raised" plantation homes are picturesque blendings of French Colonial, European, and West Indies influences. The main living floor was placed on top of an above-ground "basement," which served not only as storage space, but as protection from frequent floods. This basement-cum-first-floor was made of brick masonry. Openings, usually four across the front, had either square or arched heads. Living quarters above was *colombage*, with either weatherboard or plaster covering.

On these "raised" houses, West Indies-style double-pitched roofs extended over the galleries, creating a shaded area that allowed windows to be left open when it rained. Air was "conditioned" by means of high ceilings that allowed the hot air to rise and the heavier, cool air to settle. Floor plans, as in Creole cottages, did not allow for hallways; instead, side-by-side, parallel rooms opened onto the gallery through French doors. Windows and doors had shutters, usually vertical board shutters on the lower level, and louvred shutters on the principal floor. Fireplaces were placed on interior walls, and chimneys rose up through the steep roof to accompany the dormer windows which peered through the front and rear pitch.

Some claim that **Madam John's Legacy** at **632 Dumaine** is even older than the Old Ursuline Convent. Built for Don Manuel Lanzos in 1788–89, immediately after the great fire, it is an excellent example of the French Colonial style with West Indies accents. The **Pitot House**, 1440 Moss Street, was built in 1799 and is another good example of a plantation home, as is its neighbor, the **Old Spanish Customs House** nearby at 1330 Moss.

CARRIAGE HOUSES

Many of the stately two- and three-story mansions in the French Quarter are *porte-cochère*, or carriage houses, dating from the early 1800s. These brick masonry and stucco houses were often painted pastel yellows, blues, greens and pinks. Facades have two windows across the lower level and a carriageway that leads from the street along a flagstone "driveway," past double parlors, and then through an archway into the rear courtyard.

Creole townhouses feature arched lower level openings with spectacular fanlights and curvilinear muntins behind vertical iron bars. Individual railings beneath windows at the third and fourth level and a continuous rail on the second level are typical of this period and can be seen on many French Quarter carriage houses and townhouses. The **Pharmacy Museum**, at 514 Chartres Street, built in 1837 as both a residence and pharmacy, is a good example. The two-story pink stucco **Bosque House** at 617 Chartres is a *porte-cochère* house that has been considerably altered, but it is notable for the monogrammed "B" worked into the second-floor iron balcony.

A "balcony," by the way, is supported

underneath by brackets, or consoles, while a "gallery" is supported by colonettes. The earliest ironwork in New Orleans was wrought-iron. This "worked" iron is less elaborate than the later cast iron, with its intricate swirls, scrolling, foliations, and curlicues. The cast-ironwork of the **LaBranche row houses** (*circa* 1840) at Royal and along St Peter is some of the most beautiful in the city, as is that of the Pontalba Buildings on Jackson Square.

PONTALBA BUILDINGS

James Gallier, Sr was the original architect for the red brick, twin **Pontalba Buildings** which line Jackson Square. Begun in 1849 and completed in 1851, these galleried buildings were financed by Countess Micaela de Pontalba. (Her father was the wealthy Don Andres Almonester y Roxas; note the initials "AP" in the galleries of these buildings.) The **1850 House**, at 525 St Ann, in the Pontalba Buildings, contains beautifully restored rooms, and is a fine example of a mid-19th century townhouse. There is a formal parlor and dining room on the second floor, bedrooms on the third level, with kitchen, pantry, and servants' quarters in the rear extension. The wooden balcony along the rear of the house looks down on a fine brick courtyard.

GREEK REVIVAL

The modest little **Thierry House** at 721 Gov. Nicholls Street in the Vieux Carré – designed in 1814 by Henry Latrobe – is believed to have sparked the Greek Revival fever, which a few years later swept the city. Simple and unassuming, its basic style had evolved, by the 1850s, into impressive masterpieces such as Gallier Hall and the US Custom House.

The nearly world-wide enthusiasm for classic antiquity began after the excavations in Pompeii and Herculaneum and with the late 18th-century archaeological findings in Greece. Ionic, Doric, and Corinthian columns, paneled entrance doors with Greek key or crossettes surround, low-pitched roof and ornamental molding and dentils, rectangular transoms, and classical capped pilasters are trademarks of the Greek Revival style. Also, in marked contrast to earlier Creole designs, door and window openings were always flat-topped, rather than the dramatic arches favored by the late 18th- and early 19th-century architects who practiced in New Orleans.

The early 1830s saw the beginning of the Golden Age in New Orleans, a period of prosperity and economic growth that continued until the Civil War. Outstanding architects working in New Orleans during this exciting period included Jacques Nicholas Bussiere dePouilly, graduate of the Ecole des Beaux-Arts, who arrived from Paris in 1833; James and Charles Dakin, and James Gallier, Sr, who came from New York and began practice here in 1835; James Gallier, Jr, famous son of a famous father, whose home at **1132 Royal Street** is one of the city's showplaces; and Henry Howard, whose work includes the palatial **Nottoway** plantation in White Castle, Louisiana.

Gallier Hall, at 524 St Charles Avenue, is perhaps the most important work of Gallier, Sr. Built between 1845 and 1850, it has Ionic columns supporting a pediment with delicately carved figures of Justice, Liberty, and Commerce. The **US Custom House**, 423 Canal Street, was designed in 1848 by Alexander T. Wood, who died before completion of the building in 1880. This colossal granite structure has pediments on each facade supported by huge Egyptian-style fluted pilasters.

The "**Marble Hall**," the building's business room, measures 125 feet by 95 feet, and is 54 feet high. Each of the 14 marble columns supporting the ceiling has a capital relief of Juno and Mercury, and above the North Peters entrance are two life-sized bas-reliefs of Sieur de Bienville, founder of New Orleans, and Andrew Jackson. This building, and especially its Marble Hall, is one of America's most stunning Late Greek Revival structures.

It was during this Golden Age that American, as opposed to Creole, townhouses began to appear in New Orleans. Side and center hallways replaced carriageways in these newcomers' homes, and red brick facades were favored. The **Hermann-Grima House** at 820 St Louis, built by architect William Brand in 1831, is of Philadelphia brick and resembles the Georgian-style architecture prevalent on the Eastern seaboard.

The Victorian Age came marching in,

bearing pointed Gothic arched windows with diamond-patterned lights; ornate Italianate mansions inspired by the Italian Renaissance; the mansard roofs and bull's-eye dormers of the Second Empire; the fussy busyness of Eastlake and Queen Anne-style houses, with all kinds of spindlework, wooden beads, turrets, and trim. A dazzling array of architectural styles can be seen in New Orleans' **Garden District**, detailed in this book's chapter on that area.

The turn of the century saw the appearance of the work of Henry Hobson Richardson. A native of St James parish, Richardson spent his childhood in Louisiana, was graduated from Harvard in 1859 and spent five years in Paris, where he attended the prestigious Ecole des Beaux Arts. By the time he died in 1886, he was considered one of America's foremost architects, and certainly his style is distinctive. His rough-textured stone structures have exotic Syrian arches, deeply recessed windows, and broad arcades. The **W.P. Brown House**, 4717 St Charles, is one of the most impressive Richardson Romanesque houses in the city (Favrot & Livaudais, architects, 1902–05). Other fine examples of this bold and interesting style are at **3804 St Charles**; **the Howard Library**, 601 Howard Avenue; and the **Confederate Memorial Hall** at 921 Camp Street.

NEW ORLEANS SPECIALS

Mention must be made of the *entresol*, the camelback, and the "shotgun" house, all examples that feature prominently on the streets of New Orleans. An *entresol* (in French: "mezzanine") is a combination commercial and residential building which appears on the outside to be a two-story house, but has a half-story storage space, lighted by elegant fanlights, between the first and second floors (see an example of this style at **238 Bourbon Street**).

A "camelback" (**917–919 St Peter** and its neighbor, **921–923**) is a house with one story at the front and a two-story rear, rising like the humps of a camel. "Shotgun" houses can be seen almost everywhere in the city and come dressed in a variety of fashions; however, the floor plan is always the same, whether the house is a "single" or a "double" – that is, it develops in a perfectly straight line from front to rear. Hence its name: a shot discharged in the front room would travel through every room in the house.

The "Steamboat Houses" at **400 Egania** and diagonally at **503 Egania**, downriver from Bywater, are in a class of their own (*see picture on page 229*.) These twin houses were built by river-boat captain Milton Paul Doullet for himself and his son. They look like steamboats which might have floated over the nearby levee. The identical houses have three decks, exterior double stairs dropped like gangplanks from the second tier, pilot-houses topside, and huge wooden beads, graduated in size and strung like great necklaces between slender posts. These fanciful houses will appeal to fans of architecture everywhere.

NIGHTLIFE

New Orleans is a 24-hour town, which means there are no legal closing hours. There are clubs and bars that stay open around the clock; others that don't rev up until midnight or after; and still others that close down around 1 a.m. or 2 a.m., or whenever business slacks off. Because there are few rules regarding closing time, it's best to call your destination to see if it's still open before heading out bar-hopping at 4 a.m. (Bar-hopping at 4 a.m. is not at all uncommon in The Big Easy).

Closing hours are somewhat loose, but you can usually count on a two-drink minimum, especially in bars that feature music. Don't be shy about asking about prices and policy before going inside. Many nightclubs and discos have a cover charge; if you are calling in advance it's helpful to check current prices.

The terms "pubs, bars, and nightclubs" tend to blur in this town. There are bars with great music, and great bars with no music at all. A nightclub can be anything from a funky dive to a sleek club.

BARS

Absinthe Bar, 400 Bourbon St, French Quarter, tel: 525-8108. A musty, loud, and lively spot that revs up around midnight and features rock, soul, and jazz till the early hours of the morning.

Bayou Bar, Pontchartrain Hotel, 2031 St Charles Avenue, Garden District, tel: 524-0581. Sophisticated, up-market piano bar for soothing sounds.

Benny's Bar, 938 Valence, Uptown, tel: 895-9405. A funky, dress-down place for downhome blues and rock.

544 Club, 544 Bourbon St, French Quarter, tel: 523-6611. R&B saxophonist Gary Brown and his band have held forth here for ages, playing great Top 40 hits and soul classics.

Jimmy's Club, 8200 Willow, Uptown, tel: 861-8200. College kids and young rockers flock in for loud, live rock.

Lafitte's Blacksmith Shop, 941 Bourbon St, French Quarter, tel: 523-0066. Ancient bar that's an ages-old favorite of artists and writers; pianist/vocalist Miss Lilly Hood has a loyal following of locals who love listening to (and sometimes singing along with) her show tunes and standards.

Napoleon House, 500 Chartres St, French Quarter, tel: 524-9752. A venerable institution of higher imbibing, wildly popular with local and visiting artists and writers. Taped classical music and great atmosphere.

Pat O'Brien's, 718 St Peter St, French Quarter, tel: 525-4823. One of the world's best-known bars, Pat's has three bars, including a raucous piano bar and a splendidly beautiful courtyard. This is where the now-ubiquitous Hurricane originated.

Sazerac Bar, Fairmont Hotel, CBD. Handsome up-market bar that's been a favorite watering hole of politicos and high-rollers since the 1930s.

DANCE CLUBS

Bronco's, 1409 Romain St, Gretna, tel: 368-1000. Cowboy hats and jeans are in order for this Texas-style honky-tonk; free country/western dance lessons some nights.

City Lights, 310 Howard Ave, Warehouse District, tel: 568-1700. Glitzy disco popular with young professionals; features 1950s to 1980s music. The City Lights Dance Troupe performs almost every night.

4141, 4141 St Charles Ave, Uptown, tel: 891-9873. Handsome multilevel disco where dressed-up young professionals dance till the small hours.

Mudbug's Saloon, 2024 Belle Chase Hwy, Gretna, tel: 392-0202. Wildly popular place with a huge dance floor for Texas two-stepping and such; top-name entertainers such as Willie Nelson and Emmy Lou Harris are frequently on the bill.

Palladium, 2645 Causeway Blvd, Metairie, tel: 837-8017. A younger crowd is attracted to the live music and good dance floor here.

NIGHTCLUBS

Chris Owens Club, corner Bourbon and St Louis Streets, French Quarter, tel: 523-6400. Virtually a New Orleans icon, Ms Owens is a sexy, sophisticated lady who does a Las Vegas-style show.

Lulu White's Mahogany Hall, 309 Bourbon St, French Quarter, tel: 525-5595. The stomping grounds of the Dukes of Dixieland; cozy bar with doors flung wide onto Bourbon Street.

Maple Leaf Bar, 8316 Oak St, Uptown, tel: 866-9359; 24-hour concert line tel: 866-LEAF. Casual, popular with all ages for its live music and friendly crowd. Good every night, but the Cajun night dances (usually on Thurs) are not to be missed.

Michaul's, 701 Magazine St, CBD, tel: 566-0515. A great place for live Cajun music and dancing.

Mid-City Lanes & Sports Palace, 4133 S. Carrollton Ave, Mid-City, tel: 482-3133. Combination bowling alley and dance hall, featuring every Friday night "rock and bowl" to live music.

Mulate's, 201 Julia St, Warehouse District, tel: 522-1492. Live Cajun music, food, and dancing in the New Orleans branch of a popular club headquartered in the heart of Cajun Country.

Palm Court Jazz Café, 1204 Decatur St, French Quarter, tel: 525-0200. Traditional jazz played by some of the city's best musicians is showcased in this handsome café that became an overnight sensation after its 1989 opening. Always crowded; moderately priced Creole and Cajun food.

Pete Fountain's Club, Hilton Hotel, 2 Poydras St, tel: 523-4374. Home base of New Orleans native and clarinetist Pete Fountain; a sophisticated club on the third floor of the Hilton. The famed musician is often out on tour; call to see if he's appearing.

Preservation Hall, 726 St Peter St, French Quarter, tel: (day) 522-2238, (night) 523-8939. In a class by itself, the Hall is neither pub, nightclub, nor bar. Internationally renowned, it's virtually a shrine (albeit a funky one) to the preservation of traditional jazz. This seedy spot is where all the old-time jazz legends play. Not to be missed, but don't expect creature comforts. There isn't a bar, but you can get a go-cup next door at Pat O'Brien's and bring it in.

Snug Harbor, 626 Frenchmen St, Faubourg Marigny, tel: 949-0696. Local and nationally known artists play jazz, R&B, blues, and you-name-it in this long-time favorite of the young and the not-so-young. Very casual. Good steaks and burgers are served in the adjoining café.

Tipitina's, 501 Napoleon Ave, Uptown, tel: 897-3943 or 895-TIPS. Oozing with atmosphere, this laid-back club is the place for classic New Orleans-style rhythm and blues, as well as traditional jazz, Cajun, rock, and zydeco. Local artists and nationally known touring performers play Tip's. This is where the Neville Brothers perform when they're in town. Enormously popular place, with bars and dance floors upstairs and down.

CABARETS

Can Can Cabaret, 340 Bourbon St, French Quarter, tel: 561-8057. Tame and touristy (it's geared toward families with kids). Features lots of legs, ruffles, *frou-frous*, and canned music.

GAMBLING

In 1991, Governor Roemer signed a bill legalizing river-boat gambling on the Mississippi River. Now that the bill has passed the public should be allowed to wile away their dollars sometime in 1993.

New Orleans has high-rolling plans for its riverfront areas, including the construction of *The Queen of New Orleans*, a 2,500-passenger vessel docking at the foot of Canal Street, and the building of an even larger sternwheeler vessel which will operate from the Toulouse and Bienville Street wharves by the French Quarter.

SHOPPING

WHAT TO BUY

Few visitors leave town without at least one box of **pralines**; gift boxes can be found in candy and souvenir shops all over town. **Chicory coffee**, *beignet* **mix**, and **spices** are also widely available. New Orleans and south Louisiana **cookbooks** are quite popular. Several places ship **New Orleans food**; one shop – Bayou to Go – is located at the airport, where you can pick up your alligator along with your plane. The New Orleans School of Cooking, which has a retail shop in the Jax (Jackson) Brewery, also ships New Orleans foods and spices.

Other souvenirs include **Carnival masks**, which are also prominently featured in many shops; these range from small ceramic decorative wall masks to gaudy and elaborate face masks of leather, feathers, sequins, and beads. Mardi Gras and Jazz Fest **posters** are also hot items. The city is notable for its many **antique stores**, which range from the very chic and expensive to funky little poke-around places. **Jazz records** and tapes, **second-line parasols**, **Panama hats**, and **bisque dolls** dressed in frilly antebellum garb are other popular items.

Let's Go Antiquing (tel: 899-3027) is a shopping service whose expert on antiques provides customized shopping tours and helpful counseling.

SHOPPING AREAS

The Central Business District has several posh shopping malls on Poydras and Canal streets. **Canal Place** (333 Canal St) includes Saks Fifth Ave, Laura Ashley, F.A.O. Schwarz, Gucci, Godiva Chocolatiers, Benetton, and Esprit among its 40 or so stores and boutiques. On the third level there is also a health club, barber and beauty shops, a post office, a food court and four first-run cinemas. The New Orleans Centre (1400 Poydras St) has Lord & Taylor, Macy's, Ann Taylor, Gentlemen's Quarter Ltd, Rapp's Luggage, and Sam Goody Records & Tapes, as well as a host of other shops and several restaurants. Riverwalk (foot of Poydras St at the Mississippi River) has more than 140 shops, including The Sharper Image, Abercrombie & Fitch, Banana Republic, The Gap, and Victoria's Secret, as well as the shops of 60 or so local merchants, a large food court, and several upscale restaurants. The CBD's rapidly expanding Warehouse District is noted for art galleries, most of them specializing in contemporary works by regional artists; Julia Street is known as Gallery Row. When you visit it you'll see why.

The French Quarter is awash with shops, ranging from those housed in tiny hole-in-the-wall places to handsome Creole townhouses to the Jackson Brewery Corporation's three malls: The Jackson Brewery, the Millhouse, and the Marketplace, all three of which contain a vast array of boutiques and restaurants. In the Jax Brewery (as Jackson's is often called), the many shops include Crabtree & Evelyn, DeVille Books & Prints, Hats in the Belfry, Alexia, and the Riverside Newstand.

Adjacent to the Brewery, the Millhouse also has a slew of shops, including Aca Joe's, The Limited, Benetton, Fudge Time, and Bergen Galleries. A short walk away, the Marketplace is home to, among others, Bookstar, the Hard Rock Café, Chico's Clothing, and Morton's of Chicago Steakhouse. A block downriver of the Jax Brewery, the French Market, anchored at the upriver corner by Café du Monde on Jackson Square, has within its arcades and colonnades an assortment of specialty boutiques, candy shops, ice-cream parlors, and open-air cafés with Dixieland bands holding forth. (There are frequent, free jazz concerts in Dutch Alley in the French Market.)

Just downriver from the French Market are the open sheds of the Farmer's Market, where farmers have been bringing their produce to town for more than 160 years. Rows of bins are loaded with pecans and fresh produce. On weekends, a huge flea market is spread out around the Farmer's Market; locals and tourists love to poke through and look for "treasures."

Royal Street is famed for exclusive and very expensive antique stores, many of which carry exquisite 17th-, 18th-, and 19th-century furniture, jewelry, and decorative pieces. Notable among the stores are Rothchild's, Henry Stern, Dixon & Dixon, Moss Antiques, M.S. Rau, Keil's, Manheim, and Waldhorn's, all of which are on Royal Street between Canal and St Ann Streets. Chartres Street also has a fine selection of up-market antique stores, including Lucullus, Charles Cooper, Blackmoor, and Boyer Antiques & Doll Shop.

Magazine Street has scores of antique stores housed in once-grand Victorian mansions and little Creole cottages. The Magazine Street Merchants Association publishes a handy guide, available at the New Orleans Welcome Center, that details six miles of stores, boutiques, and restaurants.

Uptown, away from the Quarter, Riverbend and Uptown Square are popular for shopping sprees. Both shopping centers contain shops and boutiques of mainly local merchants, many of which are fascinating. East New Orleans, the Lakefront area, and Metairie have sprawling concrete malls with major department stores, such as Sears Roebuck & Co., Dillard's, and J.C. Penney.

SHOPPING HOURS

Most downtown department stores are open Monday to Saturday 9.45 or 10 a.m. till 5.30 or 6 p.m. Some shopping malls in town are open daily from 10 a.m.–10 p.m. or 9 a.m.– 9 p.m. Hours vary greatly in French Quarter shops; many of them are open seven days a week. As a very general rule they're open 9 a.m. till 5.30 or 6 p.m.

EXPORT PROCEDURES

The up-market shops and department stores will arrange for goods to be mailed and shipped abroad.

Louisiana Tax Free Shopping (LTFS), based on Europe's VAT, provides refunds of Louisiana State tax and, in some cases, local sales tax, to international visitors on items purchased in Louisiana from participating retailers. Only those merchants displaying the LTFS sticker participate in the program. International visitors with a valid passport and a roundtrip international travel ticket of less than 90 days' duration qualify for sales tax refund. It works like this: When making a purchase, visitors show their passports and request a receipt and tax refund voucher. They then pay the full price, including sales tax, for the purchase and receive a receipt along with the voucher. At the LTFS refund center located at the airport, the vouchers can be redeemed upon presentation of the voucher, receipt, passport, and travel ticket. Small refunds will be made in cash; larger refunds will be issued by check and mailed to visitors at their home address. If purchases are made by credit card, a visitor may elect to apply the tax refund as a credit on his or her credit card.

COMPLAINTS PROCEDURES

File complaints with the Better Business Bureau (tel: 1539 Jackson Ave, tel: 581-6222) or the Chamber of Commerce (301 Camp St, tel: 527-6900).

CLOTHING CHART

Women's Dresses/Suits

American	Continental	British
6	38/34N	8/30
8	40/36N	10/32
10	42/38N	12/34
12	44/40N	14/36
14	46/42N	16/38
16	48/44N	18/40

Women's Shoes

American	Continental	British
4½	36	3
5½	37	4
6½	38	5
7½	39	6
8½	40	7
9½	41	8
10½	42	9

Men's Suits

American	Continental	British
34	44	34
—	46	36
38	48	38
—	50	40
42	52	42
—	54	44
46	56	46

Men's Shirts

American	Continental	British
14	36	14
14½	37	14½
15	38	15
15½	39	15½
16	40	16
16½	41	16½
17	42	17

Men's Shoes

American	Continental	British
6½	—	6
7½	40	7
8½	41	8
9½	42	9
10½	43	10
11½	44	11

SPORTS

PARTICIPANT

Bicycling: During the day, some of the French Quarter streets are closed off for pedestrians and cyclists. City Park and Audubon Park are also ideal places for cycling. Bikes can be rented at French Quarter Bicycle & Stroller Rental (410 Dauphine St, tel: 522-3101); Bicycle Michael's (618 Frenchmen St, tel: 945-9505); and the City Park Casino (tel: 483-9371).

Boating: Canoes and paddle boats can be rented at the Casino (tel: 483-9371) for easy boating on the pretty lagoons of City Park. Sailing on Lake Pontchartrain is a favorite summertime activity. Catamarans, sailboards, and powerboats can be rented at Sailboats South (tel: 288-SAIL). North of Lake Pontchartrain, the Bogue Chitto and Tangipahoa Rivers are great places for canoeing and tubing. For information about rentals in that area, check with the St Tammany Parish Tourist & Convention Commission (tel: 800-634-9443).

Golf: The city has many lush public golf courses. Among them: an 18-hole course at Audubon Park (473 Walnut St, tel: 865-8260); four 18-hole courses, plus a 100-tee double-decker driving range at City Park (1040 Filmore Ave, tel: 483-9396); and an 18-hole course at the Joe Bartholomew Municipal Golf Course (6514 Congress Dr., Pontchartrain Park, tel: 288-0928).

Hiking: Backpacking hikes are organized from time to time by the Louisiana Nature and Science Center (tel: 246-9381).

Horseback Riding: Organized trail rides are arranged at Cascade Stables in Audubon Park (tel: 891-2246).

Jogging: Audubon Park has a 2-mile jogging track that runs beneath a canopy of live oak trees; there are 18 exercise stations along the way. Other popular jogging places are the Mississippi River levee, especially Uptown at the great river bend, and in City Park.

Tennis: The Audubon Park Tennis Center (Tchoupitoulas at Audubon Park, tel: 895-1042) has 10 tennis courts. City Park Wisner Tennis Center (Victory Ave, tel: 483-9383) has 39 courts. The Joe Brown Tennis Center (5603 Read Blvd, tel: 246-7414) has 12 courts. The Rivercenter Tennis & Racquetball Club (New Orleans Hilton Riverside & Towers, 2 Poydras St, tel: 587-7242) has 10 courts.

SPECTATOR

Baseball: The city has no major or minor league franchises; however, locals do turn out to cheer the teams of Tulane University and the University of New Orleans.

Basketball: During the week preceding the annual Sugar Bowl shootout, the Superdome is the venue for the Sugar Bowl Basketball Tournament. The Dome also hosts the men's NCAA Final Four when it's played in New Orleans. The women's NCAA Final Four is played at UNO Lakefront Arena. Colleges and universities that play home games in gyms and fieldhouses around town include Delgado Junior College, Dillard, Xavier, Southern University, Tulane University, and the University of New Orleans.

Football: The main venue is the Louisiana Superdome. The New Orleans Saints of the National Football League play home games in the Superdome on Sunday afternoons and the occasional Monday night. The season begins in September and runs through December, culminating in January with the Super Bowl. On Saturday afternoons the Tulane Green Wave plays home games in the Dome. In November, the Bayou Classic pits Grambling University against Southern University in a tough annual grudge match. On New Year's Day, the annual Sugar Bowl Classic features top-flight collegiate teams. New Orleans has hosted more Super Bowl games than any other city in the nation.

Golf: In the spring the English Turn Country Club (Hwy 406, East Canal, Westbank, tel: 394-5294) hosts the USF&G Golf Tournament, a PGA event that attracts top professional golfers from around the world.

Horse Racing: The city's two race tracks provide thoroughbred racing the year round. The season at the Fair Grounds (1751 Gentilly Blvd, tel: 943-2200), the nation's third oldest track, opens Thanksgiving Day and runs to mid-April. At Jefferson Downs (Williams Blvd, Kenner, tel: 466-8521), night racing begins in April and continues till November.

Running: Thousands compete each April in the Crescent City Classic, which begins in Jackson Square and ends in Audubon Park. Other organized runs include the Mississippi River Bridge Run (August); the Witches Run (October); the Thanksgiving Day Classic (November); and the Corporate Run (December). For further information, contact the Greater New Orleans Runners Association (tel: 454-8247 or 340-7223).

Tennis: From time to time the Virginia Slims Tournament is played in New Orleans, bringing top-name professional women tennis players to compete at the UNO Lakefront Arena (tel: 286-7222).

SPECIAL INFORMATION

CHILDREN

New Orleans is an ideal place to vacation with children. Among the attractions that appeal to children are the Aquarium of the Americas; Audubon Zoo; Blaine Kern's Mardi Gras World; City Park's Storyland and amusement park; the Louisiana Children's Museum; the Musée Conti Wax Museum; and the streetcars. The Children's Corner at Le Petit Théâtre du Vieux Carré presents several children's productions during the season. And, apart from its more exotic aspects, Mardi Gras is made for kids. In fact, for locals Mardi Gras is a family event. The whole family becomes involved in planning and making costumes, and family picnics on the neutral ground along the parade routes are festive occasions. As the parades pass, parents hoist kids on their shoulders so they'll have a better chance of grabbing the "throws" enthusiastically tossed from the floats.

In addition to the attractions, the Greater New Orleans Tourist & Convention Commission publishes a coloring book for kids that's both entertaining and educational. The book, *New Orleans for Kids*, is available free of charge at the New Orleans Welcome Center in Jackson Square.

GAYS

New Orleans has a sizable population of gays, most of whom reside in the lower French Quarter. Gay Pride Day is celebrated in the Quarter with great panache, as participants parade in elaborate, eye-popping costumes. On Fat Tuesday, the annual French Quarter gay competition for best costume is one of the most popular and exotic events of the Carnival season. If you spot a male gotten up like a glamorous Las Vegas showgirl and surrounded by an entourage, he's almost certainly headed for the stage at St Ann and Burgundy street. Follow them and be prepared for an adventure in erotica.

On a less exotic note, the Gay Men's Chorus performs concerts at various times and venues around town.

The AIDS Hotline, 929 Bourbon St, tel: 522-2437, provides counseling and assistance.

ELDERLY

The American Association of Retired Persons (1909 K St NW, Washington, DC 20049, tel: [202] 662-4850) offers its members discounts on air fares, hotels, car rentals, and sightseeing attractions, as well as the AARP Motoring Plan. Members, who must be age 50 and over, pay a small annual fee.

Mature Outlook (6001 N. Clark St, Chicago, IL 60660, tel: 800-336-6330) also offers hotel and motel discounts, as well as a bimonthly newsletter. On-the-spot membership is available at participating Holiday Inns. Mature Outlook is a subsidiary of Sears Roebuck & Co.

Saga International Holidays (120 Boylston St, Boston, MA 02116, tel: 800-343-0273), an agency specializing in tours for people age 60 and over, offers a selection of package tours.

DISABLED

Mobility International USA (Box 3551, Eugene, OR 97403, tel: [503] 343-1284) is an international organization that coordinates exchange programs for the disabled and provides information on accommodations, study programs, and other helpful tips.

The Information Center for Individuals with Disabilities (Ft. Point Place, 27–43 Wormwood St, Boston, MA 02210, tel: [617] 727-5540) puts out a list of travel agents who specialize in tours for the disabled.

Travel Industry and Disabled Exchange (5435 Donna Ave, Tarzana, CA 91356, tel: [818] 368-5648) publishes a quarterly newsletter and a directory of travel agents that specialize in travel arrangements for the disabled.

The Society for the Advancement of Travel for the Handicapped (26 Court St, Brooklyn, NY 11242, tel: [718] 858-5483) issues, free of charge, access guides specially written for disabled travelers.

The Council on International Educational Exchange (CIEE, 205 E. 42nd St, New York, NY 10017, tel: [212] 661-1414) issues an International Student Identity Card (ISIC) that entitles the bearer to reduced fares on local transportation; discounts at museums, theaters, and sports events; student charter flights; and other attractions and benefits. To qualify for the card, applicants must be full-time bona fide students. The ISIC is also available in Canada for $10 upon application to the Association of Student Councils, 187 College St, Toronto, Ont., M5T 1P7. Council Travel, a subsidiary of the CIEE, is a US student travel agency offering low-cost charters and student tours. For information about the agency, contact the CIEE headquarters in New York.

The Federation of International Youth Travel Organizations (81 Islands Brugge, DK-2300 Copenhagen S, Denmark) offers travelers under age 26 the Youth International Educational Exchange Card (YIEE), the benefits of which are similar to those of the International Student Identity Card. In the US, the YIEE card is available from the Council on International Educational Exchange (*see above*); in Canada, from the Canadian Hostelling Association (333 River Rd., Vanier, Ottawa, Ont. KIL 8H9, tel: [613] 476-3844).

The Educational Travel Center (438 N. Frances St, Madison, WI 53703, tel: [608] 256-5551) is a student travel agency specializing in student fares, bookings, and tours.

FURTHER READING

HISTORY & POLITICS

The Blue Book: Harlotry in General in New Orleans, by Semper Idem. Heartman's Historical Series, no. 50, private-print edition, New Orleans, 1936.

The Earl of Louisiana, by A.J. Liebling. Louisiana State University Press, Baton Rouge, 1960.

A History of Louisiana, by Alcee Fortier. Goupil & Co. of Paris; Manzi. Joyant & Co., 1904, c. 1903, New York, four volumes.

The American Sector (Faubourg St Mary): Vol. II. 1972.

The Creole Faubourgs: Vol. IV. 1974.

Faubourg Treme and the Bayou Road: Vol. VI. 1980.

Jefferson City. Vol. VII, 1989.

A History of Louisiana, by Harriet Magruder. D.C. Heath & Co., Boston, 1911.

History of New Orleans, by John Smith Kendall. Lewis Publishing Co., Chicago, two volumes, 1922.

Huey Long's Louisiana Hayride, The American Rehearsal for Dictatorship, 1928-40, by Harnett T. Kane. Pelican Publishing Co., Gretna, La., 1941.

In and Around the old St Louis Cathedral of New Orleans, by C.M. Chambon. Philippe's Printery, New Orleans, 1908.

The Life of Andrew Jackson, Major General in the Service of the United States: Comprising a History of the War in the South… to the Termination of Hostilities before New Orleans, by John Henry Eaton. M. Carey and Son, Philadelphia, 1817.

Louisiana, A Narrative History by Edwin Adams Davis. Claitor's Publishing Division, Baton Rouge, third edition, 1971.

New Orleans City Guide, written and compiled by the Federal Writers' Project of the Works Progress Administration for the city of New Orleans. Houghton Mifflin Co., Boston, 1938.

New Orleans in the Gilded Age, Politics and Urban Progress, 1880-1896, by Joy J. Jackson. Louisiana State University Press, Baton Rouge, 1969.

New Orleans Yesterday and Today, by Walter G. Cowan, John C. Chase, Charles L. Dufour, O.K. LeBlanc, and John Wilds. Louisiana State University Press, Baton Rouge, 1983.

Old New Orleans, by Stanley Clisby Arthur. Pelican Publishing Co., Gretna, La, 1990.

Origins of the New South 1877–1913, by Comer Vann Woodward. Louisiana State University Press, Baton Rouge, 1951.

The Rudolph Matas History of Medicine in Louisiana, by Rudolph Matas, edited by

John Duffy. Louisiana State University Press, Baton Rouge, two volumes, 1958.

The Saffron Scourge: A History of Yellow Fever in Louisiana, 1796–1905, by Jo Ann Barrigan. Ph.D. dissertation, Louisiana State University, 1961.

Storyville, New Orleans, Being an Authentic, Illustrated Account of the Notorious Red-Light District, by Al Rose. University of Alabama Press, 1974.

The Streetcars of New Orleans by Louis C. Kennick and E. Harper Charlton. Pelican Publishing Co., Gretna, La, 1975.

Ten Flags in the Wind: The Story of Louisiana, by Charles L. Dufour. Harper & Row, New York, 1967.

ARCHITECTURE

Historic Garden District: An Illustrated Guide and Walking Tour, by Isabel Sanders, and Cindy Schoenberger. Voulez-Vous, Inc., 1988.

New Orleans Architecture: Volume I, The Lower Garden District, by Samuel Wilson, Jr. and Bernard Lemann. Friends of the Cabildo and Pelican Publishing Co., New Orleans, 1971.

New Orleans Architecture: Volume II, The American Sector. Essays by Samuel Wilson, Jr. and Bernard Lemann. Authors and editors: Mary Louise Christovich, Roulhac Toledano, Betsy Swanson, and Pat Holden. Pelican Publishing Co., Gretna, La, 1972.

New Orleans Houses: A House-Watcher's Guide, by Lloyd Vogt. Pelican Publishing Co., Gretna La, 1985.

FICTION & GENERAL

A Confederacy of Dunces, by John Kennedy Toole. Grove Press, New York, 1980.

Feast of All Saints, by Anne Rice. Random House, New York, 1979.

Frenchmen, Desire, Good Children and Other Streets of New Orleans, by John Churchill Chase. Macmillan, 1949.

Gumbo Ya-Ya (A Collection of Louisiana Folk Tales), compiled by Lyle Saxon, Edward Dreyer, and Robert Tallant. Pelican Publishing, Gretna, La, 1987.

Interview with a Vampire, by Anne Rice. Knopf, New York, 1976.

In the Land of Dreamy Dreams, by Ellen Gilchrist. University of Arkansas Press, 1981.

Lives of the Saints, by Nancy Lemann. Knopf, New York, 1985.

The Moviegoer, by Walker Percy. Avon, New York, 1961.

New Orleans, by John R. Kemp. Windsor Publications, Woodland Hills, Ca, 1981.

New Orleans Unmasqued, by S. Frederick Starr. Edition Dedeaux, 1985.

Encyclopedia of Southern Culture, edited by Charles Reagan Wilson and William Ferris. University of North Carolina Press; sponsored by the Center for the Study of Southern Culture at the University of Mississippi, 1989.

Vampire Lestat, by Anne Rice. Knopf, New York, 1985.

Voodoo in New Orleans, by Robert Tallant. Pelican Publishing Co., Gretna, La, 1983.

Encyclopedia of Witches and Witchcraft, by Rosemary Ellen Guilley. Facts on File, New York/Oxford, 1989.

The Witching Hour, by Anne Rice. Knopf, New York, 1990.

USEFUL ADDRESSES

TOURIST OFFICES

The main office of the **Greater New Orleans Tourist & Convention Commission** is in the Superdome (1520 Sugar Bowl Drive, New Orleans, LA 70112). The tourist commission operates the **New Orleans Welcome Center**, 529 St Ann St, in Jackson Square, which has a wealth of free maps, brochures, and advice about the city. There is also a tourist desk at New Orleans International Airport, located near the customs desk.

The Tourist Commission's **Information Gateway** (tel: 525-5000) provides 24-hour recorded information about the arts, sports, climate, time, tourist attractions, and so on.

Hospitality Hotline (tel: 522-9200) provides information and tickets for events around town, and delivers tickets to your hotel. Operating hours: daily 10 a.m. till 6 p.m. Information is available from 6 p.m. till 10 p.m. by telephoning 587-0871.

CONSULATES

Argentina
World Trade Center
Tel: 523-2823

Brazil
650 Poydras St
Tel: 588-9187

Chile
World Trade Center
Tel: 523-4368

Colombia
World Trade Center
Tel: 525-5580

Costa Rica
World Trade Center
Tel: 525-5445

Finland
1100 Poydras St
Tel: 523-6451

France
3305 St Charles Ave
Tel: 897-6381

Great Britain
321 St Charles Ave
Tel: 524-4180

Greece
World Trade Center
Tel: 523-1167

Guatemala
World Trade Center
Tel: 525-0013

Honduras
203 Carondelet St
Tel: 522-3118

India
201 St Charles Ave
Tel: 582-8000

Italy
630 Camp St
Tel: 524-2271

Japan
One Poydras Place
Tel: 529-2101

Korea
321 St Charles Ave
Tel: 524-0757

Mexico
World Trade Center
Tel: 522-3596

Monaco
Pan American Life Insurance Bldg
Tel: 522-5715

Paraguay
International Bldg
Tel: 522-7424

Philippines
World Trade Center
Tel: 525-5225

Norway
650 Poydras St
Tel: 522-3526

Spain
World Trade Center
Tel: 525-4951

Switzerland
1620 Eighth St
Tel: 897-6510
Thailand
335 Julia St
Tel: 566-0888

Uruguay
#2 Canal St
Tel: 525-8354

Venezuela
World Trade Center
Tel: 522-3284

Yugoslavia
910 Turquoise St
Tel: 288-6202

ART/PHOTO CREDITS

INDEX